The Cézanne Conspiracy

Terrence James Coffman

Author: Terrence James Coffman

Editor: Nell Thorpe

Contributors Deane Nesbitt & Clifford Chieffo

Copyright © 2018 by Terrence James Coffman 123 N. Center Avenue, Jefferson, Wisconsin 1985862603

Terrence James Coffman

Caution, professionals and amateurs are hereby warned that **The Cézanne Conspiracy** is fully protected under the copyright laws of the United States of America and subject to royalty. All rights including professional amateur Motion picture, Radio, and television broadcasting and the rights of translation into foreign languages are strictly prohibited. Permission must be secured from the author, Terrence James Coffman 123 Center Avenue Jefferson, Wisconsin 53549

The Cézanne Conspiracy

My name is Céline Roulin. I have been in the gallery business for over twenty-five years and I've known my fair share of artists. I'm an admirer of creative men. Maxfield Connor is the only non-Frenchman whose paintings I represent. He has been exhibiting his work in my Paris gallery for over twelve years.

If not for men like Max, it would be a boring world. Creative people function differently than most others. Maybe that's why you Américains stereotype them so easily. Max is a painter of immense talent. He is a philosopher of sorts and a man with a passionate heart. He is in love with life and all things French. For a time we lived together in New York. I fell for his Southern American accent and the twinkle of his blue eyes. I knew it would be impossible to hold on to him forever. But that was never my intention. He is a friend, and from time to time, we still share my bed in Paris.

His paintings are metaphors, never to be interpreted as impressionistic or abstract. And although he has been proficient in many styles and genres he abhors being categorized. He paints from the heart, not the head. He is an intellectual, but he prefers to be in touch with his soul rather then his mind. He often told his students how Cézanne pondered for hours, days, and weeks over a single brush stroke, analyzing the effect it would have on the great impressionist's composition. Max believes his own painting should take no more than five hours to complete. He said, "Painting is like dancing; you're only dancing when you are not thinking of the steps or how to hold your partner."

I first met Max at the Sidney Janis Gallery in New York City. I was a young junior curator who had started pursuing my career at the Galarie des Arts. I was part of a team putting together an exhibition of Willem de Kooning paintings for his first major show in Paris. We were in a meeting with Mr. Janis and his son Carroll when I heard a commotion. The receptionist was arguing with someone in the gallery. Carroll excused himself to see what was causing the commotion. I heard a voice yelling, "I am an artist, a great artist! Mr. Janis will want to see my work."

We could hear Carroll arguing with someone. There was a crash. Sidney, who at that time was not a young man, jumped to his feet and ran towards the gallery. We followed him. There were drawings spewed across the floor. The "great artist" was gathering up his drawings and stuffing them back into his portfolio. Carroll told the receptionist to call the police. Sidney said, "Wait." He motioned for the intruder to follow him back to the office. The door was closed. We were all concerned. The receptionist paged Mr. Janis, he said he was fine and asked her to bring two coffees. We waited for over an hour. Carroll paced the floor and finally the office door opened. Sidney emerged with his arm around Max's shoulder. He told the shaking receptionist to set up an appointment for Max to meet him before the end of the month. As she was going through the calendar, Max looked at me and winked.

At the end of the day, we left the gallery. The plan was for my boss and me to go back to the Plaza Hotel, have dinner and then go through the slides Sidney had given us of de Kooning's work. As we walked out the door onto 57th Street I heard a shrill whistle. Someone must be hailing a cab I thought. Then I heard it again and saw Max across the street, waving for us to come over. He was handsome and we were both young. My supervisor smiled and said, "He's not interested in me. Go ahead, join him. I'll sort through the images tonight and we can meet in the morning and decide which pieces we want Monsieur Janis to ship to Paris." If you are wondering, yes, I slept with him that night and many more nights over the years.

That's how we began. Later I was hired as a consultant by Sidney Janis Gallery. My roll was to act as a liaison between Sid's gallery and several European art institutions. Max never became one of Sidney's artists, but Sid did employ him for a while doing framing and driving the gallery truck delivering paintings to rich snobs and big corporations. Max could barely afford to stay in Manhattan. He lived in his studio on the third floor of an old warehouse building on Hudson Street in Tribeca.

In those early days, as I was learning the gallery business, I traveled back and forth between Paris and New York monthly. One month in Paris, the other in the "Big Apple." It was convenient for me to live in his loft. We shared the rent, and we shared each other. It was delicious. He was my first sexual partner. I had remained a virgin through my school years. I was petrified by the notion of being naked in front of others. It was an obsession that kept me out of physical education courses in my teens, and later resulted in me being assigned to a single occupant dorm room with a full bath at the University. Most of my classmates thought I came from a rich family. I did not.

I was also a loner, in part because my need to be perfect required me to study harder than the other students. Unlike my schoolmates, there was no time for parties or boyfriends. It was not because I was unattractive; to the contrary, I was pretty. The boys wanted me, that's for sure. I was 24 when I met Max; he 10 years older and quite experienced with women. I was fragile. He was patient and gentle. He had never been with a lady quite like me. He loved my body. Max showed me that I was beautiful. He helped me to learn to feel confident about myself. He also tolerated my need to scotch tape reminders on almost every surface in the loft. He put up with my late night journaling and accepted other foibles of my personality.

This was a man who loved me for who I was.

We lived together on the Lower East Side for almost three years. But during that time period, Max came to Paris only twice. It was impossible for him to afford both a New York loft and a Paris garret. After I was appointed as the director of a small museum on the rue Mouffetard in the Latin Quarter, it became more difficult for us to see each other. I was no longer going to the States to work with Sidney. I knew Max was frustrated. He was always broke and on the edge of losing his studio. He had begun to see other women. I wanted him to move to Paris. He was unable to make up his mind. I gave him an ultimatum. That may have been a mistake, but who knows? Fate is a fickle friend. We can only live in the moment. Wouldn't it be nice if there were parallel universes where, like a pair of shoes, we could try on different lives?

Max and I went in different directions after that, but his art, and my love for it, has always been our connection. I worked as a curator, and finally opened my own gallery in Paris. He landed a teaching job in San Francisco. That's where he met the French sculptor Robert Chéron.

Now Robert resides in Marseille. Years ago, when Robert and his Latvian wife lived in the US, he was teaching art restoration and sculpture at an art school in San Francisco. That's where he met Max. Max taught painting, drawing and an art history course on the meaning of symbols. Max and Robert became fast friends and were popular among the graduate students. The older faculty resented them and, as a result, someone on the faculty erroneously reported to immigration officials that Robert was employed at the school without a work visa. The investigation found that his paperwork was in order, but there was a problem with his wife's. She had over stayed her tourist visa. More damaging, however, was that Robert's wife's father had ties to the Russian KGB. Robert was forced to return to France.

Max quit teaching after three years. He hated the politics of faculty, the narrowness of their views and he could see that if he remained a teacher he would never be the artist he was capable of being. A monthly paycheck can be a dangerous captor for an artist.

He moved back to the east coast, to Boston, then eventually to Washington DC. His first big break came when one of his paintings was included in a major group show at the Guggenheim and another, a year later, at the Venice Biennale. *Art News* and *Art in America* reviewed his one-man shows. In one of the reviews, Max mentioned to the critic that he was going through a period of discontent with his work. Max told the writer that he felt he was a prisoner of his own success. "Everyone," he said, "expects me to paint the same image over and over. I feel like Frankie Avalon having to sing the same old song at every concert. I cannot be an artist like that. I need inspiration, a change, but right now I don't know where my work is going."

Soon after that article appeared, Max's old friend Robert Chéron, who is also in my stable of artists, wrote Max that he should move to France to paint. Robert also contacted me and suggested that I also encourage him to leave the States. So I wrote to Max, advocating that he would have more creative freedom and inspiration by being in Europe, especially if he chose to live in

France. Our encouragement was just what Max needed. It was to be an adventure, a time to paint under different skies, to experience a new landscape, and most importantly, to push his work in new directions

Max agreed. To live in France would be an exciting undertaking, a dream fulfilled. Every artist, from van Gogh to Picasso, right down to Max, has had the fantasy to live in Paris or the south of France.

Max decided to take a ship rather than an airliner. I suppose he needed to ease his transition by flowing with the sea. He arrived in Le Havre, France, and boarded a ferry bound for Holland. He had always wanted to see the landscape that influenced the Dutch masters. He chose it as the first place to plant his boots in Europe. As the boat passed Antwerp, the North Sea sky combined with the sepia tones of the Dutch earth giving him an impression of what Rembrandt and Fans Hals must have seen every day of their lives. He breathed in the salty sea air of Amsterdam. Disembarking the gangway he set foot on the cobblestoned streets of the old city. Spring was in the air; he removed his heavy navy blue pea coat and threw it in the first trash container that he came upon. He had kept it for years, wearing it ever since art school. That coat preserved him during the cold days of New York. It was tattered, stained with paint and there were holes in the pockets. His life was moving into a new direction, it was time to shed the old for the new. The coat was a symbol of the past.

He quickly fell in love with the red brick public buildings and private homes. Walking along the old canals, he was in tune with the houseboats moored against the stone walls. Like his own image, they were reflected in the water. The floating homes each bore the personalities of their owners. They gently bobbed in the wake of the small boats and barges that traveled the canals. It was spring, and the small gardens that lined the city streets were filled with poppies and daffodils. He booked himself into a 1620 restored hotel. His first meal was in a small Indian café. The smells of coriander and cardamom smiled much sweeter in Amsterdam than on "Curry Row" in the East Village or Jackson Heights in Queens. Afterwards he walked to the red light district.

The next morning he hiked through the surrounding countryside and saw windmills and greenhouses filled with tulips. It reminded him of a scene that van Gogh once painted. Later in the day he returned to the city and immediately went to the

Rijksmuseum. There, he was consumed by the beauty of Flemish and Dutch art. Portraits of ruby-faced women in the most intricate lace; still life's of fruit and flowers; paintings with tulips of every variety, Rembrandt tulips, Parrot tulips in yellows and reds popping out of black and blue gray backgrounds, flies and salamanders squirming over marble table tops, glass shimmering next to silver and delft, all created by hands so skilled that no camera could ever capture their realism.

After six months of roaming and sketching in Holland, Max arrived in Paris. We were together for two glorious weeks. Robert found him a residence in Provence that was in a small artist's community in the heart of the Luberon Valley. Max was excited about the prospect of living in an artistic community in what some call "van Gogh Land." I would have preferred Max to stay in Paris, but at least he would be in France and we could see one another often. I fantasized that our once romantic relationship would be rekindled. Just like in New York, we would be together again. After all, Paris was only two hours from Provence. What could possibly stop us from being lovers again?

****

Max took the train to Provence. I kissed him goodbye at the Gare du Nord station in Paris. My plan was that, after he settled into his new home, we would see each other soon and regularly thereafter. Robert was to come up from Marseilles to meet Max at the train station just outside the old walled Papal City of Avignon. Max came on the fast train, Robert on the slow commuter line. Max waited for an hour. He set on the hard wooden bench outside the door of the station. *Welcome to Provence* the sign said. Welcome indeed to the heat, Max whispered under his breath.

They met at the station. It had been a long time since they had seen one another. They were older and grayer, but both still handsome. They embraced, and as is the French custom, Robert kissed each side of his friend's face. They smiled and chatted the whole way as Max drove the rented Peugeot to the hilltop village of Lacoste.

Lacoste is a picture postcard kind of place. The narrowed- streeted hilltop village overlooks a magnificent valley that sweeps for miles towards a distant mountain named Mont Ventoux. The Provencal sun is brilliant, almost too bright for a foreigner. Robert told Max that it would take time for his American eyes to adjust to the constant cloudless sun drenched landscape, but once it happened, the clarity would be magnificent. "You will see color more intensely than you have ever dreamed of." Robert had managed to lease a two story stone house for Max. When they arrived it was late. The keys to Max's new home were hidden under a brick near the door. They walked through the first floor of Max's new place; it was sparsely furnished and the kitchen was outdated and small, as was the bathroom. But no matter, in time Max would find all the necessities needed to make his space workable as well as comfortable.

They walked up a narrow staircase leading to the top floor. There was a small bedroom and across from it a tall door. When Max opened the door he expected to find a second bedroom; instead his jaw dropped open. He took a long deep breath and then threw his fist upward toward the ceiling. "Yes," he screamed. The master bedroom had been converted into a magnificent studio. There, in a newly constructed vaulted ceiling, were skylights which let natural light in and two small exhaust fans that would draw out the fumes of oil paint and turpentine. The windows had been removed, allowing plenty of wall space to hang his artwork. Most exciting to Max was the track lights mounted to the ceiling. The studio was perfect.

It was late and beginning to get dark outside. They

emptied the small trunk of the car and carried in their bags. Luckily they had stopped along the way to eat. Robert had brought two bottles of very good champagne to celebrate Max's new place. They sat on the threadbare couch and talked until midnight about Max's future in France and all the things they could do together in Marseilles, Provence and Paris. Max slept on a rug that laid on the stone floor and Robert passed out on the couch. Max was lucky that scorpions didn't sting him.

✢✢✢✢✢✢✢✢✢✢✢✢✢✢✢✢✢✢✢✢✢✢✢✢✢✢✢✢✢✢✢✢✢✢✢✢✢✢✢

On his first full day in Lacoste Max rose early. Robert had decided to sleep in, so Max explored the streets of Lacoste alone. The first thing Max needed to do was to find coffee. He didn't have to go far; the Cafe du Sade was just around the corner from his new residence. He sat outside on the small patio. The owner was an affable fellow. He asked Max if he was a tourist. Max said no, he was a new resident.

"Welcome, which house are you living in?"

Max wasn't sure of the street name, but describe the building.

"Que, I know the house. It belongs to Monsieur

village."

Max smiled; he liked the woman. "I'm not famous and I have no patience or desire to teach."

"Ahh, then you are a real artist, oui? The croissant is free, it is my welcome gift to you for coming to our famous village." They both laughed.

The woman knew how to cultivate clientele. Max was to become a regular customer. He didn't need to worry about the calories of croissants and pastry, walking up and down the steep lanes of the village was going to burn off every ounce of fat in his body.

****

Centuries ago, Lacoste had been a place for debauchery. The Marquis de Sade's summer home was there. Avant-garde writers and artists had been coming there for hundreds of years, and true to their natures, their morals and behavior were far from the norm of the typical Catholic Provencal farmers.

Just after World War II, Pfriem, the legendary American surrealist, moved from New York City and bought several 400 year-old buildings in the village. Decimated at the end of the Second World War, the French economy made it possible for Bernard to pay practically nothing for the properties. Robert had negotiated the lease with the surrealist for the studio and residence where Max had come to live and paint. After living in the village for six months, Max offered Pfriem a considerable amount of money to buy the place. The old painter refused. At first, Max was afraid he'd lose his studio, but eventually he learned legal issues surrounding Bernard's purchases were tied up in the French courts. Being what it is, the French bureaucracy could keep the issue in limbo for another 30 or more years. So Max settled in. I told him not to worry about our French ways of doing things; it was not worth losing sleep over. Whatever was meant to be would come to pass regardless of Max or Bernard. French bureaucrats despise Americans, so neither one of them would have a say as to the outcome.

Later that day, after Robert woke up and found Max sitting on a stone wall drawing, Robert insisted they do some sightseeing. The two took a drive to the nearby village of Roussillon. Roussillon is where the color ochre is mined; the rusted red and yellow soil has been used to make paints for over 2,000 years. Walking through the woodland pines and dust filled earth was a mystical experience. The ground in places was mustard yellow, sienna orange and various shades of umber. The town was old and all the buildings made of stucco stained brown, red and yellow. This was the place where the Archangel Gabriel battled against the fallen angels and the ground became forever colored by their blood.

The two friends ate in a small outdoor café and enjoyed a meal of fresh rabbit cooked in curry sauce with minced apricots.

Robert is a very slim, tanned Frenchmen. He has a thin sharp pointed roman nose and light blue eyes that remind me of blue glacial ice. His fingers are long and his hands strong. After all, he is a sculptor. Robert grips a chisel like a vice, and in the other hand, he holds a hammer in such a way that he can deliver a blow with precise striking force. He cannot afford a mis-hit the chisel for fear of breaking his hand. His hits to the steel cutting tools that shape granite and marble are impeccable. He can find a human figure, a pear, an animal or anything, real or unreal that might be hiding itself inside the stone. His father was a monument carver and carved names and dates on tombstone. He taught his young son to do the same. But as a young man, Robert wanted more for himself. He aspired to be Rodin or Michelangelo. Now, 50 years old, he has come to accept that fame may elude him.

"I've missed you my friend." Robert said as he pulled the meat from the bone. "We never ate like this when we were art teachers in San Francisco. In those days we were just young poor artists and didn't give a shit about gourmet food. Well, maybe when we weren't smoking joints." They both laughed.

"We were wild back then," continued Robert. "All we really cared about was painting, screwing and getting high."

Max smiled and took a moment reminisce. "It's true, and sometimes I wish those days were not so far away. It seems so long ago and yet here we are together again. Who among our old friends would believe we'd be sitting in Provence with the warm sun on our backs pulling apart rabbits and living and working in the place were Picasso, Cézanne, Gauguin, van Gogh, Matisse and other great painters worked?"

Robert leaned back in his chair and took a long drink of beer. Leaning forward, he said to Max, "You are going to be inspired. There are no art critics or gallery owners that are vultures here. Paint what you want, paint what is true, my friend."

Max was quiet for a few moments. Then shaking his head in agreement, he recited the following words. "Lavender... Sunflowers... Monet... Cézanne... Pastis... Hares... Cicadas... How could I not find inspiration here?"

From a small cotton sack, pulled from his shirt pocket, Robert pinched sweet-smelling tobacco between his thumb and finger. He sprinkled it over the middle of brown smoking paper, rolled it, and then lit it. Taking a long drag, the Frenchman peered toward the ochre cliffs saying, "Let's you and I go drawing tomorrow."

The next morning Robert drove them to his favorite village, Ménerbes. The two found an orchard of peaches on the outskirts of the small village and sat side by side on a rock wall. Robert had a leather bound sketchbook and a box of colored pencils. He removed his cap and laid the pencils in it. Unlike Max, he wasn't used to sketching outdoors. He was a sculptor. He carved directly in stone. He found his figures by chipping away chunks of rock to reveal figures, animals' even fruit and vegetables.

"Max, I used to love drawing, but somehow over the years I stopped working outdoors. You've stayed with it, good for you! When I was drawing in the fields, I sometimes thought I could feel God near me.

Max took a long drag on his cigar. "Yes, I understand how you felt. When I'm drawing in nature I often feel His presence. Ideas come to me, drawing flows without labor and time seems to disappear. I plan to spend the summer working every day in the Vaucluse valley with God looking over my shoulder. I am so grateful to you for convincing me to come to Provence, and to Céline for advancing me the money to start my new life. I'm certain I will make good paintings here in Lacoste. The Luberon will inspire me, I'm damn sure of that."

The following day Max took Robert to the train station in Avignon. After promising to return soon, the two embraced and Robert climbed aboard the train to Marseille.

****

The Lacoste studio has been an ideal working space for Max. The wide oak floors were made in the days when large trees grew in the French forests. The house/studio is located down a passageway between his stone building and his neighbors. It is a cool oasis from the blazing sun and sometimes he sits on the stone steps leading to his door to drink coffee, pastis or wine while refining a sketch or watercolor. He works day after day outside in the intense heat and sunlight. With only a straw hat for protection from the sun, he carries his easel and paint box for miles to that perfect place, the one that calls to the artist to paint. At day's end Max usually takes a cool shower, followed by an hour nap and then he goes to one of three cafes to enjoy a Provencal meal and a jug of Luberon wine. Afterwards, he will sit back in the chair and taste the sweet licorice flavor of Pernod mixed with the pungent aroma of his Cuban cigar.

Early in the mornings, before the sun scorches the earth, he rises to paint. By mid-afternoon the heat becomes too much for him to work out of doors, but in the long, light-filled evenings he returns, sets up his easel at the top of the village, and draws views of the valley that extend as far as his eyes can see. Whenever he comes to Paris he brings stacks of drawings to my gallery. I recently exhibited Max's intricate drawings of the small farms surrounded by fruit trees and vineyards. In my opinion his drawings and watercolors surpass the renderings of Monet and Cézanne, and they even rival that of van Gogh. I sell his work like no other artists in my stable. Customers think he must be French. My best buyer swears he's not an American. "Only a Frenchman," he told me, "can capture the soul of a French farmhouse."

Maxfield has always been attracted to flirts, so he is easy to seduce. I should know, I was the first one to truly entice him. I was not his first sexual experience, however, I was the woman who most excited him. I'm attainable and unattainable, amusing, fashionable, and innovative. I am an intellectual, but when needed, I know how to be superficial, shallow or appear naive. I can deliver pain and accept pain. I have nothing to prove and much to give. I know how to provoke a man; I also know when to be careful. I have always been a woman with a purpose. I know how to manage. I perform and excel at anything I undertake. For Max, that was essential. He also liked the fact that I am six feet tall. I have no problem being objectified by men, or for that matter, women. I am unashamed. I am a skillful lover with attributes most men deny, but secretly desire. It is a part of my personal toolbox. I am elegant, always look good and speak intelligently with firmness and truth. When humor is needed, I am funny. With Max I have never been disrespectful. Yes, we sometimes argue, but neither of us ever held a grudge. I enjoy hearing what he has to say, what he thinks and what he paints. I admire creative people; they usually have no hang-ups and are less prone to be judgmental. That's vital to me.

Sex is essential to both of us. When it came to

Max, I knew how to dress for him, touch him, speak with him, how to hint for what I needed. I wore the right perfume and it sat his pheromones on fire. I knew how to cross my legs in such a way that he would get a glimpse of his possibilities. I knew how to whisper in his ear, I knew when to close my eyes so the shadow colors would make him think of Cleopatra. I could touch his strong thighs and run my finger from just above the knee to the edge of his manhood. I knew how to use silence to get what I needed, how to lead where I wanted him to go. I was clever like a cat. I knew how to make him feel guilty. It was easy to love him, easy to be angry with him and easy to forgive him.

He has always been respectful with me, even when he gets drunk or mad. In the old days he was generous when he could afford to be and understood my moods, needs and desires. He believed then, and still does, that I am the best gallery director in the art world. I have never known a better sexual partner. Even though we are no longer a couple, we do get together from time to time. He still touches me in ways that are tender. He stimulates me like no other and I always climax when we're together.

During the time we lived together in New York, not

once did we have an argument that unglued us. It was not because of any horrible act of deceit or disrespect that we split up. It was simply was that our time and space was not meant to be exclusive or forever. We will always be friends; we will always love one another. I can count on Max. He can count on me.

There have been a few other women in his life. He was married for a brief time, but that ended because she was unfaithful. He had a few short-term girlfriends. It wouldn't surprise me if he visited a brothel or two. I don't fault him for how he may, or may not fulfill his sexual needs. I am no prude. I am French.

Since taking up residence in Lacoste he's met a woman. I admit, I am jealous and reticent about him getting involved with someone so quickly. I admonished myself, thinking, Céline, you have no hold on this man, no right to be possessive. Be happy for him. I did tell Max not to get attached to quickly; after all, he is handsome, romantic and an artist. There are many women who would enjoy his company. Provence provides the sweetest and most delicious fruit in all of France. He has the opportunity to sample, and then choose, the perfect match for his tastes.

Max often goes to the village of St. Rémy to draw

the craggy peaks of the Alpilles. On one of his forays, he stumbled upon Les Baux de-Provence, an ancient hill top town that dates back over 5,000 years. Because of its spectacular views, it became one of his favorite sites to draw. During medieval times, the town was known as the "*Court of Love*." Here, troubadours composed passionate poems in praise of the well-bred aristocratic ladies. In return, the poets would receive a peacock feather and a kiss.

While sitting at a small outdoor café for lunch in Les Baux, he saw Françoise for the first time. Max described her as stunningly French. Immaculately, yet provocatively, dressed as only Parisian women do. He told me he was immediately captivated. According to him, her make-up accented the natural light peach tint of her skin. Earthy grey eye shadow created the perfect contrast to her sapphire blue eyes. He said the woman's blonde hair was pulled back in the style of the traditional French Braid.

As he described their meeting he was seated behind her watching her hand sensually fingering a glass of wine. She was wearing a citron-green sundress. The back of her neck and arms were tanned. Her silver bracelet caught the sun reflecting its light on the stone wall of the café where a kitten jumped hoping to catch the light in its paws. She laughed and turned the bracelet so the reflected light danced in different directions for the cat to chase.

Françoise must have felt Max's eyes on her; she turned to see him smiling. He pointed at the young cat and said, "You've found a nice friend."

She replied, "Oui il est si joli", but Max did not understand, while his French was improving daily, his understanding of the language was still rudimentary. She repeated in English, "Yes, he is so cute."

Max nodded to her. He told me that when she turned toward him her eyes and perfectly shaped mouth instantly captured him. He thought, how wonderful it would be to kiss her. Max was snared.

She fiddled with her table napkin, patted her lips and put it back on the table. "You are American?"

Max noticed the imprint of her pink mouth on the white cotton. "I am."

"Where in America do come from?" He liked the sound of her voice.

"South Carolina," he replied.

"I have been to America many times, mostly New York City and Miami but never to your Southern states, maybe someday you can take me there, oui?"

Max was caught off guard by the boldness of her proposal. After all, he thought, she doesn't know me. I could be a killer, a rapist or some kind of pervert. Why does she trust me?

She patted the chair next to her, "Come, join me."

He took his glass of Pastis and the decanter of water and sat beside her.

"You like Pernod?" She asked.

Fingering his glass he winked at her. "I am in love with most things French and especially fond of this."

She glanced to see if he was wearing a wedding ring. "You are not dressed like an American tourist. How did you come to enjoy Pastis? Most Americans I have met do not have such refined tastes."

"I am an artist, most my clothes are spotted with drips of paint." He pointed a few out to her, the yellow on his shirtsleeve, purple splatters across his jeans and a few specks of pink that had splashed on his sandals. She noticed a plop of green on his ear. She pointed at her own ear and laughed. He took his napkin, curled it around his finger and dipped it in his glass of water then rubbed the paint away. "I must have missed that one. As for the Pernod, yes, the Impressionists loved it as well. I heard it influenced van Gogh's paintings."

She pushed her coal colored hair back behind her ear and laughed, "If you would like, I can take you to Isle d'Sourge where you can buy real Absinthe. Pastis, or Pernod, is nothing like the real thing. I have a friend who owns a shop in Sourge. He discreetly sells old bottles of the Green Fairy."

Max smiled and tried a bit of French. "Oui that would be magnifique."

Maybe his feeble attempt at our language paid off. Françoise's quickly replied, "Shall we go now?"

"Do you have a voiture?" She said."A what?""An automobile." She laughed."Oui, Oui. I have a small Peugeot," he said."Bon, My car is in the garage. I live in Paris, but each summer I come to Les Baux to stay. It is a beautiful village and soon I will come to live here year round."

He reached for her hand, and for what seemed like minutes, but probably were only seconds, she clasped both her hands around his. He introduced himself. "I am Max de Carolina, and you are?"

"Je suis Françoise de Paris."

She threw her head back and laughed. "You are a funny man. Most American men I meet do not have a sense of humor.

The young kitten moved back and forth leaning herself against Max's leg

"It is a pleasure to meet you Françoise.""Le plaisir est le mien. It looks as if the kitty likes you." "Is she yours?""No, she is homeless, maybe you should take her home." Max shook his head, "Maybe."He was drawn to the woman, their connection was instantaneous. As they drove to Isle d'Sourge the conversation in the Peugeot was animated and easy. He told her about his paintings.

"I also paint," she said. "But I am just an amateur."

I like the fact that Max shares his conversations word for word.

They talked about making art in Provence. Max looked at her hand and saw the wedding ring. She noticed and said, "I am married to a politician; we are separated. Right now divorce is problematic."

Max wondered why she still wore the ring. Affairs can be nice with a married woman he thought, but dangerous with the spouse of an elected official.

He threw caution to the wind. Hell, this is France he told himself; affairs, mistresses and lovers are a part of the culture here. Even the French president has a lover and no one cares. All the French want from their leaders is that they meet their governing responsibilities successfully. They are not looking for role models.

Max leaned forward. "I'm new to Provence. Would you be open to showing me where the best vistas are? We could paint together."

He was Odysseus; she was the Siren who sang and smiled. And like the temptress she was, she asked, "What will I get in return?"

"I can teach you. I was once a professor of art."

Laughingly she put him in his place. "I am not the foolish star struck university student you may have taken liberties with in your past. I am quiet proficient in several ways. There are many things in my repertoire where I excel. I have talents, a number of them you might enjoy. If I agree to be your artistic tourist guide, you may learn some new things from me. We can negotiate later, but right now we need to get to Isle sur la Sorgue. Where is your car parked?"

The tranquil town on the river Sorgue is surrounded

by water that winds its way around shops, restaurants and cafes. In some places there are canals that run off in different directions through the city center. It was Market day in Isle sur la Sorgue. The green open park spaces and narrow streets were crowded by farmer's stands, booksellers' tables, cheap tourist art hung on pegboard, and all the kind of stuff you'd expect to find in a small French market. Both vacationers and locals push, shove and compete for bargains, and in some cases, necessities. Françoise bought fruit, vegetables, cheese and sausage. She told Max that the red peaches and Cavillon melons were in season. He looked at them saying, "We have cantaloupe back in the US and our Georgia peaches are the best in the world."

She pushed the tip of her tongue just far enough to moisten her lips, at the same time teasing him with the idea of what a French kiss could really be. "You must try our melons, they are the sweetest thing that will ever touch your lips," she proclaimed.He pulled out a pocketknife from his knapsack and cut a

sliver to sample. It dissolved on the tip of his tongue. As the juice ran down his cheek she wiped his chin with her finger. She took the droplet and put it on her tongue, saying, "Sinful isn't it?"

A farmer stepped from behind the table boasting, "These melons are the favorite of Parisians. Alexander Dumas requested the mayor of Cavillon to send a crate of our melons for a special dinner he was hosting in Paris? After the meal, Dumas wrote a letter to the village congratulating us for growing the most sensual melons in the world. For the last hundred years, we have been sending the first pick of the melon crop to the Dumas heirs."

Françoise took Max to a wine shop on the rue Jean-Jacques Rousseau. The bells on the back of the door jingled and, from behind a beaded curtain, a man with a long mustache poked his head out, only to say he'd return in a moment. There was a scurrying sound from the back room and Max heard a woman giggle. When he came back, the shopkeeper saw Françoise and spread his arms wide. They embraced, kissed each other's cheeks several times and conversed in French. Max didn't understand a word. Françoise introduced Max to Paul Malassigné. The Frenchman shook the American's hand. In broken English he said, "You are a lucky man to be with such a spéciale woman. Madamé Françoise is my best customer. She is known by everyone here as, '*The Most Beautiful Woman In Provence*'. She tells me you are an artist like herself and that you want to taste the "Green Fairy." It just so happens I have a source. And, because she is after all, '*The Most Beautiful Woman In Provence*', as well as my best customer, I will give you a taste of heaven. But, you must promise me not to tell a soul where you found real Absinthe. The gendarmes would put me in prison and throw the key away," he laughed.

Françoise looked at him skeptically, "Oh come on now Paul, you've paid off the captain of the gendarmes, the mayor, the city council and even your neighbors. You have no worries, they are all in your pocket."

The short shopkeeper crossed his arms and moved his head from side to side saying, "Oui, that may be true, even so, one must still be careful. What if some snoopy Parisian reporter comes sniffing around? The press would love making us Provencal's look like we are as loathsome and corrupt as the people from Marseille. I am just a humble shopkeeper trying to squeak out a living."

Humble!!! Françoise chuckled, "I could find a better word, how about, "Plein de merde?" (Full of shit) As for your meager existence, how would you explain the Ferrari parked in the shed behind this shop?" I have seen it, remember? Let's see, you might tell them it belongs to your girlfriend. Certainly not your wife, because you told me she doesn't know about your expensive racecar."

From behind the curtain came a muffled chuckle. Max looked at Françoise; she cupped her hand over her mouth to keep her own laughter from spilling out. The shopkeeper lowered his head and said nothing.

Monsieur Malassigné reached under the counter and produced a dark bottle with no label; he placed three small glasses on the countertop and a pitcher of water. He then reached for a jar of sugar cubes on the shelf behind him. Françoise smiled, touched Max's hand, then whispered in his ear, "Watch, Paul will mix it the old way, just like Cézanne

Malassigné poured the yellowish green absinthe into each glass to about a third full. He then put three sugar cubes on a large flat spoon with holes in it. He placed the slotted spoon over the top of the glass and poured a small amount of cold water slowly over the sugar to dissolve it. The sweet water dripped into to the glass of the Green Fairy and as it did, the Absinthe took on white cloudiness, which the shop owner called, "the louche." He picked up the glass and swirled the liquid then added the remaining remnants of sugar on spoon. Leaning down, this shopkeeper placed his pointy nose over each one of the glasses and smelled the herbal aroma of anise and fennel. He looked pleased, "We will let the sugar soak for a minute or two. I want the flavors to blossom. Then I will add more water to release the bouquet."

"So while we wait, Monsieur Connor, tell me about how you met '*The Most Beautiful Woman in Provence?*"

"I was having a quiet lunch in Les Baux and this woman interrupted me."

Françoise smiled. "No." Raising her voice an octave she said, "THIS... scruffy American, was starring at me. I could feel his eyes soaking me in like the sugar in your Absinthe. He told me he is a painter. Paul, my rule is not to become intimate with artists,"

Malassigné laughed, "Too much competition for you Madamé?"

Françoise whispered into the shopkeeper's ear, turned and then looked at Max saying. "A woman needs to keep her secrets. I don't want you stealing my painting or drawing techniques, or for that matter, any of my skills. I might, if I think you have potential, let you participate with me in the exploration of other creative talents that I possess." She kissed Max on the cheek and laughed.

The shopkeeper coughed, pulled his handkerchief from his pocket and blew his nose. "Madamé

Françoise, no one is as talented as you."

She looked at Max and winked, "You see why Malassigné is my favorite shopkeeper?"

The proprietor handed one of the glasses of Absinthe to Françoise. "Madamé, please taste."

She breathed in the fragrance, smiled, put the glass to her mouth and took a sip. "Parfait," she said.

A huge grin came over the shopkeeper's face. He handed Max a glass, took the other for himself and raised it towards the ceiling saying, "Pour la belle Françoise."

When Max told me this part of the story, he said, "I felt a tinge similar to an antiseptic sensation on my lips. When the absinthe touched my tongue I thought of licorice sticks and caraway seeds. Before I swallowed it, I let the liquor float between my gum and teeth. It filled my throat with a smooth fresh feeling and it has a much different flavor and color than Pernod. It was pure magic."

He was probably right. The bottle of absinthe Monsieur Malassigné served them must have been produced sometime prior to 1915. Its detractors, mostly social conservatives, were able to have it banned. They claimed Absinthe made people crazy and triggered epilepsy and tuberculosis. One temperance critic decreed it caused men to become ferocious beasts who beat their wives and children, thus destroying French society, and the future of the country. Max was lucky to taste the real thing.

The three finished their drinks and the shopkeeper handed Max the bottle. "Monsieur, long ago my grandfather sold absinthe to Cézanne and many famous artists. Françoise tells me you are famous, so I make a present to you, Oui."

Max reached for his wallet and the shopkeeper said, "No, no I cannot accept your money. Françoise is a dear friend and besides, she likes you. *The Most Beautiful Woman In Provence*" always has her way in France."

As they walked out the door Max asked what the shopkeeper had whispered to her. Françoise threw her head back, combed her hands through her hair to untie her french braid. She tossed her head from side to side releasing the strands of her Cleopatra thick tresses. Max described her movements to me as sensual. He said she replied. "Paul believes you are a lucky man to be with such a beautiful woman."

"He's right," Max confirmed."Are you hungry?" He asked.She smiled, "Maybe a bite of cheese and some crackers would be nice."They crossed the street and sat on a bench. Max told her to

wait while he ran down the boulevard to the small grocery shop. When he returned, Françoise opened the grocery sack and removed the goat cheese, sausage and bread. Taking the baguettes, Max pulled a pocketknife from his knapsack and cut them lengthwise to make two sandwiches. As Françoise finished assembling the sandwiches, Max uncorked the wine and poured it from the bottle into two plastic cups.

She shook her head, "Only an American would drink wine from a plastic glass!"

Afterwards she and Max moved off the park bench to sit in the grass by the river. Max retrieved his sketchbook and box of pencils from his sack and began to sketch Malassigné's shop. She laid back, closed her eyes and soaked in the warmth from the sun and fell asleep. An hour later Max nudged her, she sat up, looked at his drawing and said. "Very good, you're much better than I thought you'd be."

Max smiled.

Malassigné and a large dark-skinned Algerian looking woman exited the shop together. Françoise waved to them. He waved back. After they disappeared behind his building, Max heard the roar coming from the engine of the shopkeeper's fancy racecar and listened as the sound of the engine faded as it exited the village. Max walked across the street, placed the drawing in the postage slot of the absinthe seller's door.

As Max told me the story, it was getting late and Françoise told Max that she had to go; she was worried about him driving the narrow road that winded its way down the steep cliffs surrounding Les Baux at night. When they reached the village he walked her to a small stone house not far from the café where they first met. He asked if she wanted to have dinner, but she said she had to meet someone and it would be best for him to leave town before the sun disappeared. Max asked her, "Can I see you again?"

"Oui, I would like that." As if a southern American woman, she curtseyed.

"Can I kiss you?" He asked.

She smiled and came close to him. Max said the kiss was intoxicating.

She asked for his phone number. Max thought it odd, usually the man asks for the lady's number. But then he remembered; when in France do as the French do. He wrote his number down and handed it to her.

As Max headed for his car he saw the homeless kitty. He picked her up and she rubbed her face against his. He gently placed her on the passenger seat, and then walked to the driver's side door, opened it and slid in. Françoise removed her scarf and placed it on the seat beside the kitten. The small creature curled herself up into a ball around it, purring as Max gave a wave to Françoise and drove off towards Lacoste.

****

I had introduced Maurice Michelin to Max years before my friend moved to France. Maurice is an heir to the French tire maker. His old villa is part of the family estate. Monsieur Michelin has restored the gardens to their original splendor. There are exotic plants from the Sahara, native flowering trees, an olive orchard and even a small vineyard that supplies grapes for his own private label wine. He is in his early 70s and has nothing to do with the company that bears his family name. Funneling huge sums of money to him, his inheritance flows through Swiss banks and undisclosed investments. It has allowed him to become a significant art collector of both American Abstract Expressionists and French Impressionism. He's purchased several of Max's paintings from me.

His other passion is sports cars, especially racecars. He is not married, never been married. It is rumored he was romantically involved with the heiress of an American cola company who had a summer home nearby. Whether it's true or not, I don't know, but I have my doubts, because every time we met, he was with a considerably younger Italian man, quite fit, quite tan and very handsome.

Maurice has been a long time client of mine. In 1967 Max was living in Washington D.C.; Michelin lived in Saint Remy. Maurice chartered a jet and together with me, and his friend Mario, we flew to New York City where he bought two small Jackson Pollock ink drawings from the Janis Gallery. We then went to Washington DC to visit the Philips Collection. That's where he met Max. I had asked Max if he would like to join us for lunch with Marjorie Phillips. Maurice had met both Marjorie and her husband Duncan in Paris. As collectors, Duncan and Maurice paths had crossed many times and they developed a friendship. Mrs. Phillips was familiar with Max's work. She had first seen his paintings at the Franz Bader Gallery where she purchased a small watercolor for the Philips Collection. After lunch, the three of us walked to Max's studio near Dupont Circle. Maurice was immediately taken by Max's work. He bought three paintings. We were lucky to be able to fit them into the small jet that was taking us back to Paris. Since that time Maurice has purchased other works by Max. Michelin was impressed by the way Max drew, so impressed that he commissioned Max to do a series of etchings. When I told Maurice that Max was moving to Provence, he was thrilled and proposed Max paint in his gardens. The commission was good for Max. It has allowed him to pay the expenses of his studio in Lacoste.

The day after Max met François she called him. It was a short conversation.

Max told her he was driving to St. Remy to draw in the gardens of a rich client. "Who." she asked."Maurice Michelin"

There was a pause, and then Françoise asked, "You know this man?"

 "Yes, he owns several of my paintings and a bunch of drawings and prints."

She laughed. "Well then, you must be a real painter." "Did you think I was an amateur?""No. I admit I have heard of you. Have you been to

Maurice's villa yet?""Yes," Max replied. "Last week I painted a view of his peach

orchard.""Hummm...I love peaches. Did you see the beautiful

Cézanne over his fireplace?" "I did. It's exquisite."

Françoise whispered into the phone. "A friend of mine found it in an attic near Menerbes and sold it to Monsieur Michelin for a large sum of money. I accompanied my friend to Michelin's Villa. Ever since then, Maurice has asked for my opinion before he buys a work of art."

"Call Maurice, ask him if you can change your appointment? Tell him Françoise Gemmer, *The Most Beautiful Woman In Provence*, desires to meet with you. Michelin will understand."

After Max hung up the phone with François he called his patron. "Apparently we have a mutual friend, Françoise Gemmer from Les Baux."

"Oui, I am well acquainted with her. She is a beautiful woman, very talented and has given me valuable guidance regarding art. Her advice to me has proved to be quite lucrative. I am not surprised that you know her. You must have met her in Avignon or at an art event."

was mentioned in the article simply as, "the wife." I will send you some newspaper clippings. You may find them interesting."

Max asked me if I had ever seen the Cézanne over Maurice Michelin's mantle. I had not. It must have been a recent acquisition. Then he told me how Maurice came to acquire it. I thought it odd. Michelin always bought major works through established dealers like myself. I first met him when he came into my Avignon gallery and bought three of Max's paintings and a large sculpture by Robert Chéron. Over the years I helped him build his collection. It wasn't an exclusive relationship; I knew the other dealers Maurice worked with and sometimes I worked with them to secure major pieces of art for him.

Françoise told Max she had a meeting in Apt in the morning, but could see him in Saint Rémy that the afternoon. "I know the village well, I can serve as your personal guide so to speak. Let's meet at Durand's chocolate shop, I am in love with his orange confitures."

As she was about to hang up the phone, he said, "I forgot to tell you, I brought home that little kitty you were playing with at the café."

"Bravo, have you given her a name?""Yes, Putty

Tat,""That's a strange name, where did you come up with that?" Max laughed, "You know, Tweety Bird and Putty Tat." Françoise had no idea what he was talking about. I did, it was

a famous American cartoon about a cat and a bird. I remember seeing the cartoon film in an exhibition at the Museum of Modern Art in New York.

Françoise's comment was, "Give her a nice French name."

The rendezvous went as planned. Max told me the chocolates were outstanding. He compared them to Bloomingdale's near the Lexington subway station and Varsano's Chocolates on 6th Avenue in New York, "They are not overly sweet, small, and very expensive, but worth every franc."

After feasting at Durand's, Françoise took Max shopping. She told him she needed a scarf and a floppy wide brim cap to keep the sun from her face. As they were walking along window- shopping, she complained, "I'm disappointed with the quality of merchandise here, these shops apparently cater only to tourists. Everything is cheap and probably made in Vietnam or China. I will have to go to Avignon or Nice to find something decent."

As they rounded the corner, she grabbed Max's

arm and pulled him into a pharmacy. "I need some lipstick and sunscreen."

While he was looking at postcards, he glanced over to see her put a toothbrush into her purse. How odd he thought, why would someone of her stature do that? They left the shop and Max asked, "You couldn't find what you needed?"

"No. They only carry L'Oreal and I won't put that merde on my lips.

Max thought he might ask her to stay the night in St. Remy. Unbeknownst to him, Françoise was ten steps ahead of him; she had packed the Carine Gilson negligee that she purchased in a shop on rue de Grenelle in Paris. Over a dinner of trout smothered with slices of truffle, she whispered into his ear that she wanted to stay the night with him. They did not linger for dessert. In the darkness of the candle lit hotel room, their lovemaking was gentle and slow, her sighs sensual. He thought her tongue on his neck, behind his ears and in his mouth was delicious.

In the morning they went to a nearby boulangerie where they indulged in sweet rolls with Moroccan coffee. There was only one other couple in the shop, and they were obviously German. It was an easy deduction for Max. They were dressed in leather, and a motorcycle was parked out front of the bakery. Françoise whispered to the waitress who was pouring her coffee, "Je déteste les Allemands, ils sont tellement désagréable. La plupart d'entre eux sont laid à regarder et ne ont pas de classe." (I hate Germans; they are so rude. Most of them are ugly to look at and have no class).

In perfect English the woman snarled, "Uncouth, rude, crude. I agree, they are a bad lot."

Max lowered his head, sipped of his coffee and took a quick peek at the Germans

There was a small dog running around licking up crumbs from under the four round tables in the small front room. The pup may have belonged to the waitress who pretended to be too busy sweeping up the floor to refill the Germans' coffee cups. Maybe the dog's owner was the baker in the back room, punching his chunky fists into the dough on a rickety table. The table legs banging on the uneven oak floor made Françoise smile. She leaned

across and whispered in Max's ear, "Our waitress said all this racket will make the Krauts leave."

It was not the noise that got the Germans to leave; it was the dog peeing on a nearby chair. The overweight male Kraut rose from his chair and tried to kick the dog, but lost his balance and then fell flat on the floor. His wife helped him up. They left without leaving a tip and the waitress yelled, "trous ass " (ass holes).

The waitress asked Françoise if there was anything more she or Max required, Françoise requested more coffee, thanked the woman and asked if they might have it pored into a paper cup. Françoise took Max's arm and led him to the door. With coffee in hand, he managed to push the door open with his behind. He took a deep breath of the succulent Provencal early spring air and then kissed Françoise on the cheek. They crossed the tree-lined road and entered a small garden park filled with bear's breeches and iris, wisteria and bougainvillea climbed up a stone wall that once had been the side of a house. The primrose was in bloom, its yellow flowers enticed Max to open his knapsack and take out his sketchbook and watercolors.

They sat side by side on a green iron bench and he began to draw. His book was already half filled with images of olive trees, mountaintops and ancient Roman ruins. Françoise watched him take a pencil and lightly draw the outlines of a twisting woody wisteria vine fixed to the grey stones of the old building. The rocks came from one of the quarries that used to supply the Luberon villages with building materials and jobs. He sipped his coffee and a drip fell from his mustache onto the rag paper surface he was working on. Françoise jerked when she saw the coffee splatter on the drawing. Max told her it was all right, the coffee stain would blend in when he added watercolor. She took a paper handkerchief from her shoulder bag and blotted his mustache. He laughed; she frowned.

As he worked on his piece, she asked questions about his life. He spoke of growing up in South Carolina and his father and mother's love for each other. He spoke about Robert and me. He talked about his studio in California, the galleries that represented him in Atlanta, Chicago and New York City. He told her about the important Corcoran Biennial where his work hung alongside America's most important painters, the one man show at the Brooklyn Museum, the awards he won and the art publications that featured articles about his work. He told her he had never married, fathered no children and never been arrested.

"Clean as whistle. No complications, that's good. Very good, that's what I want in a man!"

Françoise disclosed little of her background or her life in Paris. Max had a feeling there were secrets.

She mentioned little about her own artwork and nothing about the Louvre. Max thought it odd when out of the blue she said, "My husband says my desires are abnormal" Max felt she was hinting at something intriguing.

"I enjoy my time alone. Often I dress up and imagine I am with lovers, alone in my bedroom. By myself, I act out the most luscious fantasies. Do you think I'm perverted?"

Without hesitating, Max replied. "I am not one to form opinions as to what is perverted or not. To each his own."

"I like that in a man; I liked it in Picasso."

A few days after they had visited Saint Remy, she invited him to dinner at her place. Max told me she lived in a small apartment over a café. The building, he thought, could have been 400 years old, or maybe even older. He said he had gathered flowers from a garden near the Goat Gate in Lacoste. He thought about bringing wine, but decided on the aperitif Génépy because it was made from flowers of the Alps. Max, you see, is a romantic.

When Max arrived at her apartment, he noticed a bag hung on her door latch. He removed it and several pieces of mail fell on her doorstep. He thought it odd. In small villages throughout Provence, mail deliveries do not come to the residence; one simply walks to the post office each day or so to get the mail. As he picked up the pieces he found two hand-addressed envelopes to her, one from Sotheby's and the other from Christie's. He put them under his arm, intending to give them to his hostess.

Max rang the doorbell. He heard her running down the stairs. She opened the heavy oak door and threw her arms around him. He handed her the pieces of mail. She thanked him, took his hand in hers and led him up the stairs.

Max told me she was wearing a short black dress and sandals. Knowing Max, he probably observed her anatomy from behind. Like most women, she no doubt chose to walk in front of him, understanding and expecting him to observe one of her desirable assets. As for Max, I can attest to his prowess. Max is tempting; his tall, thin, yet muscular physique, is a turn on. Even when a girl knows better, he is impossible to resist. And, after all, he did bring her the most expensive aperitif along with her mail.

He gave her the bag with the magazines and a few Paris newspapers and handed her the letters.

"You may want to open these two." He handed her the ones from Sotheby's and Christies International. "Looks like the big auction houses are interested in your work."

She snatched them from his hand, "I wish; but no, they are just ads."

Max handed her the aperitif. She squeezed his arm, "How did you know? Génépy is my favorite."

Françoise poured them each a glass of wine. She showed him around her apartment. Max said the furnishings were a blend of antiques and modern. The antiques were French and the modern furniture, Italian. She offered him a seat and sat across from him. She asked what he was working on. He told her he had spent the day on a large oil painting. "What of," She asked.

"My impression of the valley below Lacoste."

She re-crossed her legs and rubbed her hand back and forth across her thigh. "Did you use photographs to work from?"

Max lifted his eyes to hers. "No, I never work that way. I absorb the landscape into my being. It is more honest that way."

"I don't understand," she said. "How is it more

honest?"

"Because the landscape I see flows into my soul. If I were to make a painting by copying a photograph that I took, that would be easy. But then, why not just leave it be as a photograph? I am looking for true impressionism. Not the impression of what lies before me, but that which resides inside me."

"I would like to try to paint your way. Will you teach me?"

"I used to be a college teacher. It almost corrupted me. I left teaching to save myself. If you want to work alongside me, and watch how I work, then that will be fine. You may ask questions. I may, or may not, answer them. Sometimes, it's best to find your own answers. The quest itself is far more important than the outcome. But I am not a teacher any longer. You will lean more from watching me than you will from talking. I will not critique your work. If this is acceptable, then join me in the studio and fields."

"I would like to try this. Yes, let's do it."

She titled her head, sniffed the air and smelled the aroma of the ratatouille cooking in the kitchen. "*Excusez-moi s'il vous plait.* Make yourself comfortable, I have a few things on the stove to attend to."

She started to walk away, stopped, turned, and began pointing as she said, "Oh, I am sorry, I have some art books you may like to look at. They are on the shelves of grand-mère's old bookcase. And also, la toilette is down the hall to the right."

He asked. "Where is your studio?""It is across from my bedroom.""I'd like to see your work.""My studio is locked. It is my sanctuary, my vault of secrets.

It is off limits to any one but me."Max walked around her living room. Most of the pillows and carpets looked to be Persian. The plaster walls were covered salon style with ornately framed traditional paintings. There were several framed photos of Françoise. Some were obviously professionally taken. There were no pictures of children, men or pets. When Max told me about this, he wrote, "This was a good sign!"

On the outer wall, next to the window facing the street, was a small oil painting that caught Max's eye. It was a garden scene, and the setting looked familiar. He recognized the place where it had been painted. The view was of a pine grove near Aix. He bent down closer to look at the details. The texture and the brushstrokes were recognizable. He touched the painting and softly ran the palm of his hand across the surface. He bent closer for a better look and, on the lower right side of the painting, he saw the signature of Paul Cézanne.

Françoise came back into the room to announce that dinner was ready. Max turned, "Wow! I just touched a Cézanne."

She smiled. "Yes, you have touched a famous artist's work. And now, Monsieur Max, you are about to taste a great chef's masterpiece."

Françoise's apartment was small, so the kitchen served as the dinning area. They sat across from each other. Max said that Françoise set the table beautifully. In 1898, Monet designed his own dinnerware. Françoise copied his idea. She also used white porcelain plates, but instead of the blue edge and a yellow rim she had reversed the colors.

The fresh eggplant, zucchini, bell peppers, and tomatoes she bought at Les Baux's Saturday market made for a perfect ratatouille. Max told her that as far as he was concerned, it could be the entre. However, as she lifted the top from the meat server and unveiled the Beef Bourguignon with its aroma of sirloin, cognac, onions, carrots, butter and wine Max said to her. "This is a culinary orgasm."

She ate like a bird. He had three helpings.

After she cleared the table she poured coffee and took a pie out of the oven. It was a pecan pie. "I thought you might be missing your Carolina home," she said.

My friend was in the clutches of a woman he believed to be beautiful, maybe even a great chef, and on top of that, she admired art and artists.

With aperitif glasses and the bottle of the Génépy, they retired to the living room. He asked her a number of questions about herself. He was prodding and she played coy. Sometimes smiling, maybe yes, maybe no, she avoided telling him anything that could reveal who she was, or what she was.

Finally, she put her finger over her lips and said. "Questions, questions, questions. You Americans ask too much and say too much. Mystery is exciting. Secrets can be enticing. I think for now, you should just enjoy. I will let you know what you need to know. Besides, I want you to explore me, discover what excites me. I will lead you on a voyage to places you never imagined existed."

She took him into her bedroom. Three days later he returned to Lacoste.

He began to stay at Françoise's place once or twice a week. Just as often, she'd show up at his studio/apartment. They made it a point to be apart for at least two days a week. The arrangement was mostly Françoise's desire. She told Max she had many chores to do, friends to see and she needed time to be alone with her work. Max understood. He liked to have time for himself as well. The odd thing was that when he went to her Les Baux apartment, she would not show him what she had been working on. He asked her why. She told him to stop asking. "I will show you when I want to. Don't ask me again."

That was their first major quarrel. Max stayed away and didn't call her for two weeks. She telephoned him crying, "I miss you. Can you come over? I will make you a good American hamburger with chips."

"You mean French Fries." He said.

She hung up. Five minutes later she called him back, "Oui, frites."

Max wrote me about the incident, "When I returned she was insatiable, I was worn out, but she kept wanting more from me. My cock gave out; my tongue was so sore the next morning that I couldn't even eat breakfast."

I am sure you're wondering why Max sometimes talks to me like a sailor. Why do I put up with it? Well the truth is, when we lived together in New York City there was an old World War II Navy veteran named Willy Smoot who lived in a rent controlled flat on the floor above Max's studio. He was always coming down to see what Max was painting. He could be a pest at times but, for the most part, we both enjoyed his company. He asked Max good questions about what, and why, Max painted the things he did. They were simple yet profound questions, which drew out of Max explanations and helped Max clarify his vision. I think Willy made Max a better painter.

Willy Smoot was crusty, his language salty. He was honest. If he didn't understand a painting, he'd tell Max. Willy had no aptitude for art speak or phony art world intellectual bullshit. There was no fooling him. His bluntness could be misconstrued by a less assured artist, but from the very beginning of his career, Max was committed to finding his own voice. Trends and fads were never an influence on his style. When Willy died, I knew how deep the loss was for Max. I made a pact with Max that we would always speak about art with the same directness and colorful language that Willy Smoot employed. When he spoke like Willy, or I did the same, we both understood the honesty of our words.

I like talking like Willy; it brings out the masculine side of me. There's no need to blush and nothing to hide.

****

Françoise is coming to Max's studio more and more. She stays the night and sometimes will be there for week. Usually she works on watercolors and drawings. Every once in awhile she asks him what he thinks of piece. He doesn't bite. Far too many times he's experienced her anger when he makes a suggestion or points out a weakness. He doesn't trust her. After all, she is the toothbrush bandit.

Whenever he stays at her apartment, her studio door is locked. He's learned not to ask her, what she's been working on. He made that mistake once but never again. She was so angry that she slapped him. He walked out of her place and drove back to Lacoste. He did something once, I don't know what it was, but she cut his penis off by withholding sex for a month. When Max told me about it, I didn't use Willy words to respond, I just kept quiet. If I had tried to talk sense into Max it would have only served to place a wedge between us. My hope is that Max will end the relationship, but I fear that won't happen. She will just go to Lacoste, say she's sorry, promise it won't happen again, and then crawl into bed with him. She fucks him in so many ways!

They are back together, but it won't be long until her behavior will change. She will become frigid again. She'll pull away and he will lose himself in his work. She'll get angry and he will sulk. When she becomes amorous again, he'll take advantage. It's their pattern, and it's unhealthy.

Not long ago she suggested they go to Aix. Max knew the town was where Paul Cézanne was from. He looked forward to going to the place that inspired *"The Father of Modern Art"* as art historians like to refer to Monsieur Cézanne. It was not a long way from Lacoste and the drive was beautiful. Françoise was in a good mood and Max felt upbeat and still high from a night of intense sex with her. Françoise acted as navigator. She directed him to drive the back roads through Lourmarin and Le Puy-Sainte-Réparade where they stopped at two vineyards along the way. They decided to have lunch before they began working. Françoise knew of a place that she swore was the best eatery in the area, Chez Madame Berne. They shared a large bowl of thick beef stew washed down with red wine from a vineyard near the foot of Sainte-Victoire. Afterwards they settled in the hills just east of Aix-en-Provence to draw. The earth was red and wild rosemary and thyme was everywhere. They set up to work on a plateau that was covered with sand-colored stone remnants from the old abandoned Bibémus quarry.

Max told me he was more interested in sketching the scrubby woods and rocks around him. Françoise chose to draw the mountain. After sitting for almost three hours he decided to stretch. He rose from the flat rock from which he had been seated and walked over to where Françoise was comfortably ensconced in the folding chair she had brought. I suppose she was so entrenched in her work that she didn't hear him coming up behind her. Max looked over her shoulder and saw a magnificent Cézanne pinned to the cardboard drawing block sitting in her lap.

When she realized he was standing there she was startled and flinched. "Why are you sneaking up on me?"

He apologized and told her how magnificent the drawing was. He couldn't tell if she was pleased or upset. Finally she regained her composure. She reached over the arm of the chair, and with her latex gloved hand, picked up the sketchbook sticking out of her duffle bag. She pulled out two more Cézanne drawings that were between the empty white pages. She showed them to Max.

He was flabbergasted. "Françoise, these are amazing." She replied, "I know. I am good aren't I?"

****

Not that long ago, I think it was late June, Françoise went to Paris for a week see her lawyer. At least that's what she told Max. So I came to Lacoste. I stayed at his place. He slept on the couch downstairs and I was ensconced in his bed upstairs. His scent on the pillow brought back memories. I longed for him to come upstairs, to let me wrap my legs around his thigh and kiss him, love him and fall asleep beside him. But that won't happen anytime soon. The bitch blinds him, so I convinced myself the reason I was there was to see how his work was progressing. Max's show was scheduled to open in a year. His painting was going well, his colors and forms brilliant. The exhibition will be a huge success for both of us. However, I'm worried about Max and what this woman might do to him.

I love Provence; I love the color blue and the smell of lavender fields. On the day I had to catch the train back to Paris we spent a beautiful morning together. He had brought a carafe of coffee and Puits d'amour pastries stuffed with red currant jelly from the Boulangerie. We sat on a wall half way up the hilltop near the Goats Gate overlooking Bonnieux. Max was working on a drawing of the distant pastures and vineyards laid out across the valley below us. There were no shadows on the wheat fields; the grove of cherry trees nestled below us and just beyond, off in the distance, I could see the orange tiled roofs of farmhouses reflecting the summer sun. It was so romantic.

I didn't say a word to him, just watched as his hand sketched receding lines on his paper representing the furrowed strips of earth in between the rows of lavender plants. Time was slipping away. As much as I wanted to stay and soak in the scene of Max and his fields, I had to get on the bus to Avignon in order to catch the train back to Paris on time. We kissed. It was not the same long, lingering, repetitive kiss that I remembered during our life together in our New York Tribeca loft. Sadly, that had vanished long ago. And yet it was a kiss that reminded me to continue to be patient. Eventually, Françoise will disappear. She'll leave for greener pastures and he'll become mine again.

Before we left the house I wrote a note to Max. "I'll see you in Paris. Love, Céline." I put the note card to my lips and left a lipstick impression of my kiss. I placed it on his pillow, closed the bedroom door behind me and walked outside to where he was waiting in his car.

After I left, and before Françoise returned, Max spent a few days in the village of Saint Rémy. He wrote me a letter saying, "This morning I sketched the convoluted trunks of olive trees that have been twisted by the suffering of the earth, or those who screamed behind the walls of the *Asylum for the Alienated*, that hospital where Vincent van Gogh was confined. For me, it is sacred ground. If I were a Muslim, I would go the Mecca, but I am an artist, so I go to the place where *Starry Night* was painted."

"I am sitting in an olive grove across from the Roman ruins of Glanum. I have set myself up to work under the tree that has the widest span and the most shade. My intention is to make a drawing that will capture the twisting limbs of the olive trees. I'm not interested in the leaves of the trees, nor do I care much about the olives themselves. No, what fascinates me are the gnarled trunks that have the character of old grandfathers. Stretching and twisting sideways in all directions, the branches spread outward and up toward the sun. Slender green shoots from last years pruning have begun to form a canopy. The openness of each tree is so well trimmed that a swallow can fly through the tree without brushing its wings against a branch."

"I removed an over-ripe melon from my knapsack, a corkscrew and a bottle of local wine I had picked up in St. Remy at the shop next door to Nostradamus's house. Before I started drawing, I had opened a book of van Gogh's letters that I bought from a bookseller in the village. Some of them were written to his brother Theo during his confinement in the asylum across from where I'm sitting. I can hear the raspy songs of cicadas in the trees. Vincent must have heard them too. I feel sweat running down the ridge of my nose, just now I watched it drop on this piece of paper I'm sending to you."

On one of their many drawing excursions Max and Françoise went to Arles. The two walked inside the ancient Roman ramparts surrounding the old city. They ate dinner at the popular Café La Nuit on the Place du Forums. Streetlights illuminated the café where tourists stood in line for an hour or more waiting to be seated. It was the same place van Gogh and his friend Gauguin often went. Max and Françoise were seated outside under the yellow awning. They enjoyed fish with tapenade, carrots and potatoes and for dessert they shared chocolate noisette. Max said the food was meant more for tourists than locals. The hotel where they stayed was close by. It was a 15th century building built upon Roman ruins from the time of Constantine. After their meal they strolled along the Alychamps, the Roman cemetery where crypts line the walkway. It was late evening and the moonlight made the poplars, cypress and pine trees visible in the night sky.

Their hotel room was romantic. They closed the double doors to the balcony and Françoise tied Max to the bed. She teased him, she tortured him, he licked her, but she never touched him. She climaxed and then left the room. Two hours later she returned and untied him. She told him she had taken another room in the hotel and closed the door behind her. Max told me he was not upset, he said he masturbated and his ejaculation hit the ceiling. GOOD BOY MAX!! WISH I WERE THERE TO CATCH YOUR CUM WHEN IT FALLS.

****

As Max told the story, the next day he and Françoise walked three miles in the blazing

Provencal sun to the drawbridge over the Canal Bouc. It was similar to the one van Gogh painted, the one where two lovers stroll hand in hand over a yellow bridge. Max sat in the high grass along the canal bank and drew a view from the south looking north toward Arles. Françoise walked a ways further and sat alone with a piece of paper and a pencil and began to draw the bridge tender's house.

Max stared at the bridge and imagined Vincent standing beside him painting the scene of the lovers on the bridge. Vincent was tense; a pipe was tightly clamped between his tobacco stained teeth. Max noticed that one tooth was missing. Sweat was dripping off the end of his nose. His paintbrush was moving constantly between the palette held in his hand and the canvas that rested on a rickety easel. The easel was tied down to pegs that the Dutchman

must have hammered into the soft earth. Every once in awhile he coughed and spit into the canal.

"Vincent, take it easy, it's hot out here."

Without looking at Max, van Gogh shouted. "Hot! It's always hot in Arles. If you can't take the heat go back to wherever you came from."

"Your painting is coming along nicely, you don't seem to be struggling with the composition and your colors are flowing nicely."

"What do you know about struggle? You've never gone hungry, you sell your work"... Vincent looked at Françoise. "You have a girlfriend. I bet all your teeth are still in your mouth and there's money in your pocket! You're not an outcast. You're already famous, I'll be dead before anyone knows my name."

As Vincent continued his tirade, a splash of yellow oil paint hit Max's cheek. "They call me a madman. You know what I'm going to do soon? I'm going to slit my throat. The crows will try to stop me; I'll get a gun and shoot them. Maybe I'll shoot you. How would you like that?" Vincent walked away and disappeared into a field of sunflowers.

Max got up and walked to where Françoise was working. She was unaware of Vincent's presence, she probably heard Max mumbling and thought nothing of it. Sooner or later she'd catch on to his hallucinations, and like most of the people who spent time with him, she'd think he was mildly schizophrenic too. I knew better, Max is gifted.

Max told me that she folded her drawing so that he couldn't see what she had done. She grabbed his shirt and pulled him down. He started to ask her if he could see what she had created. She hushed his lips, pushed him down prone into the tall grass, unzipped his pants, pulled out his cock and began to run her tongue up and down on his stiff shaft. Just as he was about to explode she rolled off of him and began to cry. "I can't," she said.

Sweating, and still hard as a rock, he put his forehead in his hand and pleaded, "Why, why do you do this?"

"Don't ask me."

Max repeated his question, but this time with more authority. She didn't like that.

Her mood changed. She became angry. "Don't ask me questions. I will tell you things when I want to. I hate men who ask questions. If that's the kind of man you are it will be over between us."

They walked back to the city in silence. The rest of the day she remained distant and very quiet. She refused dinner. That night she remained in her room. Max walked the streets alone. A dark-skinned young girl propositioned him.

Max called me from a pay phone and asked where he could spend a thousand dollars for a meal in Arles.

I said, "Are you drunk?"

"No, but I'm going to be. I can't talk now, just tell me the best place to take a beautiful woman."

"Who, Françoise?""No, fuck her!"I remember saying, "Good, than I suggest Le Criquet." "Is it expensive?""V ery""Good!" He hung up.

Le Criquet was crowded. The guests were dressed to the hilt in fine clothes and the women wore their most expensive jewelry. Their fingers sparkled like the fine champagne on the tables. Heads turned when they saw the scruffy painter and the scantly dressed Vietnamese girl. Max said the whispering in the room was like the humming of the bees. Max tipped the maitre d' 200 francs. He smiled; my guess is that he was amused to have a vastly different kind of customer than the snobby want-to-be aristocrats he was used to showing to the tables. He took Max and the girl to a table window and handed my friend the menu. Max told me later that I was right; it was a very expensive place. The sommelier came and discussed the wine list and at first made a suggestion that was clearly top of the line. The man probably thought he was embarrassing the painter. Max said, "très bien."

Max and Aimée enjoyed an incredible meal. He learned a bit of her history. He wasn't sure how much was fiction or what was truth. My friend decided to believe every word she said. He paid 700 francs for the meal and left a 300-franc tip. Max walked Amie back to where he met her. A week earlier I had sold one of Max's paintings for a considerable sum, so, as you Americans like to say, he was flush. Max handed her a check for 5,000 francs and said, "Go home to your own country, take care of your family. This is not the life for you."

She cried, thanked him, kissed him, asked him if he was Jesus, and promised to go home to Vietnam. He kissed her cheek and walked away whistling.

The next morning Max rose to the soft knocking on his door. It was Françoise. She crawled into his bed and snuggled close to him. "I am sorry for last night. I just am frightened that I might be hurt."

"Hurt by whom, me?"

She put her finger to his lips shushing him. He presumed, she was talking about him, hurting her. After all, he was always the one to get blamed when she felt wounded.

Exhausting his manly reserves, she fucked him over and over again. He was convinced she was insatiable. She was insatiable for something much more than sex.

The next day they visited the Abbey of Montmajour, a medieval church built atop of a hill that sat on an island in the middle of sea marshes. The marshes had long ago been filled in to create pastures for farmland. The abbey was stunning and provided almost endless views of the fields below. The only thing on the horizon was the city of Arles. From its high ground, Vincent van Gogh painted the fields with a train and wagon off in the distance. Looking east, Max drew the view of farms sitting in fields of sunflowers and wheat. With their orange tiled roofs, the small farmhouses were settled upon crisscross fields of citron green and yellow. Beyond, under clear cobalt skies stood the cliffs of Alpilles and the familiar village of Les Baux.

Françoise took Max's sketchbook from his lap and led him to the church. The sanctuary was empty. Statues of saints, and even the altar and pews had been looted and taken away long ago. Only the shell of the once magnificent building remained. Its stone walled, domed ceiling and granite floors echoed with the sound of their footsteps. Thier whispered voices bounced and echoed in surround sound.

Max said he sang Don McLean's song *"Vincent."*

I've heard Max sing that song many times before. If he weren't an artist, he could have been a singer in a band or a church choir. The sound of his voice must have been magical, the acoustics in a place like that resonate and reverberate. I once heard a child singing in the Cathedral Notre Dame. It wasn't a performance; it was just a young girl entertaining herself. I felt I was listening to Édith Piaf, that's how good it sounded.

Max told me Francoise began to dance and he thought of Isadora Duncan. He said "*The most beautiful woman in Provence* spun and twirled across the expanse of stone flooring. I was mesmerized by the flow of her sundress. It was like looking up into the sky and watching fast moving clouds cross from the west to the east. At times her movements were ethereal, and at other moments, provocative."

She pulled him to her and ran her hand up his thigh and touched him. He became aroused and she could feel his firmness. Like a tango dancer in a Montmartre dance hall, she pushed him away and then teased him back towards her. They were alone; she took his hand and drew it up under her dress. The sound of her orgasm bounced off the church walls. I guess both God and Satan smiled.

God created sex to procreate, but the devil uses it to

drag souls into hell.

The next day they returned to the Arles drawbridge. As Max told me, Françoise struggled with a difficult perspective view of the bridge and erased and erased until she got it right. The old lady who lived in the bridge tender's house came out to tell her to put something on her head to protect her face from the sun.

"You are so young and pretty, you don't want to become an old wrinkled woman like me do you?"

As if Francoise were a beauty pageant judge, she smiled, placed her fingers and thumb on the old woman's chin, then gently turned her head from one side to the other and said. "No, I don't see any winkles that mar your skin, I only see the lines of a life well lived."

The old woman blushed and went back into the bridge tender house. She returned with a straw bonnet, placed it on Françoise's head and tied the blue and yellow ribbon under Françoise's jaw. The old woman kissed Françoise on the lips, and like a schoolgirl, the old maid skipped, yes actually skipped, back inside and closed the door shut.

Françoise showed her drawing to Max. He told me he held it in his hands and for almost a minute and was unable to say anything. He was stunned. He said it was as if he were looking at a Rembrandt. Finally he turned to her and said, "Françoise, this is beautiful. It's as good as any Renaissance drawing or Dutch Master piece I've ever seen."

She was flattered. She tilted her head and said. "You're not the only one who can draw!"

From that point on he recognized she was far more talent than he had first realized. It was obvious to Max; she had skills and abilities far beyond an amateur. His respect for her as an artist changed. He wrote telling me how incredibly talented she was. What did he think? He knew a woman could be both beautiful and talented at the same time. Max was not a sexist. He was an admirer of Georgia O'Keeffe, Lois Mailou Jones, Joan Mitchell, Frida Kahlo and thought Helen Frankenthaler was the best painter in modern times. Over the years we had many discussions about the history of art and women. For centuries the art world was ruled and dominated by men. Okay, there were a few woman painters who reached prominence, Elizabeth Vigée Le Brun, Gentileschi, Ruysch, Marie–Gabrielle Capet and maybe a few we know in history, but that doesn't compare to the vast number of men who made their living and reputations as so called "Great Artists!"

Historically societies consigned women to the crafts. Yes, Berthe Morisot and Mary Cassatt received respect, but it seemed that 19th century art critics relegated them as secondary to their male impressionist compatriots. But then, that shouldn't be a surprise; all the art critics were men.

Returning to his studio the next day, Max and Françoise spent the night together. They had dinner at the Café du Sade and then sat on the stone wall that overlooked the valley of the Vaucluse. They had a bottle of wine from one of the cooperatives near Avignon. They watched the swallows catch the evening insects as they flew back and forth between Bonnieux and Lacoste.

Looking out towards the expanse of the valley below, Françoise was staring at the view. She told Max she was thinking of the earlier conversation about her marriage.

She whispered, "I need beaucoup amour,"

Max liked the sound of that. He told me he said, "Don't we all."

She licked the tip of her forefinger. "For me, lovemaking must be erotic, if it isn't, then it's boring. I don't have patience for boring."

Such talk can make a man either dumb or eloquent.

Max was more prone to the latter.

Max told her he agreed and said, "Yes, we artists are provoked by sensual observation. By nature we are voyeurs, are we not? We are sightseers, recorders, and follow few rules. We are also carnal creatures. Have you ever run your hand across Rodin's sculpture *The Kiss* in the Hôtel Biron, if not, you should. Mark my words; it will bring you to an orgasm."

According to my friend, she kissed him and then lowered her head saying, "There are times when I'm afraid of who I am."

Max probably squinted, that was one of his facial clues that I came to recognize when he was perplexed. I can image the quizzical tint to his voice when he replied, "Why?"

He told me that within a nanosecond, her demeanor changed. "For a moment," he said, "She clenched her teeth then yelled at me."

"Stop. I don't want to talk about it." She screamed.Max had experienced her abrupt changes in mood before. He knew enough to back off. He couldn't help but wonder what had set her off, or what she might be withholding. They returned to the car and drove back to Lacoste in silence. There was no sex.

He told me. "If I didn't know it was summer in Provence, the coldness in the room would have frozen me."

At dawn, with his cup of coffee in hand, he left the studio and walked to the stone terrace to watch the sun rise over the valley. Birds were singing, and from some distant farm in the valley below, a rooster crowed. Max loved to watch the sun burn away the morning mist. Since coming to Lacoste it had become part of his routine, coffee in the morning, a splash of cream, a teaspoon of sugar and the sunrise.

By nine he would be drawing in the fields. At three in the afternoon, back to the house to eat and take a siesta, then into the studio to refine what he had drawn in the valley below the village earlier in the day. At nine, as the sun was disappearing, he stopped the creative flow to have dinner. One or two nights a week he'd cook something simple to eat, but on most evenings he felt he owed it to himself to have his meals in the village or drive to his favorite restaurants in Bonnieux or Menerbes. Depending on how tired he was, or how driven by creative energy he felt, he'd either go to bed or stay up late into the night painting. Oftentimes, the coolness of a Provencal summer night was the best time for him to work on oil paintings.

For Max, painting was like dueling with swords. He'd plunge his brushes into mounds of oil paint squeezed from large tubes of color onto the glass palette that sat upon a table by the side of his easel. Then, scooping up the globs of colors, he would mix blues, yellows, and shades of red together or lay greens, purples and yellows into white pigment in the middle of his palette. From there he would add safflower oil, a dash of water, a drop of Japan drier and a small amount of damar varnish and begin blending the colors to the exact tone and consistency that he felt compelled to create. Loading his paintbrush with color, he'd turn and charge the canvass on the easel. Max would attack and splash the color on to the canvas, paint would fly across the white cotton duck surface and splatter on his walls, floor and self. In his battle with the canvas his brush strokes where thrust with power and conviction. The ox and squirrel hairs of his brushes, loaded with color, would sweep, twist, turn, push, drag, and pull color to create forms without conscious thought into skies, trees, villages, fields and mountains. Sometimes the easel would shake and the painting would topple towards him, but Max was too nimble, too quick to be caught by the flying canvass. A painting could take an hour, a day, weeks or months, to be resolved to his satisfaction. And when done, his paintings were sublime.

Like most other summer days, Max began the day with drawing. But this time he chose not to leave the village. He sat on the wall near Marie's boulangerie. It was extremely hot, sweat beaded on his forehead and dripped down his nose. His arms and hands were moist and he knew the sun would win this battle; he'd soon be forced to return to his house and studio where his 5 electric fans made living in Provence bearable. But at that point he figured he could take a couple of hours to work outside. Max began to draw an image of the swallows over the little chapel on the hill. He drew the swallows swooping down from above the building and the gardens below. The drawing had a mysterious perspective. It was as if he were a part of the flock, a bit distant from the others, observing, watching, but never landing.

Françoise found him and came to his side. She asked if he would drive her home. During the ride she touched him and laid her head on his shoulders. He didn't say anything just enjoyed the experience. She kissed him, ran her hands through his hair repeating his name three times.
"Max...Maxfield...My Maxfield."

When they reached Les Baux she kissed him,

saying, "I will see you in a few days. I have a meeting with a colleague."

Max asked whom. She replied, "A colleague?"

She titled her head and coquettishly smiled, "Are you jealous?"

"No, of course not, just wondering. I didn't know you had a "colleague." Is this a business associate?"

"Oui, he is in the art trade.""Is he a dealer?"She cut his questioning off. "Sort of. Look I have to go now.

I will see you in a few days."They kissed. She smiled. He left confused, curious and pissed by things he didn't know were happening.In early August, Max called to tell me Françoise had filed divorce papers. From what I had read in the papers, (and passed on to Max), her husband's secrets were about to be revealed. I assumed Françoise needed to get as far away from him as she could. Allegations against him concerning secret bank accounts in Russia had been leaked by an anonymous government source to the le Monde reporter, Jean Legris. None of the details had been released, only that improprieties were suspected. However, there must be something to them because

Françoise's husband resigned his office in the Ministry of Finance.

Max told me she rarely spoke to him about her husband. Once he made the mistake of asking her about him and she got angry. Very angry. She threatened that if he asked again, she'd end their relationship. After that, Max never asked anything about him. Max told me he had inklings that there was something strange, something hidden. Maybe even something forbidden.

****

Off and on throughout the summer, Françoise would stay at Max's studio. She would return to her Les Beax apartment for a week or so each month, but most times without Max. When he asked her why he couldn't accompany her, she replied, "A woman has her secrets."

There were many days when the two of them woke early and headed into the countryside for inspiration. Françoise always wore latex gloves when she worked. Max thought it odd, especially working outside in the heat Provence. He once asked her why she always covered her hands.

She told him that it was to protect her nails. "I pay a steep price to make these hands look nice for you. Only Chanel for me."

She created drawings, watercolor sketches and a few oil paintings. Just like Max, the lavender and wheat fields, sunflowers, vineyards and quaint villages captivated her. Max didn't say it her, but he did tell me her work was tight and too realistic for his taste. Her imagery was safe, he said. And yet she had skills comparable to Rembrandt and Frans Hals.

When he first began working with her, he came to the conclusion that a man should never make assumptions about a woman, especially a French woman. But despite her experimental sexual nature, her work wasn't always expressive or passionate. Sometimes she asked Max for advice. He would tactfully demur, suggesting she go to a library or museum to look at various artists he thought would inspire her. When she requested a critique, he'd usually counter by asking what she thought of her piece. "Long ago" he said, "I learned it was better for students to find their own answers." It was also clear to him that if he said the wrong words, at the wrong time, she'd chop his head off.

As summer was coming to a close they visited Gordes, a popular summer town perched on the face of a cliff. The village was known for its several galleries and quaint tourist shops. They went there to visit a gallery that had contacted me about lending them a few of Max's small drawings. Even though I was planning a large exhibition of his work at my Paris Gallery, I went ahead and approved putting a few of his pieces in the Gordes gallery space. I felt it would be a good venue to promote what I was planning regarding his one-man show in Paris.

Max said the Gordes opening was well attended and he was most grateful for the opportunity to meet several other artists working in Provence. He said the majority of other artists in the show were from other countries and only spending the summer there to market their work to the tourist trade or the wealthy part- time residents living in the south of France. Most of the people attending were either Japanese art lovers enamored with impressionism or rich Europeans who had second homes in Provence. He mentioned that he met an elegantly dressed Russian man who seemed quite interested in this work. The gentleman's English was almost unintelligible so the conversation was difficult. However, it was clear, that of all the artists in the show, the Russian was interested only in Max's work.

Max alerted me so that I would be watchful should he appear at my gallery in Paris. "Céline you will easily recognize him, he is rather muscular and has a deformed ear."

I had not attended the opening. I chose not to because I was uncomfortable with meeting Françoise. Max was smitten with Françoise; according to him, she was the woman of his dreams. It was hard to hear him say that. Obviously, he had forgotten that he had once said the same thing to me! The idea of jealousy is repugnant to me. I didn't want to be jealous. But, after all, Max had been my greatest lover. I secretly wanted him back, and as much as I wanted to tell him that, I didn't!

It was foolish. I know that now. But at the time I was afraid of being rejected. I was not some immature college girl who hadn't had experience with love and men. I should have screamed at Max that I was better for him than she was. I had far more to offer a man than a typical woman could. I was over fifty years old...successful...smart...attractive, (gorgeous as a matter of fact). It was not that I needed him! I was self-confident. I had been married. It didn't work. Too bad, not my fault and that's my truth. I've had my share of lovers. Some were just for sex and others because I cherished them. But dammit, why did I blow it with Max? FUCK! Why did he blow it with me?

I should have done something, but I didn't. Drawings get erased, people shouldn't.

A few days after the event he called me. He was pleased. All but three drawings were sold. During our conversation, he informed me he was planning to come to Paris. We needed to plan his upcoming show and he also wanted to deliver a portfolio of new watercolors to me. He mentioned he was not bringing Françoise. That was good, we had to organize the show and distractions would be ill advised. There were critics to court, magazine ads to design, the reception to plan, and the invitation lists of collectors, cultural ministers and professors from the École des Beaux-Arts to compile. He asked if he could stay at my apartment. I of course said, "Yes." It was a glorious week. It felt like the old days in New York. Me and my lover staying in bed till noon, coffee at a museum's café or taking a walk through gardens, discussing art and movies into the late afternoon, maybe a play after dinner or an evening of nightclub hopping. The next day the same thing and the day after that, a repeat. It was hard to see him leave, but his painting and obsession with "*The Most Beautiful Woman in all of Provence*" drew him back to the village of Lacoste.

Fall came and Françoise didn't go back to Paris. Winter brought the stronger Mistral winds to the Vaucluse. At times they blew so hard that Max could not set foot outside, not even to run to the bakery for his favorite pastry. The windstorms raged for days but every once in awhile they stopped to rest. Most days it was impossible to work outside so Max refused to go outside. Putty Tat wouldn't go out either. The Mistral gave Max time to frame drawings and watercolors. He also completed 7 large abstractions based on the views he sketched during the summer.

For the most part, Françoise stayed at her apartment. The drive up and down the mountains between Lacoste and Les Baux was treacherous. Her small car could easily be flipped by a gust of wind. It was not safe to drive when the Mistral carried pieces of houses, farm buildings, trees and even an occasional cat or stray dog tumbling across the narrow road. On good days she would come to his studio, on calm nights he'd drive to Les Baux and spend the night. Sex was less frequent, shopping sporadic and anything outdoors was, as Max called it, "A pain in the ass."

Because of the wind, Max often found himself

staying at Françoise's apartment for two or three days. The same was true for her at his place. There was a difference though. She could work in his studio, but he was not allowed into hers. This vexed Max and increased his curiosity as to why she was so secretive about the room; the door was always locked. He could sit in her kitchen and sketch, but he had to be neat and that cramped his style.

One day, while working for hours on a pen and ink drawing in his studio, Françoise said to Max, "I don't have a style of my own. I'm a better copier of other artists' works."

She held up her sketch paper and he was not completely surprised to see that she had perfectly rendered a Picasso-like drawing of her and Max and Pablo in a three way romp. It was suffused with sexuality and came effortlessly out of her head.

Max told me about it, saying, "If someone saw it in a gallery they'd swear it was done Pablo Picasso."

He told me Françoise took the drawing out of the sketchbook, ripped it into several pieces and then threw it into the wood burning stove, saying, "Not good enough."

Max raised his forearms, turned the palms of his hand towards her and with an almost shocked expression asked her. "Good enough for what, for whom? I don't understand."

She smiled, "For me, of course. What did you think, for the Louvre, for the National Gallery of Art in your own country?"

"It would have been nice to hang in my studio or your apartment. A memento of our sex life together with Picasso."

She laughed. "I don't think so, your neighbors would disapprove. They already think we are perverts."

"Perverts! I could care less what people in the village think. There are several artists who live in this village and they would find it amusing. But most of all, my friend Robert would really enjoy it."

"You've spoken so many times to me about Robert. When am I going to meet him? He sounds like such an interesting man."

Max began to think about her desire for a threesome. There was a momentary tinge of excitement, but then the idea of having sex with his best friend and Françoise was not fitting with his side of that fantasy. It was repulsive. Max always thought of sex with a stranger as being exciting. Someone unknown, maybe a person with a different nationality or racial background, a stranger met on the street or in the bar. That was more to Max's liking.

When Max wrote me about this episode, I was not shocked. We had experimented once in a similar way. I found it enjoyable, but not surprisingly, it scared the hell out of Max and we never did it again.

Max paused for a moment to think about his friend's attributes and just what to reveal to Françoise. Max had reached a point with Françoise where he was less open regarding his personal life. He also felt at times it was best to keep her in the dark as to what he was up to. After all, Françoise was not always forthright with him. "Well, he plans to be at my opening in Paris. I think you'll like him. I hope you like him. Like Céline, he is a best friend. I trust him like a brother; there are no secrets between us. He's extremely talented and as I told you, he's done lots of work for the Louvre. He's a devoted family man, but also a bit of a rake. He has a great sense of humor, drinks a little too much and seems to always be in need of money."

Françoise kissed Max on the cheek, "I look forward

to meeting him."

Winter in Provence that year was typical; the whistling winds kept the skies blue and the nights cold. More often than not, the gales blew for days on end. When the winds blew especially hard and fast, Max closed and latched the wooden shutters to keep the dust from rolling across the floor. The shutters rattled and it was hard to sleep at night or read a book or even listen to music on the radio. There were times when making art became impossible. The banging sounds from outdoors had Max running to the door where day after day he obsessively looked outside for damage. Constant interruption is not conducive for contemplation, so his painting suffered. But as spring got closer, the winds became less frequent, less intense, and the village's people and their pets began to venture outside. For Max, who had just experienced his first winter in Provence, spring allowed him to escape what he referred to as his house arrest.

In February he saw his first bee and heard a bird singing in the cypress tree near the boulangerie. By March, a lawn mower sputtered in someone's yard, and in the valley below Lacoste, cows mooed in fields of emerging green grass filled with daffodils. He walked out his door to see a bird sitting on the budding twig of an almond tree near the Goats

Gate. He swept up the debris left by the wind in the corner of his garden wall. It felt good to be outdoors. The air was now clean and fresh and a breeze, not a storm, moved it about. His neighbors could re-plant, prune or just sit in the sun and smile.

As spring came along, Max and Françoise needed to unwind, to enjoy the excitement and pleasures of village life again. Being confined in the two small communities was difficult for Max, but more so, especially hard on Françoise. She was, after all, used to spending the fall and winters in Paris. I can't image myself being in the south of France for so long without getting out. Provence is a nice place for Parisians to visit, but it's really more for foreign tourists and sightseers. There is much to enjoy there in late spring and especially during the summer months, however, its primary attraction is the countryside and it's quaint villages. The landscape, as opposed to a cityscape is what it offers. It fits Max's needs well. He is an artist, influenced by the same milieu that inspired van Gogh and Cézanne. There are other parts of France that have also had a significant influence on art. Certainly the areas around Brittany, Pontoise and the Barbizon provided vistas, and still do, which influenced Pissarro, Monet, Gauguin and hundreds of other artists of prominence and thousands of wannabes.

On a warm May evening they decided to drive to Avignon for dinner. Françoise called the commune "The City of Popes." Seven centuries ago Bertrand de Got was elected Pontiff. He refused to go to Rome, choosing instead to install himself in a Dominican Convent in Avignon. Seven Popes governed the Catholic Church from there until 1417, when of the seat of the Papacy returned to Rome.

There was a restaurant, the Bistrot Roquette, on the left bank of the Rhone River not far from the spot where Vincent van Gogh painted his first star filled night scene. The owner and chef, René Boulle, was a close friend of Françoise's, he loved to kiss her cheeks. René was known throughout southern France for his sauces and his use of the finest meats. Whenever Françoise called to say she was coming to his place, she would tell him to have snails and rabbit fricassee with morel mushrooms ready for her. The poor man had to stockpile morels just for her. She knew they were expensive and that he would not charge what they cost him; she didn't care. For dessert, both of them usually had chocolate mousse with caramel. I have been there many times myself with my gallery clients, so I know the caramel was warm and the mousse chilled. Perfect. Meals at René's are ecstasy, the next best thing to an orgasm.

On their second visit to Rene's restaurant, which may have been toward the end of May, they had their choice dinner once again. Afterwards, Max and Françoise went to a nearby hotel for a nightcap. They were sitting having a drink at the bar when Françoise began to tease both Max and a well-dressed Russian gentleman who was sitting beside her. She enjoyed being coquettish with him. Max found her playfulness erotic. There was no doubt she sent a signal of wantonness to their newfound friend. The man invited Françoise and Max to go to a party at a nearby château. Françoise asked which one. When he said the Château Rouge, she quickly agreed, saying to Max, "I have been there with Monsieur Michelin. Max you will love the owner's collection of paintings. I once accompanied Maurice to the Château. He sold one of his Picasso drawings to the owner, a Russian oligarch named Boris Volkov."

The Russian fellow smiled saying, "Yes, Volkov is my employer. But I would not describe him as a Oligarch. He is far more.

Max described what happened next. Before they left the hotel he excused himself saying he had to use the pissouir. Max told me that by the time he unzipped his pants he was so aroused that his cock was as hard a teenager. Pissing helped only a little bit to alleviate his firmness. Lucky for him his sport coat obscured his boner. When he came out of the pissouir he saw Françoise leaning close to their new friend. Her skirt was high, her legs crossed, and his hand was on her thigh. As Françoise looked over the man's shoulder, she saw Max walking towards them. She smiled at Max, he smiled back and she bent her head slightly so she could lick the Russian's ear. When Max reached them, he embraced Françoise, and said to the man who might become their shared lover, "We should party together." I knew what kind of party Max meant!

Françoise smiled and purred, saying, "Let's go!" The three left the bar, the valet brought her newly purchased Renault to the curb. Max took the drivers seat and Françoise sat on the passenger side. The Russian sat in the back and said to her he would guide them the Château. Max put his hand on her thigh, she pressed her foot on the accelerator, he shifted gears, and the Renault roared off. The car sped down Rue de la Republique, took a fast left onto Rue des Lices and then a right on N570.

As they were stepping out of the car Françoise whispered to Max that their companion's name was

Gosha. Holding both men's hands, Françoise walked between the two. They walked up the stone steps and entered Boris Volkov's opulent but tasteless home. Immediately, a server approached them with a tray of Zavalinka martinis and caviar. The music was pounding; the vodka flowed.

As the three were moving to the dance floor, a woman approached Françoise. It appeared to Max that Françoise knew this woman. Gosha asked Françoise to dance, but she declined and grabbed the woman's hand and the two hijacked the dance floor. They moved provocatively together. The other couples stopped dancing and cheered Françoise and her partner on. It was clear they were titillated by each other and encouraged by the audience. Max was aroused, but at the same time jealous. He was confused by the duplicity of his erotic feelings.

When the music changed to a slow beat, Françoise and her dance partner exited the dance floor and walked to the bar holding hands. Gosha put his arm around Max's shoulder and whispered in my friends ear, "Say au revoir to your lady."

Boris walked towards Max and Gosha. Volkov extended his hand to the other Russian saying, "Glad to see you made it Gosha. How was the drive up from Marseille?

Gosha muttered something in Russian. The chateau's owner nodded and patted the man's cheek. Volkov then turned toward Max saying, "You are the American painter who lives in Lacoste."

Max was caught off guard. Perplexed, he asked, "How did you know?"

"I have my spies. After all, I'm Russian."

Volkov looked towards the bar. With vodka in hand, he pointed his pinky finger towards Françoise and her dance partner, "I see Françoise has found a playmate."

Max felt uncomfortable looking at the Russian. Volkov had thin eyebrows and wore his obviously lightly dyed blond hair in an almost shaved fashion. His light blue eyes were so colorless that Max felt like he was looking at a vampire. There was a scar running from just below his ear to the edge of his lip. He was heavy, but not fat. One ear was misshapen and stuck out further than the one on the opposite side of his head. There was a purple mole on the side of his neck and the gray hair from it appeared to be a cousin to the three that protruded from his nose.

Volkov pointed to the remaining dancers. Max

noticed the thick gold rings on two of his fingers. One had a serpent sculpted from a ruby mounted on an onyx stone. The other, a square block of platinum engraved with the hammer and sickle of the old Soviet Union. "It seems my friend Domino and Françoise have ignited my guests. Look at how they all now dance so deliciously. I must say this looks to me like we will have a very successful party. It will be the talk of Avignon."

Gosha excused himself saying, " Please, excuse me, but I must try the herring and black bread, and of course, the shashlik. It is good to find real Russian food in this part of France."

Volkov shook his head understandingly. "When you go back to Marseille, tell our friends there that we are making great strides towards influencing our culture on the Provençale's."

He turned towards Max. Pretending to be disappointed, he made a face and said, "Our two beautiful ladies will talk about fashion, food and maybe gossip about us as lovers, or other things they have in common."

He smiled. "So, lucky for us, we can spend some time looking at other beautiful creations. Allow me to show you my art collection."

As they walked down the hall his words quickened. "I have several paintings that I am sure will intrigue you. Come, I want you to see the Monet watercolors I recently purchased. I also have a rather beautiful Cézanne still life that was painted in Aix. There are a few Picasso's and two nice Henri Matisse drawings and, of course, some of my own countrymen's work."

Excitedly, he pointed out several Kandinsky's. "I am one of only two Russian private collectors who own a Marc Chagall. I even have a Naum Gabo sculpture from the time he was living and working in Berlin, long before he settled in America in '46."

He paused for a moment, "I understand, Mister Connor, that you were once an art teacher. Did you know Gabo taught at your country's famous university, Harvard?"

Max knew the answer, but he didn't say a word.

Max had a friend, Clifford Ragnetti, who was Gabo's studio assistant in the early 60's. Later, Cliff went on to write the first definitive book on silkscreen printing for artists. As a young artist, he would visit the Manhattan galleries to see what Larry Rivers, Joseph Albers and Robert Rauschenberg were doing with the medium. Besides frequenting Sidney Janis Gallery, he often could be found nearby in the galleries of Leo Castelli and the Marlborough. On one of his tours, Ragnetti wandered into the Janis and met Max who was helping to install an exhibition of Andy Warhol's photo silkscreens of Marilyn Monroe. Cliff introduced himself and they engaged in a conversation about the emergence of serigraphy as a technique for painters. Max had pointed out that up until recent times, silkscreen had been mostly used for commercial applications. Cliff agreed and reminded him that screen-printing began in China a thousand years ago. He went on to tell Max that it was only recently in the early 1900's that printers began experimenting with photo-reactive chemicals. Max and Cliff were both proponents of the emerging recognition that serigraphs were an important means of artistic expression.

In those days the staff at the Sidney Janis was small. Max had become a part-time employee enlisted to hang exhibitions. Not wanting their conversation to stop, Cliff offered to help Max hang the show. The two labored most of the day putting eye hooks and wire on the backs of the artwork and hammering nails into the plaster walls, talking the whole time about the merits of each piece as they placed the masterpieces on the white walls of Mr. Janis's gallery.

When they completed hanging the show they walked from the storefront gallery on West 57th Street down 7th Avenue to Leo Steiner's Carnegie Deli. It was one of Max's favorite places to eat and Cliff had never been there. They each ordered a corned beef and pastrami sandwich. In those days, Steiner cured the meat in the cellar of his restaurant.

Max told Cliff to order extra rye bread. Cliff asked why. "You'll see when the sandwich gets here."

The place was packed with customers. There was a line of people waiting to get in that was a block long. Max assured Cliff that the line would move quickly. When they got in, Max and Cliff were seated at a long table beside tourists and regulars. In front of them was a crock of huge pickles to nibble on while they waited for someone to take their order. The service was fast and the place loud. Bowls, saucers, coffee cups and dishes banged as waiters and waitresses carried trays laden with Reubens, corned beef, cheesecake, Hopple Popple, nosh, "egg and oy" and salami. The yelling of staff and the accents of every borough in New York City combined with languages from all over the world. Carnegie Deli was a calliope of un-tuned sound.

Occupying a small corner table was the comedian Woody Allen and across from him sat a skinny blond girl. Woody was chattering away. She wasn't laughing. She just sat there in silence, pushing a spoon round and round in circles in the teacup in front of her.

When the meal was placed in front of Cliff he was shocked at the size of the sandwich. There was so much meat between the slices of bread that he could barely get his mouth around it.

Max laughed, "Now you understand why I told you to ask for a side order of rye bread. You can take half that pastrami and corned beef off your sandwich right now. When we're finished eating, and ready to go, have the waiter wrap your leftovers with the extra rye bread and then tomorrow you can have it for lunch."

"No, I'm eating the whole thing now!" It was clear to both of them that they shared similar tastes in artists and food.

From that time on, Max and Ragnetti were friends. When Max introduced him to me, I immediately liked him. At that time Cliff was just starting a career as a restorer of old paintings and was beginning to acquire a reputation for his knowledge of historic painting techniques. He had a beautiful redheaded girlfriend. As couples, we often went to gallery openings together, and of course we enjoyed a follow-up dinner at one of the many "Cheapie Chinese Restaurants," as we liked to call them. Other times we'd go to Carnegie's and talk about art and artists. Of course we also raved about the incredible food and enjoyed ogling whatever celebrity of the night was sitting at the corner table.

Clifford Ragnetti had taken Max to meet Gabo in his studio in Connecticut. Max remembered being awed by the man and his work. Max felt Gabo did not see himself as a Russian artist. He was no more a Russian artist than de Kooning was a Dutch artist or Hans Hoffman a German artist. They were artists, period! Where they were born had little to do with their vision, or their greatness.

The gift of creating does not derive from a nation, continent or a physical place, it comes from the muses, and the muses transcend the earth.

****

Volkov placed his meaty hand on Max's shoulder and led him through a cavernous tapestry filled hallway. Volkov pointed out three works of centuries-old Parisian tapestries made by Nicolas Bataille plus a Royal Beauvais factory piece depicting a hunt scene. But the one he was most proud of was a piece he claimed was made in St. Petersburg during the time of Peter the Great.

The clicking sound from the heels of the Russian's Saint Laurent boots on the marble floor was rhythmically out of tune with the drone of the pulsating base guitar coming from the ballroom. As they moved away from the dancing crowd of partygoers, the music and laughter faded. In a large living room filled with opulent furniture and paintings, they stood in front of an unusual Cézanne ink and wash drawing. Max thought it was out of character with what he knew about the artist's style.

Cézanne was an introverted man born and raised in Aix. His father was a prosperous banker who wanted his son to study law. Despite his father's demands to become a lawyer, he chose to become a painter. When he was a young man Cézanne moved to Paris where he studied with Camille Pissarro. He tried to make a living in Paris as a painter, but failed.

He returned to Aix and enrolled at the art school there. His father got him an appointment as a banker, but he was not suited for the profession and returned to Paris to work full time as an artist. He tried to enroll in France's most prestigious art school, the École des Beaux-Arts, but failed the entrance exam. He was disappointed, but not defeated.

Under the tutelage and influence of Pissarro, Cézanne worked beside the great French master in the fields surrounding his home, the village of Pontoise. It was through Pissarro that Cézanne met Doctor Paul Gachet, the homeopathic physician, art collector and amateur printmaker. For a time, Cézanne lived at Gachet's home in Auvers-sur-Oise. While he was influenced by the Impressionistic style of Monet and Pissarro and their insistence on painting outdoors, Cézanne, at that time, was far more interested in working in his studio on still lifes and portraits.

As he matured, Cézanne refocused his style away from Impressionism. He married and had a son. But what really made a difference in his artistic development, and the genius he was to become, was the inheritance of his father's estate. He became free from worrying about money, which allowed him to make art on his own terms. Selling paintings to provide for his family no longer mattered, only his uncorrupted, groundbreaking vision laid before him. Landscape painting became more and more important to him and the beauty surrounding his home village of Aix was the perfect source of inspiration for him.

He worked painstakingly slow. Each well-placed brush stroke was methodically thought out. Sometimes it took him hours, or even days, of contemplation before he placed his color-tinged brush onto the surface of his canvas. Every shape or form, created by his brushstroke, had to be in perfect harmony with the others. It was like creating a puzzle, and all the pieces had to fit perfectly together.

Cézanne was not an Impressionist. He was the founder of modern art. Picasso said of him, "He was like the father of us all." Matisse described him as, "The God of painting." He was, as Bonnard decreed, "The painter most powerfully armed in front of nature." His work inspired Cubism and abstract impressionism. The artists of the 20th Century became his disciples. Painters such as Matisse, Picasso, Mondrian, Braque, Morandi, Kahlo, O'Keeffe, de Kooning, Diebenkorn, Frankenthaler and even Anselm Kiefer, Lucian Freud and Damien Hirst were all his protégées.

In a boastful, almost arrogant voice, Volkov asked. "What do you think? I bought it from a dealer who knew that I would pay a substantial ransom for an authentic work by one of the most important and influential artists of modern times. He found it in a most unusual way. You might even say, unscrupulous manner. But then again, isn't that the way so much art is bought and sold?"

Max was hesitant; he didn't like Volkov, but the Russian was the host so he was somewhat coy with his reply. "It is a view of Mont Sainte-Victoire. It's unusual because in the 1890's Cézanne rarely drew a scene before he did a painting. The drawing is also very polished for a sketch. I would have thought he would have done something quickly, rougher, and less detailed. What do you know about this drawing? What is the provenance of the piece?"

Volkov sensed Max's skepticism so he gave more detail than maybe he should have. "The oil painting of Mont Sainte-Victoire is in the Hermitage Museum. The sketch I have was confiscated by a Russian soldier at the end of the Second World War. He liberated it and other Nazi artifacts from an SS bunker in Berlin. The drawing of the mountain was put in a box with other souvenirs and forgotten. Some sixty years later, after the old man died, his grandson was cleaning out the veteran's house to get it ready for sale. In the attic was the old man's footlocker full of war plunders. The stupid boy thought the rusted Nazi helmet and flag, as well as the German Luger, could make him some money. He looked at the drawing, thought it ugly and pitched it back into the trunk. Thinking the gun and helmet, plus some of the other stuff might be of value, the boy called a local antique dealer to come look at the items."

"It just so happened the dealer was a supplier of mine. My friend went through the footlocker, and as expected, he said he found the typical relics of war, but nothing of significant value. German Luger's can be found in almost any antique shop and helmets are common as well. But then he unrolled the drawing. He said he almost shit his pants when he saw Cézanne's signature. It was all he could do, to not let out a gasp. The boy must have sensed something in my comrade's smile. So the kid asked if it was any good?"

My friend shrugged and, like you Americas like to say, acted as if he couldn't give a shit about the piece. Like a piece of trash, my friend threw the drawing into the trunk, saying, "It's nothing more than a worthless sketch by some untalented Nazi."

He told the boy he'd buy the footlocker with its entire contents. "I will pay fifteen hundred rubles for the kraut helmet and gun. I also want to keep your grandfather's medals, draft notice and discharge papers. The rest of the stuff is junk and I'll dispose of it for you."

"What about the old newspaper articles?" the boy asked.

"They aren't worth anything. Everything now is on microfiche or computers. I'll throw them out with the drawing and other trash. Unless you want to keep them?"

"My friend is a crafty dealer. Make them think something is rubbish and you can steal a magnificent prize. My associate pulled out the cash and handed it to the unsuspecting teen-ager. The greedy bastard was overjoyed, took the money and probably bought his friends and himself enough cheap vodka to last a month."

"My contact told the kid not to tell anyone about the box or its contents. "When I resell this stuff I don't want to pay taxes or possible fines on this deal, and you sure as hell don't want to share your fortune with your brothers. Just tell your папа you took the shit to the dump and it cost you three rubles to dispose of it. Tell him to reimburse you. Fuck, you're a man now and you can use a few more rubles in your pocket."

Max was a man of conscience. Volkov, and probably most of his associates, were vultures. It was difficult for Max to hide his disgust. "I assume you have signatures of the boy and his family testifying to how the drawing came into the old man's possession? Often times these works of art were looted by the Nazi's from museums and private collectors. There is an effort to repatriate these works to the original owners."

Volkov lowered his head and slowly shook it, pretending to be sad. "Unfortunately, Monsieur Connor, the boy and his family died in an explosion from a gas leak. But no matter the monetary value, I intend to keep the drawing. There are collectors who don't buy art as a financial commodity. We do so because we wish to have an intimate relationship with genius."

When Max told me about his conversation with the Russian, I warned him that unscrupulous dealers and investors could be found throughout Europe. Forgers, art thieves and nefarious sellers and collectors have duped even the big international auction houses.

Max went on to tell me that Volkov took him into his study. As Max described it, there was a vast library of art books, ancient manuscripts and first edition books by the Great Russian authors. Volkov pulled three Monet watercolors from a safe hidden behind a group of books. He spread them on the table for Max to look at. Later, Max told me all three were stunning.

In 1883, Monet moved to Giverny and rented a house and outbuilding to serve as a studio. With help from his wife and children, the family made initial improvements to the property. His fame and subsequent success at selling paintings made it possible for him to buy the house and enough land to expand his gardens. He built a greenhouse and a large building for a studio with skylights, high ceilings and big doors to accommodate moving his large murals.

Monet was the architect of his gardens. His career brought commissions and buyers from around the world, allowing him to purchase a section of wetland and meadows and the ability to employ seven gardeners. In 1893 he designed lily ponds and the Japanese inspired bridge. Local French water lilies were planted alongside varieties of water plants from all over the world creating a variety of color as varied as his painting palette. Six years later he was consumed with painting his precious water lilies.

By 1900, and in his mid 60's, Monet's vision was becoming blurred. Within a short time, his perception of color changed. The once vibrant greens and blues of his paintings was becoming muted. Not long afterwards, his focus changed, almost unreadable to his viewers, his work became less impressionistic and more abstracted. Through his damaged eyes the world he looked upon had changed color. It now appeared to be yellow, not bright hansa yellow, but muted yellow ochre.

As Monet was approaching his 80's, surgery and corrective lenses were recommended for the cataracts in both his eyes. His friend, Mary Cassatt had had cataract surgery and it had not gone well for her. Thus Monet was reluctant to have the surgery. Finally, at the age of 82, he went ahead with having the operation done to his right eye. Monet was unhappy with the results, but eventually he began to discern violets and blues. However, even with his left eye clouded by a thick yellow cataract, he swore he would not do another procedure. Monet was never again able to use both eyes together effectively.

After that, his eyes worsened and Monet's work changed. He could no longer distinguish colors; light blues disappeared, and his tones became dark and muddy. He could no longer work outdoors. All the skills that had made him famous disappeared.

The three Monet watercolors appeared to have been done sometime around the last years of the old master's career. Color was splattered across the heavily sized hand-made rag paper. Sadly, it looked as though a child had painted each of the images.

Max told me the three pieces were unsigned. He told Volkov it was a shame the pictures were not signed.

"The issue of authenticity will be difficult. They're un-Monet looking. I suspect, you're going to be hard pressed to sell or exhibit them."

Volkov shook his head. "That will not be the case. I have someone from the Louvre, a conservator of considerable skill, especially as it relates to Monet and the impressionists. Domino is here to look at my Monet's. As a matter of fact, she is the woman your lady friend has been dancing with tonight. They were being quite familiar with one another, wouldn't you say?"

Max was not sure how to reply. The Russian smiled wickedly. "Tell me more about your lady friend."

"Her name is Françoise, she is an amateur painter. She lives in……."

The Russian put his finger to his lips. "My friend, please, let me give you a word of advice. Never call a French woman, 'Amateur'!"

Volkov took Max's arm and led my friend back to the ballroom. The squeaking sound of men's leather soled shoes on the dance floor sounded like pigs being castrated. The crowd's laughter had grown louder and shriller.

A waiter brought a tray of vodka martinis. Another offered caviar and horderves.

The Russian grinned, saying to Max, "Try the Salo, it is magnificent. Less meat, and more fat makes it best. It's like a plump woman; once you fuck her, you want more."

Volkov didn't see Max spit the dark salty fermented pork into his napkin.

Domino entered the room and tapped the back of Volkov's shoulder. As he turned, she said, "We have business to attend to."

Then, much like the snipping sound of scissors, she took a moment, and with sliced words said to Max, "Françoise. Beautiful. Lick...like parfait." Smiling, she walked off with Volkov.

Max looked into the crowd on the dance floor, but Françoise was not among the mass of swarming bodies. He went to the bar. She wasn't there. He wondered if she might be upstairs in one of the twelve bedrooms. Where was Gosha? Was her Renault still parked in the driveway? Was she sick in the bathroom? Was she outside in the garden? He worried, where the fuck was she? Then he felt her arms around him, she was behind him, her body sliding up and down, her mouth blowing in his ear and the scent of Shalimar close to his cheek. He turned, looked at her with suspicion and desire. There was something erotic yet disturbing about Françoise being with the man they had met at the hotel and the woman from the Louvre. She pulled him close; he tried to stand firm, but firmness only resided in his loins. A witch has so much power.

On the drive back to Lacoste the tension was palpable. Max asked if she knew the woman. Françoise told him she didn't. When they arrived back home she went to his bed, but he slept on his chair in the studio.

In the morning she went upstairs to the workspace. Like a cat that silently jumps into bed without disturbing its partner, she curled up onto his lap. She purred, "I am sorry for last night. I went too far. I must admit something to you. I do know the woman who danced with me. Many years ago my husband wanted me to deliver our small Cézanne painting to her so she would verify its bona fida. You know the painting; it's the one in my apartment here in Les Baux? For years it hung in our Paris apartment. When we separated, it came with me to Provence. He wanted it valued for insurance purposes and needed the museum to provide an affidavit as to its authenticity. Domino is a conservator at the Louvre. I haven't seen her for years and at first I didn't remember her. But she remembered me. I did see her on a few occasions at events in the Louvre and once or twice at gallery openings. There was one time when she contacted me to ask if I would consider repairing a damaged Dali drawing. I didn't feel qualified to touch, let alone work on, a masterpiece. That was the last time our paths crossed. I don't want you to think I have betrayed you. I am not lying. This is the first time I have seen her in years and there is nothing going on between us. Yes, it would be fun for us to have her together for sex but nothing more. I love you Max."

In spite of what she said, Max felt betrayed. Yet, he also had a tinge of guilt. After all, his complicity in what happened that night had to be equally shared. He was still aroused by the fantasy of her making love to her dance partner or of her climaxing with the Russian.

He took her home. He was tired and mad, and still a bit drunk, so he decided to stay the night at Françoise's apartment. In his condition, he was not up to driving from one mountaintop village to another. Just before falling asleep on her couch, he told himself that in the morning he'd leave and never come back. However, in the morning she came into the room, cuddled next to him and began to stroke his cock.

Truth was I was not shocked. But what really infuriated me was the stupid remark he made to me, "Françoise's kisses are intoxicating. I forgave her." No, I thought. His penis did the forgiving.

The bastard then had the audacity to tell me that he bore the responsibility. I screamed, "GOOD, then you deserve each other! Don't call me. Don't write me. I don't want to hear anymore about you're fucking asinine affair. If you're so stupid to let this woman manipulate you, than you deserve each other. FUCK you!!!"

Françoise was sinking her finely manicured claws into Max. Like Delilah, cutting Samson's hair to steal his power, her intention was to steal Max Connor's talent. From the beginning, I sensed Françoise was using Max, but I wasn't sure for what purpose. Maybe it was to hurt her husband. Max might be a pawn in the divorce game. Call it intuition, but something didn't feel right to me. Usually when I feel something is not right, I try to trust my gut.

****

It was in late May when he finished framing his work for the exhibition at my gallery. Françoise was withdrawing from Max. When I first learned of this, I became hopeful that she would disappear altogether. A month later my enthusiasm waned.

Max told me about a conversation he had with her. "Françoise what is going on with you, why are you so distant."

Françoise raised her voice, "I don't want to be in your shadow. My father forced me to help him with his projects. I do not want, no I will not, play the role of an assistant to any man again."

My friend was caught off guard; he tried to diffuse her anger. "You've never spoken about your father, or for that matter, your family. Maybe you need to tell me about him. What did he do to make you feel this way?"

Her face reddened. "You are an artist and so was he," she screamed.

"I would think that would endear me to you."

Her voice changed from a snarl to something akin to loathing. "Just stop now!"

"I am not your father," Max yelled.

Her teeth clinched. "I need to be alone. I want you

to leave."

"For how long?""I don't know. Just leave."

She slapped him. He was stunned.

Max was able to stay away from her all that spring. I was surprised and hopeful. It wasn't so much that I wanted him for myself, even though the possibility was delicious. No, I felt he needed his freedom. I had the feeling she was attempting to mine his genius. She was using sex like an excavation tool. I could do that; hell, any woman can do that. Most men, even the brilliant ones, are easily blinded by beauty and cunning. So, you put on your mining outfit, enter the shaft and you begin searching for treasure. What did she want from him? Was she a gold miner? No, she had money of her own, and after all, he was a painter. She was after something more precious, but I couldn't unearth what she was after.

The woman named Domino, who worked for the Louvre, interested me. I knew most of the staff at the museum, but this name was unfamiliar to me. I asked Max, if at Volkov's party, he had caught her last name. He hadn't. He said she looked to be North African, maybe Moroccan or Algerian. He said she was exotic, tall and thin and that she spoke with an unrecognizable accent. Her eyes reminded him of black sapphires, her dark curly hair was long and reached to the middle of her back. Like Elizabeth Taylor, she had a small dark mole above on her cheek. Her nose was thin, but slightly askew.

I asked if there was anything else he noticed about her. Anything unusual.

"She had a tattoo above her ankle."

He seemed a little embarrassed telling me. "She noticed I was staring at it; my guess is she had no idea that I knew what the symbol represented."

"Well, what the fuck was it?" I blurted out.

I don't know if Max was reluctant to tell me, or if he was waiting in some sort of dramatic pause to reveal what he knew. "It was the Seal of King Solomon's magical ring, the ring that gave him the power to command demons and speak with animals."

Summer returned early to Provence. The Mistral winds grew quiet and the bees bedded down in the flowers of fruit trees. By July, Françoise had phoned him three times asking him if they could meet. Each time Max resisted. Unannounced, she came to his studio. Her scent opened a pathway for Max to return. Maybe it was the scent of the

Shalimar perfume she wore, or the purr of her voice, that allowed her to recapture him.

He held out for as long as he could, but in the end, he was weak. He invited her to return to his studio. I was angry. Max's judgment was between his legs. How could such a gifted man be so stupid? A Frenchman would have known better. A clever French woman like Françoise can make pâté out of even the toughest yank.

They renewed what Max thought were romantic and artistic efforts as a couple, much like Pablo and Dora Maar or Mary Cassette and Degas. However, her intentions had nothing to do with romance or the stuff of legends between a woman artist and a male artist.

Later in the month, they were doing watercolors of lavender. By mid July they were painting sunflowers. Along with painting, sex had returned and it was exciting and frequent. Or so Max thought.

Arguments disappeared, and the color of Max's palette changed. He began to work with more intense yellows offset by cobalt blues blended with zinc white instead of his usual titanium white color. Françoise's paintings began to look like Paul Cézanne's work.

When he asked her why she was copying the great painter's style she replied, "I can learn from him just as I do from watching you paint."

The thought crossed Max's mind that she might be mimicking his work. "Have you done anything in my style?"

"No, you're not famous yet," she laughed.

While on a trip to Avignon, Françoise wanted to stop at a posh cosmetic boutique located on one of the city's haute couture streets to buy make-up. As she sat on a tall, leather-cushioned stool, an attractive cosmetologist applied lipstick and eye shadow to Françoise's face. The woman's body was so close to Françoise that their breasts brushed against one another. Not once, but several times. Max told me it did not appear to be accidental. He noticed how often they looked into each other's eyes. He recognized Françoise's expression. It was the same look as when she was about to climax with him. When the woman was finished applying the lip color, she hugged Françoise and handed her an envelope and bag filled with samples. Françoise pulled a small rolled package wrapped in tissue paper and twine from her bag and handed it to the woman.

As they returned to the Rue d' Annanalle Max said,

"That was interesting." Françoise smiled. "You think so, why?"

With a suspicious tone to his voice he asked, "What was the package you gave her?"

In a biting sort of way she spit out her words, "You don't care about the package. What you mean to say, but won't, is that you are worried that she may be a lover of mine."

Max made it appear he was far from angry. "That could be erotic and I would enjoy watching the two of you together, but no Françoise, I am curious as to what you gave her. What was it?"

"She is a friend of mine Max. I gave her a few small drawings, that's all."

Curious, Max inquired, "What of?" "If you must know, they were the ones that I did near Aix." "Not those incredible drawings of Mont Sainte-Victoire I hope." With a so what attitude, she replied, "Yes, I gave her the views of Victoire that I did in the pine forest." Perplexed, Max may have raised his voice a little too loud.

He was prone to do that when he was frustrated. "Françoise, why didn't you give her your versions of the scene rather then the ones you did in the style of Cézanne?"

Françoise became angry. "You remind me of my husband."

Max went on the defense. "I have said it before. I am not your husband, and,

I am not your competition!""No you are not my competition. Like you, I make money from my art! I know you think I am wealthy because of my husband, or maybe you believe I have some sort of inheritance. You are so fucking arrogant."

"I'm not arrogant!""What I do, you call copying."

 "Do you mean you are selling work that looks like others?" "You might benefit from doing the same!" she blurted. "Never, if people wish to buy copies they go to the department store, not galleries.""You are naive, Max. There are ways that a good copy can fetch a remarkable price."She turned. Max tried to ask another question. She waved him off refusing to answer any more questions.Max told me he walked away. I suppose he needed time to cool off and collect his thoughts. He told her he'd meet her at the café across from the store when she was finished shopping. Max told me he waited two hours and drank four bourbon whiskies and two beers before she showed up. She was in a better mood and it seemed to Max, that after such an ugly confrontation, she was acting like nothing had

127

happened. He didn't say anything, but he thought: What was going on? Who was the woman who took the bundle of drawings?

She showed him the things she had bought, two new skirts, a Gucci handbag and a pair of Italian heels. He said, "Nice." She ordered a glass of wine; he suggested they get a bottle. She said, "I think you've had enough." He knew he was on the verge of drunkenness so he was smart and agreed. Françoise suggested they drive to an art supply shop in Apt. "Why Apt?" he asked. "The one we usually go to in Aix has everything we need."

She put her elbow on the table and her hand on her chin, frowned and gave Max a look of determination. Max had seen that stare many times before and he knew there would be no arguing with her. "I need some special drawing materials."

It was apparent when they entered the door to the shop that the man she introduced as Antoine was more than just a good customer. Max was not sure if he was a former lover or just some sort of special confidante. Whatever he was, Max felt uneasy about him. Antoine Arseneault collected old art supplies. Max asked what inspired him to have such an unusual collection. He replied that his fascination was attributable to his trade. Françoise and Antoine shared a smile.

"I supply museums all over the world with materials manufactured during the times when artists made their paintings or drawings or prints. To be done properly, conservators do not use modern day art supplies. I am one of only a few sources in Europe who can furnish the special supplies required for such tasks. The Louvre is one of my clients, as is the Rijksmuseum in Holland and the Hermitage in Saint Petersburg Russia.

Max asked him if he knew Robert Chéron. "He does conservation work for the Louvre."

"Yes, of course, he is quite gifted, one of the few artists who conserves old statues. I have never personally met him, but I know his reputation."

"He and I are old friends. We taught together in the states. He is the one who convinced me to come to France and settle in Lacoste."

Arseneault replied, "You are a lucky man to know such an important artist."

"My friend Max is represented by Céline Roulin," Françoise inserted.

The art supplier nodded, "Then you must be an important artist too!"

"Important, well maybe someday." Max smiled.

"Well Monsieur, if you are with *The Most Beautiful Woman In All Of Provence* you must be someone special."

Max smiled and then asked. "Do you know a conservator at the Louvre named Dominique Dubois? She's a conservator at the Louvre who works with my friend Robert?"

"No, I am unaware of anyone by that name in the conservation office.

"I suspect she'd want to know about your inventory."

He snapped back. "I know everyone at the Louvre and they know me."

Max said the shopkeeper seemed to be in a rush to change the subject. He turned to Francoise and asked, "So Françoise, what can I help you with?"

Françoise smiled, that kind of smile one uses when trying to defuse an awkward moment. "Max needs a few things, but I doubt you have the brands he is use to working with, but who knows, maybe he might be willing to try a few pigments and drawing tools used by the masters."

"I had no idea there was another art supply shop in the Luberon." Max added. "It is good to know about you and this shop. I use the shop in Aix, but I still have to order supplies from the States, and that's expensive. I must say though, I am taken with the French manufacturer, Charvin. Their oil paints have the consistency of mayonnaise and the colors are exquisite. Maybe we can do business together."

Arseneault shook his head. "As you can see, I do not have a supply of modern art materials here. My wares meet the needs of a special cliental."

Paper is paper, ink is ink." Max replied.

Arrogance, or maybe professional bravado, caused the dealer to snap back at Max. "Not true."

Max didn't appreciate the challenge. Was the dealer trying to show off in front of Françoise, or was he just a pompous asshole? It wasn't worth the effort for Max to argue with the so-called expert.

Max walked away from the man and started looking at the shopkeeper's art supplies and materials of the trade. It was like walking into an 18th century apothecary shop. Cobwebs were in every nook and corner of the place, reaching high up to the wood ceiling and the beams that must have held the weight of the upstairs storeroom, or what possibly could be Arseneault's apartment.

Webs of dust and attached cotton-like tiny balls of spider eggs clung to the uneven oak floor moldings. The walls were filthy and looked as though they hadn't been painted in over 100 years. With each stride that Max took, the floors sunk a fraction of an inch and made a squeak that sounded like as if he had stepped on a mouse's tail. Dust and mildew was in abundance and so were small black scorpions.

Pigments in jars and tubes of paints with strange names for colors were sitting in baskets and cardboard boxes on old wooden tables. Rickety shelves were filled with timeworn books, badly tattered and smelling of mold. These books weren't related to art. Max thought that odd and was curious why was this man selling old yellowed books by unknown European authors? There must have been at least 100 ornate frames stacked against walls; almost all of them were in various states of disrepair. Some still had patches of tattered gold leaf clinging to the ancient walnut and chestnut woods. My friend surmised that many of the frames he was looking at were centuries old, likely planed and carved from old growth forest trees now long gone.

Max saw at least fifty jars of ink, most colors were burnt sienna or black and a few were identified as umber. All the bottles of ink were labeled with dates beginning from the 1600's and running through the mid 1800's. The shopkeeper had stacks of aged handmade papers from Italy, France and Holland. There were dried earth colors from Roussillon, finely ground aggregate dust, exotic beetles and jars of other once living creatures that had been crushed to make pigments. Max picked up and examined slices of rocks that came from all over the world ready to be pulverized into colors.

Max could see why the shop would be vital to art conservators, art preservation specialists, or the few artists left who wanted to waste their time and talent doing "*Old Master*" style of paintings. Yes, my friend could appreciate the skill of someone painting in the style and techniques of Rembrandt, but what was the point? Creativity, bringing something new into the world, is what the Universe requires.

Arseneault crept up on my friend and then startled him. "I despise the modern chemical colors of the 20th century. Come with me, I want to show you the backroom where I hoard canvas and linen. My stock of fabric goes back even further than those woven in the days of the Impressionists. One of my greatest treasures is a 250-yard bolt of Belgium linen that came from Antwerp. A Russian friend of mine found it in the attic of a historic brick factory building that was about to be demolished to make way for a high-rise apartment complex. I'm not sure how the Russian was able to get the bolt out of Holland. I knew enough not to ask."

The shopkeeper proudly showed Max wooden stretcher frames he bought on jaunts to remote property sales. He even collected the hairs of old artist's brushes, gallery labels from defunct European galleries and so much more. He had a hundred paintings that were originally stolen by the Nazis but then passed on to the French underground. When Max inquired how they came into his possession instead of being repatriated to their rightful owners or their heirs, Arseneault pulled his shoulders all the way up to the lower tips of his unusually long ears. He then held his forearms outward toward Max slowly turning his palms up without saying anything.

After the tour Max was looking around the shop, he needed a few new tubes of Cadmium red light oil paint. What he found were tubes of Dutch oil paints from the 1940's. Many of the color names were unfamiliar to him. There were no synthetic haired brushes, no mechanical drawing pens. Just lots of outdated and useless art supplies. Some of the inkbottles were half empty. When he unscrewed the tops on a few watercolor tubes they were dried up and as hard as a rock. There was nothing of value for a contemporary working artist, but for a preservationist it was a goldmine.

While Max was rummaging around, he saw Arseneault opening a door behind the sales counter. He and Françoise were about to step inside. Max began to join them; Antoine raised his hand saying, "No, you may not come into this part of the shop. It is reserved for my special clientele. I am sorry." He turned and said something in French to Françoise.

Françoise reassured Max by saying, "He wants to show me his new batch of handmade colors. Antoine's formulas are secret and he only sells them to a special clientele. Fortunately I am one."

Arseneault shook his head affirmatively. Max watched as Françoise walked down the stairs to the cellar. Max said to Françoise, "See if he has any cad colors down there. Oh, and don't trip in those heels you're wearing."

So as to not stumble, she pulled off her high-heeled shoes saying, "I won't and I will." The shopkeeper took what appeared to be an antique key from his pocket, unlocked the basement door, and the two disappeared into the room at the foot of the steps. Max heard the latch lock behind them.

After what seemed like an hour, Max grew tired of waiting for Françoise to return from Arseneault's secret basement room. My friend went across the street to a small outdoor cafe. He ordered pastis and started a drawing. When the waiter brought his drink, Max sat back and looked at the art shop. He thought about the strange owner of the supply store. Talking to himself just a little bit out loud he mumbled, "that building is a firetrap."

The waiter must of heard Max saying something and returned to Max's side, "Qui, Monsieur, what can I get you?"

A little embarrassed, Max said, "Excusez-moi, I was just talking to myself. I'm fine, but maybe in a little while, if I'm still sitting here alone, could you bring me another Pastis?"

Max thought to ask the waiter if he knew the shop owner. "No Monsieur, he does not frequent our café. He is, how do you say in English, inhabituel?"

"Inhabitable? Max suggested.

"No, that's not what I mean." The French waiter scratched his head and tried to find the right word in English." Then it came to him. "Strange."

Max shook his head, "Yes, I agree."The waiter excused himself and went back into the café.The street market was bustling with villagers and tourists. He could hear Parisian and Provencal dialects, the guttural German shoppers yelling at the vendors and the singsong tones of Moroccan merchants against the background noises of the scooping of exotic spices with metal spoons clanking against cooper pots, chickens in pens clucking, and loud gypsy musicians playing guitars and screaming at the top of their lungs, created a cacophony of market sounds.

Max said that everywhere he turned, there were incredible motifs to draw. Banners were flapping in the wind, blue and yellow Provencal scarves hung from rods dancing in front of tourists, Moroccan carpets were spread on folding tables where dealers and rich Japanese buyers rifled through mounds of rugs and haggled over prices and questionable values. Everywhere there seemed to be paintings of sunflowers, portraits of popes and peasants, lavender fields, stone churches, stone houses, stone troughs, stone walls and stone monuments to French monarchs and beloved Provencal poets.

Françoise came up behind him, looked over his shoulder and kissed his cheek. She said, "Your drawing is beautiful. It reminds me of Matisse, or that American you like so much, the California painter with the funny name."

"You mean Diebenkorn?" "Yes that's the one." Françoise told him the shopkeeper apologized for not allowing Max to come into his private sales room. "He is very French, and when it comes to French artists, he believes we need to be given preference. He only sells to certain clients. And because he finds my skills, what should I say, special…I am one of those that he sells to."

Max wondered if it was sex or something else that gave her special status.

"What did you buy from your friend?"

She pulled out three old unshapely artist brushes. She said. "Antoine told me these are weasel and squirrel hair. The hairs were sorted and mixed by hand and the heads of the brushes are hand glued to their ferrules. Aren't they beautiful?"

"Useless." Max snapped. "He just sold you crap, they will fall apart as soon as you try to use them."

"I didn't buy them to paint with. I got them because they are antiques. They will look nice in my apartment. I was thinking that I could put them on the table under the Cézanne painting."

Max apologized. "While we are here let's order appetizers, and then we can go shopping. I need a hat, also and some rouge and lipstick. You wouldn't want to see my beautiful face scorched by the Mediterranean sun would you?" Françoise then turned her face to give a profile view to Mac. I am sure my friend was captivated. Stupid man!

His brow frowned; he was not in a good mood.

"Oh come on now Max, after you take me shopping for makeup we can go to Roussillon. I need some ochre colors and, besides, my favorite restaurant is in Roussillon."

As he often did in regards to Françoise's requests, Max gave in.

It was not a long drive, but it took some time to get where they were headed. The serpentine road wove through sweet smelling olive groves and purple vineyards, then up into the mountains and passes of the Vaucluse and Luberon. Françoise drove her yellow Karmann Ghia as if she were driving in the Le Mans races. Her bag of newly purchased cosmetics rattled in the small compartment behind the two front seats. By the time they reached the village, Max was ready to call a chauffer to bring him back to Lacoste. The drive scared the hell out of my American friend. For Françoise, it was just another excess.

There was a real art shop in Roussillon, a store with

a fine stock of name brand oil and acrylic paints. Françoise purchased jars of various shades of dry powdered earth colors, the kind of colors used to paint stucco houses or Renaissance paintings. He bought tubes of color, lots of oils, enough to last him until fall. As Françoise promised, the meal of rabbit cooked with apricots, nuts and potatoes was superb. Max drove her car back to his studio and Françoise returned to Les Baux.

In making art Max couldn't lie or be diplomatic. When he painted he was in touch with his true self. It was easy for him to paint a recognizable still life or a landscape. "After all," he once old me, "it is just copying what is in front of me and that is skill; it is not art."

When he started a painting he had no idea or plan as to what would appear on his canvas. The paintings came to him from the muses. He was a conduit for what needed to be brought into the world; images flowed like rivers. "Good paintings," he explained, "are like dancing. When you think of the steps or how to hold your partner, you're not dancing. You dance only when you feel the flow of the music and then move with it free of thought or intention. This is how I paint."

When he returned to his studio, he unloaded his supplies and tore open the box filled with 61 large tubes of Charvin oil paints. Soon after arriving in Lacoste, on his first trip to the art supply shop in Aix to buy supplies, he had discovered the French-made paints. Charvin was unheard of in the States; most shops in New York or San Francisco only stocked American brands of paint. A few shops did offer English oils, but in his early career those were too expensive. When Max was the young struggling artist, he bought the tinting colors used by house painters and paint stores to make colors for walls. They were cheap, but they also took months to dry. Sometimes, even years.

As Max became more successful at selling paintings, he could afford better paints. He liked different manufacturers for different reasons. Some companies made better yellows than others, some used various binders with oils that made the paint flow in different ways. Some dried fast, some dried slowly. He said he sometimes felt like a chef seeking the perfect consistency for his palette. It was all about feel and everything about color. But with these newly discovered French oil colors he found the perfect paint. The colors, made in the French Riviera town of Cannes, were magnificent. The touch of the paint was like soft creamy butter. It reminded him of the formula de Kooning had given Max to use: safflower cooking oil, a drop of water and a small amount of kerosene. He then put the colors into a bowl with the mixture and whipped the paint to the consistency of mayonnaise. It was cheap, and since it worked for Willem de Kooning, it was good enough for Maxfield Connor.

Like opening a fine bottle of wine and pouring it into a glass to see the color and then taste test it on the palate, he took the caps off each tube of paint and smeared a tiny amount of color on a white sheet of paper. Beside each shade of color he wrote its name. There was Saint Remy Blue, (the color of the Provencal sky), Opaline Green, (as green as spearmint ice cream), Julia Pink (reminding him of the lipstick Françoise wore) and Azurin Blue, (the same blue as the Mediterranean Sea).

The new series of paintings that Max had begun were entitled *"Françoise's Garden"*. They came a week after the two had been in Aix to see Cézanne's garden. These paintings were brighter and painted with the new palette of colors. They were intense, the brush strokes calm and certain. When his friend Robert first saw the paintings he asked what was the inspiration, Max thought for a moment, then replied, "It's amazing what a beautiful woman can do for an artist."

In late September, Françoise and Max spent several days drawing in the town of Opeds. One day, after hiking to the chapel and setting up to draw, the Mistral began to blow. The chilly wind defeated Françoise and she asked to return to Lacoste. Max managed to finish a sepia drawing on yellow paper of the church overlooking the valley below. As they were walking down the steep hill, Françoise fell and cut her leg. He could tell from the depth of the wound she would need stitches so he drove her to the hospital in Avignon. Françoise was a basket case, crying and overreacting to what was a minor injury. The doctor cleaned the injury and put three stitches in her leg to close the gap. That night on the way back home to Les Baux she cried over the possibility that she might have a permanent scar on her leg.

Max told me that Françoise takes great pains to keep herself slim; she eats like a sparrow and is able to fit into dresses that only pre-teens can wear. Her looks are obsessively important to her. She exercises constantly, dances daily and fast walks for miles each day. It is almost impossible for her to stay still for long. When she sits, her leg constantly swings. Max believes there is excessive energy pulsing through her body. I suspect it could be cocaine.

According to Max, their lovemaking is inconsistent. A lot of the time she professes being tired or not in the mood. Max is frustrated. "Sometimes," he said. "She is like a cat in heat, and other moments, like a nun who took a vow of chastity. I'm confused. If I ask why, she snaps my head off."

Some nights Max is cut off, but then there are those times when Françoise can crawl into his lap and entice him to go upstairs and make a meal of her body. He tells me she is the best lover he's ever been with. How un-thoughtful, has he forgotten that I was once his lover? One day she is pushing him away, and the next day, pulling him back in. Like a fish, he is hooked on her line. He tries to swim away, but she knows how to reel him back in. He is exhausted. I want to save him, but he doesn't realize he's snagged. The bitch is using sex to manipulate him. Like most men, his brain resides in his cock. He is oblivious to what she is doing.

Max is deep into his painting, he feels under pressure to have enough work for his show at my gallery. Françoise convinced him to leave the studio and his painting behind so they could go to Pont du Gard to draw the Roman aqueduct. She completed a drawing of the stone waterway with two large poplar trees in the foreground in sepia ink on rag paper. Max said the results were astonishing. In spite of, or because of her strict diet and constant exercising her health seems fragile to my friend. He told me that after long hours of staring at the landscape under the intense Provencal sun her vision became blurred. For several days she stayed at home with the shutters closed. She would not let Max into her apartment. He was worried, he called her and offered to take her to the hospital in Nice. She refused. When Max pushed harder, she became angry. She admitted it was not her health that kept her confined in the apartment. She confessed that she was working on a painting commission for a friend. When Max asked who was the buyer, she skirted his question, replying, "It's a chance to use some of the antique colors I bought from Antoine in Apt. He has a buyer in Marseille who wants a Provencal scene that will remind him of the Impressionists."

Max said to her, "I'm happy for you. It's always nice to receive a little money from our art."

Apparently she was pissed and replied, "Pour vous n'êtes informations, son pas un peu d'argent, il est une somme considérable! (For your information, its not a little bit of money, it is a considerable sum of money!) When Françoise is angry she reverts to yelling at him in French. Max told me he hung up the phone.

Throughout that fall, their relationship had gone

from hot to cold so many times that Max is unsure which Françoise he will encounter on any day. He said it is like walking on eggshells with her. According to what Max tells me; one day she is sulking and distant, and the next she can be exultant and loving. He's beginning to wonder if she's doing drugs, or maybe she's just crazy.

I wonder if he is crazy. How can such a smart talented man be so foolish? He lets her emasculate him. The man I once lived with, and loved, is disappearing. It is up to me to free him. But it must be undertaken with caution. In order to succeed I have to enlist Robert. Can I trust him not to turn Max against me? I have dropped several hints to the sculptor, but he never seems concerned and probably thinks I am just a jealous old girlfriend. Even with Robert I have to be careful. Call it manipulation if you wish, I am intent on saving Max and if I have to be deceitful, so be it. Max is great painter and someday, if Françoise doesn't fuck him up, he will become famous.

****

In late October, Max's show opened at my Paris

gallery. I arranged for him and Françoise to arrive in a very special automobile. On the steps, outside the gallery, undeterred by the soft rain, a crowd of admirers waited. My artist and his girlfriend arrived in a restored 1928 Chenard limousine. Famous celebrities from the past, Claudette Colbert, Coco Chanel and Jean Cocteau to name just a few, had used the same car. When the limo pulled up and the chauffer opened the door, Max exited first. He was wearing a tuxedo jacket, blue jeans and cowboy boots. He extended his arm to Françoise. A diamond necklace embraced her thin neck. Her Christian Louboutin heels were the perfect match for the red Dior dress she was wearing. Stunning as she was, Max was the star. They walked through the door and I greeted Max with a kiss on his cheek. I did not do the same with her. I didn't take her hand. I didn't say bonjour; what I really wanted to do was to close the door in face. As I escorted Max to the main gallery the patrons cheered.

The critical and financial success of Max's exhibition exceeded my expectations. Buyers and critics alike were charmed. Their questions and praise flowed as fast the wine they consumed. In the crush of admirers, touching and complimenting Max, Françoise was pushed aside. Absorbed in the milieu of the moment, Max didn't notice her disappearance. I did. But I was the gallery owner so

I needed to be alongside of him. We were the center of attention. Praise and credit cards were thrust upon me. Later, when I went to my office to retrieve more bottles of wine, I saw Françoise sitting in the corner amid the coats and damp umbrellas of my guests. Two empty bottles of Dom Pérignon were at her feet. She was on her phone speaking to someone in Provencal, a dialect we Parisians don't understand. She hung up quickly. She started to stand, but fell back in the chair. She was drunk. She needed attention. I brought her to the back alley door. She sat on the brick stoop. I lit a cigarette and handed it to her. She yelled, "Keep your hands off Max. He belongs to me."

I replied, "Max does not belong to anyone."

Françoise snarled and then spat on the ground. It was clear to me she was more venomous than the vipers in the lavender fields of Provence. Drunk, she slurred her words. "I sell my work too! I make more money from my art than he does!"

"Yes, I know you do."

I walked back into the gallery; Max was engrossed in a deep conversation with the Minister of Culture and his wife. I excused my interruption and pulled Max aside. I told him that Françoise was drunk and yelling in the alley behind the gallery. Without excusing himself, he bolted for the back door. It was embarrassing. I used the cover of the "crazy artist reputation" to explain his departure to my patrons. His disappearance from the gallery only added to his persona. I actually think that I made more sales as result of his flamboyant and mysterious disappearance.

I had no idea what happened that night between them. Maybe she went to her apartment on Rue Raynouard and stayed with her so-called husband. It would have been nice if Max had shown up in my bedroom, but the fool probably went to Pigalle and found pleasure with a woman or two there.

I knew Max would resist any attempt on my part to free him from Françoise. Her hook was deep and to remove the barb would not be easy. I had friends in the Préfet de police, also powerful clients who could provide research on Madamé Françoise Gemmer.

Max returned to Lacoste. Françoise stayed in Paris. She calls Max a few times a week and they exchange letters. I am glad she's been away from Max for a few months. He tells me he was getting much more work done as a result of her not being around. We have agreed I will come visit him in at the end of March. This could be my chance to get Max back. However, there are complications regarding Françoise and they are more worrisome than jealousy or retrieving lost love.

****

It is now November in Provence and the Mistral winds are blowing almost daily down south. On less windy days Max tells me he's able to go outside and draw in the fields. He wrote me saying, "Yesterday, my hand was swirling and my entire body moved as I captured workers pruning a cherry tree near the village."

He sent me two small pen and ink drawings; one was a view of the Chateau de Sade that stood atop the village of Lacoste, the other, a sketch of a black beetle with red dots on its shelled wings. In the letter that accompanied the artwork he wrote how excited he was because our friend Robert was coming to visit him.

This month is February and, according to Max, it's cold in Lacoste. He must have forgotten his old life in New York where it really gets icy. One of his Lacoste neighbors gave him a space heater and he had it running full blast almost all the time in his studio and kitchen. At night, to save money, he shut them down and walked around wearing flannel pajamas and wrapped himself in a down comforter. Spring was a month and half away.

Robert came to Lacoste. As usual he took the train from Marseille to Avignon and then caught the bus to Lacoste. When Robert pounded on the door Max came running down the stairs from his studio. He opened the door and a gust of wind hit him in the face; Robert rushed inside and embraced him.

Max told me Robert was wearing gold corduroy pants, a burgundy red turtleneck sweater with a hole in one sleeve and a leather patch covering the elbow on the other. He had workmen's boots on his feet and a wool golf cap pulled down to cover his ears. He threw his knapsack onto the stone floor of Max's living area. He sat in Max's favorite leather chair, the one with oversized arms stained by cadmium red oil paint. Max unplugged the heating unit from the wall socket in the kitchen area and brought it into the living room. Robert took a pack of cigarettes out of his denim shirt pocket, shook out an unfiltered cigarette and began to smoke. Max went back to the small kitchen.

Max removed his French press from the pantry and began to boil water in a teapot on the stove. He put a scoop into a brown paper bag filled with Carte Noire coffee beans, measured out enough beans to fill his grinder and let them whirr until the beans were the texture of steel cut oats. He loaded the beans in the press and then poured hot water over them. He let the coffee and water sit for a few minutes. He took two coffee mugs from the one kitchen cupboard that was affixed to the wall over the sink. He slowly shoved the plunger down and the ground beans layered at on the bottom under the metal plunger disc. He let the coffee brew a little longer and a sweet, chocolate-like smell filled the room. Max poured the coffee into cups.

While Max's back was still turned, Putty Tat jumped into Robert's lap. The sculptor was startled, although he was used to cats because he and his wife had five in Marseilles. According to Robert, cats are better than children.

Max returned to the living area with the two coffees. As he handed Robert the piping hot cup of coffee Max noticed a strip of his friend's curly grey hair was shaved and several stitches were visible. Max sat himself on the cat scratched sofa and asked how Robert's bus ride went. Robert admitted that every time he came by bus to the Luberon he's scared. "That fucking road is narrow and all it would take is for the bus to swerve off the asphalt onto the loose chips of gravel and off the mountain me and the other passengers will go."

"You know Robert, you told me that the last time

you came to visit. I asked the oldest man here in the village if such an accident has ever happened and he said 'Never, but, once in a while the bus has pushed a car over the edge.' Wouldn't you rather be in a big bus and be the pusher rather than the pushie?"Max then asked. "What happened to your head?""I got into a fight; you know, there are rough places in Marseille."

Robert quickly tried to change the conversation. "Max, do you miss Françoise?"

"Yes and no. I miss the sex of course, but not her moodiness. I'm getting much more work done now, spending less money and I'm losing weight. No more expensive restaurants; I'm living on coffee and croissants."

Robert vigorously shook his head. Dandruff and marble dust spewed from the sculptor's grey curly hair and fell on the navy blue shirt he was wearing. "No way! I didn't come here all the way from Marseille to eat bread rolls!"

Max smiled and replied "I just said that to get your goat and maybe to bamboozle a free meal out of you."

"Okay, you got me. Tonight's dinner is on moi." Robert brushed the dust from his shirt and Putty

Tat watched as tiny bits of grit and loose gray hairs parachuted through the shaft of sunlight coming in from the nearby window.

The two decided to go to the Café du Sade to have dinner. Over trout, potatoes and several bottles of wine they discussed their work, the cost of making art and the challenges of being artists. Uneven income, stupid comments by critics and lack of understanding by friends, family and neighbors drive them crazy. Having to do normal living stuff like cleaning house, fixing the toilet and buying groceries took precious time away from being creative. But more so, what bothered them most, were the long hours of time when their work fought with them and, after days of effort, they came away with shit.

Robert apologized that he was unable to come to Max's is opening. Robert said he understood that it was a great success and told Max he was very happy to hear that I had made so much money for him.

"Well, my friend, you and Céline must be rolling in cash now."

"Not exactly, my art supplies cost a fortune. When I was living in New York there were many art supply stores and their prices were reasonable. I would get a discount on top of that because of the sheer volume of paint, canvas and paper that I used. Here in Provence there are only a few shops. The prices of French made products are much higher than what I paid in the US, and to import products to my studio here doubles the cost of what I would pay in the States. Do you know what a tube of cadmium red costs me now? Almost a hundred Francs! I paint large paintings; some of them are 5 x 6 feet. I don't have an exact plan about what's going to appear on the canvas. That means I'm doing a lot of experimentation and over-painting, which makes it even more costly for me. And then, on top of that, I have to store my paintings in the barn of a farmer who lives outside of town. So rent is an added expense. To transport my work to Paris or Avignon costs a fortune. This fall I'm going to try and paint in the barn again. I love painting 10 and 12 footers. When you paint that big it means lots of extenders, turps and linseed oil, not to mention a hell of a lot more oil paints. I can't find big tubes of oils locally, so I find myself having to go to Paris for them."

Robert told Max that he sympathized with him. He added his lament to the cost of being an artist. "I know how you feel. Do you have any idea what it costs me to buy a large piece of marble? And my tools, especially my chisels, they have to be constantly replaced. The one good thing for me is that I am able to take stone from the quarry located here in Lacoste at no cost. I have a Russian friend who owns a quarry outside of Marseille and he gives me stone in trade for sculptures. I own and maintain a flatbed truck that I use to transport heavy stones. I have a frontend loader; a crane and over a hundred power tools."

"Max, the sad thing is that most people don't recognize how much it costs to be an artist. In my case I do have advantages over you in that most of my work is commissioned. With my smaller pieces I can be more speculative and show them in galleries and museums. I often tell young artists to be realistic as to their expectations. When you add up the cost of the studio and supplies it's quite an investment. Sometimes they ask me how much they should charge for their work. I tell them an electrician or plumber sets a fee and we don't argue about it. It's just the way it is. Charge at least the same hourly fee of tradesman. Once you become more established and rich clients desire your work, then you can increase your prices. An artist should make enough money to make a living."

Max chimed in, "Yes, and let me add, most novice buyers don't realize that we have to pay a 50% commission to our dealers."

Robert sympathized with Max regarding shipping costs and Max was grateful that his friend volunteered to see if he could find a transport company in Marseille to help. After all, the harbor there was one of the largest cargo and container ports in the world. Maybe a deal could be struck, like a trade. "Shipping for a painting; or maybe you could arrange a night between the foreman of the docks and Françoise in return for a crate of art supplies?" I can just hear the two laughing now.

"Robert, do you remember when we were in San Francisco and the students would say, 'I need to find a style before I graduate.' I would reply to them, you can't create a style. Your style comes through your work and it will take years to develop. It will come out through honest work and a vision of your own. Do you like this singer Bob Dylan? Well there will be thousands who will sound like him, maybe even try to look like him, but his authenticity belongs only to him. I would tell them go to the library, check out a book on any artist they liked. 'When you look at their early work, you will see their paintings were influenced by the generation of artists who preceded them. For instance, look at Jackson Pollock, and you will find that he was influenced by Diego Rivera, Thomas Hart Benton, Picasso, Miro and even Salvador Dali.' Robert, my favorite artist is our friend

Richard Diebenkorn; Hopper and Matisse influenced him. I believe most artists find their own voice in middle age. So this whole idea of finding a style quickly is nonsense. Young artists have to accept that it will take a very long time for them to become who they are supposed to be."

Robert asked Max who influenced him. Without hesitation Max replied. "Vincent van Gogh because he was passionate and painted with brilliant color and power. Willem de Kooning for his abstracted landscapes and terrifying yet beautiful women. I admire Leonard Baskin for his drawing ability."

"He wasn't a bad sculptor either." Robert pointed out.

"Yes, he is fantastic. Who are your major influences Robert?"

Without any hesitancy, Robert emphatically said. "Well of course Auguste Rodin, but more so his supposed mistress Camille Claudel. Her brother was a famous writer. I've often thought it interesting how talent resides in certain bloodlines, so can cruelty. In 1913 her brother had her committed to an insane asylum. In the mid1930's, after being in the asylum for two decades, Camille wrote to a friend saying, 'I live in a world that is so curious, so strange. Of the dream which was my life, this is the nightmare.'

"Her brother Paul, whom she loved dearly, only visited her seven times during the thirty years she was confined. Her sister came once and her mother never. Nor did Rodin. She died in the asylum in 1943."

Max interrupted. "Vincent van Gogh's father threatened to put him in an asylum as well. Vincent was living with a prostitute and it was an embarrassment to his father who was a minister in the Dutch Church. I guess in those days any family member who disapproved of what their child or sibling was doing could sign papers and have their kin dragged off to the nut house."

Robert replied. "There's a few people in my family I'd like to put away."

Max sat back in his chair, lifted the wine bottle that only contained a few drops, and sprinkled what was left into his empty glass, saying, "Well, there's one or two of those in every family!"

Robert Laughed, "My father-in-law is one of those. Let's go back to your place, I'm tired and we have a busy day tomorrow."

****

In the morning the two went to the boulangerie for crepes and coffee. They took their meal to the overlook near the mairie (town hall) and looked across the valley. From miles away they could hear a dog barking. It was strange to Max that mechanical sounds stayed in the valley, but the sound of nature and animals could be heard in Lacoste. A motorcycle or tractor could be seen far out in the valley, but its noise did not reach the hilltops.

Max felt he had exhausted the motifs in and around Lacoste. He suggested to Robert that they scout out other locales for new subjects to draw. Robert agreed. They went back to the house to get their supplies. As they climbed the steep narrow cobblestone lane back to Max's place, he noticed how far behind Robert was. Robert was obviously out of shape and the steep climbs in the hilltop villages exhausted him. Max leaned against the stone wall to wait for his friend. Huffing and puffing and out of breath, Robert reached his friend and leaned against the wall beside Max. He pulled the pack of cigarettes from his shirt pocket, removed one, lit it and took a long slow drag. Max looked at his friend, shook his head and said, "Well, you dumb fuck, that's part of the reason why you can't circumnavigate this village."

Max patted his friend's cheek, turned, and continued to climb the stone steps leading to the studio. A few minutes later Robert came through the door. "Jesus, how do you do this every day? If I lived here it would kill me."

Max puffed out his chest and said to Robert, "I'm in the best physical condition I have been in since I was a kid. When you climb this hilltop day after day you quickly are whipped into shape. I'm at least 15 pounds lighter than when I arrived. Better yet, I'm more attractive to the ladies now."

I remember when Max moved to Lacoste he called me with the same complaint. In the beginning of his sojourn in Lacoste, climbing the steep hill was hard for Max as well. Now he was able to fly up to the top of the village and not be out of breath.

Max liked to draw on rag paper, mostly because of the texture, but also he liked the off-white color and the sizing that it was impregnated with. It was the sizing that allowed his watercolors to sit more on the surface of the paper so as to not fade into the paper's fibers. His bleeds and pools of color were more intense, deeper, richer and more beautiful.

He went to the kitchen, turned on the faucet and filled two jars with water. If the daylight was not too intense, he'd do watercolors; it is better to work when the sun is behind a cloud. He had quickly learned that the challenge in Provence is that there are very few times when clouds float in the sky. Working outside under direct sun and relentless summertime heat is unbearable. If he sat in the shade of a tree or a building, he usually could tolerate the suffocation of the Provencal summer, but summer was not there yet and at this time of the year he'd be able to see color without the reflection of the bright paper burning his eyes.

Max grabbed a small box of mechanical pens, pencils, and erasers, a half-inch thick sheet of hardboard and big paperclips to hold his paper against the hard surface. He didn't like drawing in sketchbooks, Max preferred single sheets of 18 x 20" Coventry rag paper. He also brought along some handmade paper that he purchased in a 400-year-old stone mill in L'Isle-sur-la-Sorgue.

After they collected their supplies and filled their canteens with drinking water, the two walked down the hill to the car park. They had only driven a few kilomètres when they saw a dirt road disappearing into the woods. There was a small sign partially hidden by untended bushes. The sign was broken and the old letters were faded, but they were able to make out the word *abbey*. As they drove up the lane, the trees and ground foliage gave way to a huge expanse of fields. Sitting in the open ground was a magnificent stone chateau. They learned later after returning to Lacoste that it was originally a Carmelite abbey built by friars who had been repatriated after the 7th crusade. The site was even older than the 12th century; long ago the caves on the side of the mountain next to the abbey had been the home of religious hermits.

The abbey was beautiful with a chapel and gardens of iris, roses and bamboo. Someone was restoring the site, but no one seemed to be around. Outside of a gated wall was an olive orchard. Max sat himself on a wall and made a sketch of the small vineyard. As the sun shifted, he moved to sit in the shade of an ancient oak tree that had just begun to unfold its leaves. There was enough shade for him to paint a small watercolor sketch of the abbey and with a view of the valley below.

Robert was not that much into drawing, but he enjoyed being outside sketching. He sat next to Max, opened his sketchbook and started to draw with a pencil. He told Max there was something almost Zen-like sitting there on the stone wall of the hidden abbey.

Max heard nuns singing. He got up and looked everywhere for them. But there was no one, not a caretaker, not a priest and no sign of restoration workers. He asked Robert if he heard the singing.

His friend replied "No, maybe there's a car parked somewhere nearby and the radio is on?"

"No, this music didn't come from any radio, I can tell you that. There was one soprano voice that was truly angelic."

They stayed for a few more hours. Robert was not up to staying out in the fields all day like Max. He suggested they leave, take a nap and then get dressed for a nice dinner somewhere not far from Lacoste. Max suggested he take a nap in the grass. Robert declined saying, "I'll be eaten by bugs. No, I want to get back to Lacoste."

So they gathered up their art supplies and drove back to the village. Max told Robert that he'd like to come back to the abbey the next day. Robert told him that he planning to return to Marseille in the morning. I'm not sure if Robert was spooked by Max's insistence that mysterious nuns were singing to his friend; I assume Robert didn't know about Max's unusual gift. It could have simply been that he had other business to attend to in Marseilles.

After they got back to Lacoste the two of them took a long nap. Very much like in Spain, it is the custom in Provence to take a siesta. Shops close, the poste shuts down and farmers leave their fields to sleep as best they can through the hottest part of the day. To compensate, they rise early in the morning and stay up very late into the night. In Provence it stays light much later than it does Paris. It's not unusual to see farmers working in the fields at 10pm.

They went to Bonnieux to eat. On the short drive from Lacoste, Robert complained that the wound on his head was bothering him.

Once again Max tried to find out how his friend injured his head. Maybe he had been hurt in some sort of criminal attack. After all, Robert indicated that it had occurred in a rough area somewhere in Marseille. Max tried to pry information about the wound out of him, but Robert refused to talk about it.

When they arrived in the village, they parked the car on the side of the hill of the narrow asphalt road that ran through the town. Robert stepped onto the street, but Max had to squeeze out of the driver side door and then duck his head to avoid a hedge of thorny bushes. He was not so lucky; one scratched his right arm as he headed for the back of his car. "Oh shit," he yelled. A bit of blood was exiting from the small wound.

As he came around the trunk Robert laughed, "Well aren't we a pair, two wounded artists, out together for dinner." He handed Max the bandanna handkerchief that was in his back pocket. "Do you want me to tie this around your arm? We don't want them to think you were in a fight with stickers do we?"

Grabbing the bandanna and patting it against his wound, he said. "You think you're funny, don't you?"

Robert put his arm around his friend's shoulder and patted Max on his cheek. "All we need is Françoise to be with us and we'd be *The Three Musketeers*."

Handing the make-shift compress back to Robert, Max smiled, slapped the back of his friend's head and said, "She wouldn't be a good musketeer; knowing Françoise, she would prefer being the courtesan to the musketeers.

Robert yelled, "One for all and all for her."

They entered the small restaurant. Ironically it was just around the corner from Françoise's apartment. The bistro was a small place and sitting outside, overlooking the vast valley and the lights of Lacoste off in the distance, must have been scrumptious. The owner of the place came to greet them with menus and complimentary wine. Françoise had introduced Pierre Parsall, the owner of the restaurant to Max a few weeks after the two lovers met. He was in his mid 60's. The bistro had been started by his father and before that, his grandfather had used the old stone building as an automobile repair shop. Pierre had beautifully renovated the building. Both the inside and outside walls were made from massive stones that had been excavated hundreds of years ago from the quarry in Lacoste. The hand-forged hinges and the huge oak door made the entrance feel as if one was walking into an old French mill or the side door of a monastery. The glass, in what looked like the original small window frames, were hand- blown, the shutters painted Provence blue and window boxes filled with yellow flowers.

They ordered a bottle of rosé and waited to open the menu. There was no rush, it was time to enjoy each other's company, but also for Max, also a chance to again question Robert about his injury.

Pierre bought a plate of grapes from a vineyard just outside of town and a sampling of local cheeses. Taking a stem of deep dark, almost black, purple grapes and then tilting his head back Max threw three of the fruit into his mouth, "Thank you Pierre, soon tourists will return and business will be brisk again. You won't even have room to seat two old artists, leisurely taking up time and space, when the line is out the door and up the street to get in here. I would imagine you're looking forward to spring?"

"Qui Monsieur Max, also to the return of the *Most Beautiful Woman In All Of Provence*. I will always have a table for you and Françoise," He bowed to Robert adding, "and of course, your friend."

Scratching the healing wound on his head, Robert explained, "I have a few very lucrative commissions offered to me by the Louvre. I need to return to my studio; all my time now will have to be spent on this project so I may not be able to visit you for a few months."

Max feigned crying. Robert punched his arm. The next day Robert slept till almost 9am. Max had to wake him so that he could catch the bus from Lacoste to Avignon and then the train returning to Marseille. As the bus pulled up to the parking lot near the boule court, Max grinned and told his friend, "Remember, on the bus, you are the 'pusher!' Only cars and motorcycles are thrown off the mountain side." The two friends hugged and Max returned to his studio to finish a painting he had started a week ago.

****

Unfortunately, Françoise returned early. And with the coming of spring, the two were once again painting together in the fields of the Luberon. I have never seen her work. All that I know about her abilities comes from Max.

He told me, "She is talented, a brilliant draftsmen, but she is mired in the past. If she were a man in the 17th century, she would have been as recognized as Rembrandt. She can draw like Picasso and paint like Monet. Her creative challenge is how to function as a contemporary artist with a voice of her own. When we work together, she tries to loosen her painting, to go into a flow, to find and say something new, but she fails. She has no vision of her own. Her greatest challenge is that she can't see beyond art history. I've tried to help her, but sometimes even a very talented person will be nothing more than skilled. Skill is important for an artist, but it is not enough. The truly great ones bring something new into the world. Françoise does not."

I decided to make a few discreet inquiries as to Françoise's history. Who was she? After all, she was married to a prominent politician. I called a few friends, but no one seemed to know much about her. They knew there were rumors surrounding her husband's finances and allegations of some sort of intrigue between him and a group of Russian oligarchs. There was nothing about his wife, except that she dabbled in art.

I have a very good friend who is highly placed in the French government. He is a Member of Parliament and serves on the committee overseeing national intelligence, secret stuff that we French don't really want to know. For good reasons, I can't tell you his name; let's just call him HP He is in a position to know my country's secrets and other frightening things that could scare the hell out of you or me.

I called him regarding Madamé Gemmer. It was just a simple request; at first he probably thought it was nothing more than a jealous former girlfriend wanting to find some answers regarding an old boyfriend. It wasn't until I received his return call that I began to suspect there might be reason for me, and more importantly Max, to be concerned.

He informed me he had spoken to a well-placed underworld source in Marseille. This stoolie told HP that Françoise's phone was being monitored by the DCPJ. When HP asked the informant why Internal Security would be interested in her, the source said he had no idea, but maybe it had to do with her husband. HP said there was something strange about the conversation; he felt the informant wanted to tell him more. Towards the end of the conversation HP heard a click sound coming from the other end of the phone; he suspected someone was listening in to their discussion. Quickly, his source asked an odd question. "Ask your gallery friend if she's seen the Cézanne painting at Maurice Michelin's home." HP said the phone then went dead.

This was the second time I heard about Michelin's Cézanne.

****

Françoise wanted to visit Cézanne's studio. Max agreed and the next day they drove to the studio in Le Beaux. When they entered the great master's workshop, Françoise pointed out that the studio of the *"Father of Modern Art,"* was filled with the same objects that appeared in his paintings; his easel, paint box, parasol and even tubes of paint were waiting there for his return.

Max asked her, "How many times have you been here?" "Maybe a hundred."Max knew she bordered on being obsessive, but he dared not question her motivation or indicate that he thought it unusual. If he did, he'd be castigated. "You must love his work," my friend said.

Françoise replied, "I admire his fame. I am in awe of how the prices for his paintings have exploded. Did you know that Sotheby's recently sold one of his landscapes for a million Francs?"

Smiling, Max said, "I hope, before I'm dead, that my work will bring such high prices."

Two women tourists were standing in the room discussing the differences between Monet's garden and Cézanne's Jardin. One of them said, "In general, I distain the "Americanized" structured garden of Monet. It is too pretty."

The other replied, "No, this garden is wild and unkempt. I don't understand why. You'd think the people who run this place would clean it up, cut down the bamboo and weeds, trim the trees and get some light in here. It's a mess, this place isn't worth the entrance fee we paid."

Françoise stepped between the two critics, Max had said. I knew what was coming. Francoise was not the kind of person to let an insult go uncontested. "Excusez-moi, obviously you have no taste; you must be Germans. Let me explain to you. Much like his paintings, Monsieur Cézanne created a modernist garden; he was ahead of his time. When you visit my country, which, by the way, is a Republic, show some respect. I have been in your so-called Fatherland. You people are obsessed with control. You pick up every branch in the forest. Not a limb out of place, everything in lock step. That fits your people's personality."

Max told me Françoise's tirade cleared the room of tourists. As they scampered towards their bus, Françoise clapped her hands. Max told me he was embarrassed. However, the museum guide grabbed Françoise and kissed her on each cheek.

****

During the rest of the week, Max returned alone to the fields below Lacoste to draw. There were sunflowers stretching all the way from Lacoste to Lumiere. He made a few quick sketches of them, but then settled in to draw the twisted and gnarled branches of trees in an ancient oak grove. He also walked all the way to Bonnieux to do watercolors of the vineyards.

Max and Françoise had another fight. She said she needed a break away from him for a week or so.

Max was more than happy to oblige. It was another one of her mood shifts. But, I have to say, Max pissed me off when he said, "Maybe she's going through menopause." Even though this woman is causing my friend to go crazy, his stupid response was just what you'd expect from a man!

Robert called a few days ago. Apparently he was on his way to Paris for a meeting with the woman from the conservators' office in the Louvre. Robert was hoping for another commission to restore several statues lining the top of the Louvre. On the way up to Paris he decided to stop off to visit Max in Lacoste. The two old friends drank long into the night talking about painting, sculpture and the mysteries of amour.

I wish I had been there to hear the conversation."What is going on between you and Françoise?"Max shook his head, "I wish I knew."Robert made a stereotypical remark. "She is from Paris. The women there are *fou* yet beautiful.""They are what?" Max asked.Robert said he pointed his finger to his head and twirled his finger in circles.Max replied. " Yes crazy. Over and over she leaves me and then comes back, leaves again then comes back, leaves, return. It's a fucked up pattern that's driving me nuts! I have no idea why she's so complicated."

I can imagine Robert pulling his callused hands through his long gray hair and then saying, "If she can't, or won't stay, with you, then you need to let her go."

Knowing how his disparaging remark must have sounded, Max reluctantly said, "Robert, I shouldn't be so harsh. I think I love her."

"You think you love her? That tells me you are not sure. Maybe she is not right for you, my friend."

I'm sure it is hard for Max to consider that he could be fooling himself. I've never thought of him as being naive, and yet he should admit to himself that her beauty and the cunning ability she has to trap him and hold him as prey is blinding him.

Robert said that after their conversation, Max seemed embarrassed. He said Max looked down at the floor, stared at a small scorpion that was looking to catch an ant and then mumbled, "You might be right Robert."

Robert said it was uncomfortable at Max's place. "In spite of the oscillating fan, it was hot as Hell in Max's house. I was constantly wiping my brow. I told Max he was intoxicated by her presence. She would make a great fisherman; she knows how to set the bait and then cast the lure. 'Françoise catches you and throws you back into the sea. When will you learn not to bite the hook again Max?' Robert tells it like it is. That's one of the reasons I have always liked him.

Robert's story unfolded. Max poured wine into their glasses and removed a Parodi from his shirt pocket. He stuck a match and the foul little cigar turned red at its tip. Max took a long drag then looked across the valley toward Bonnieux. He said he loved Bonnieux.

Robert told Max, "You love the village across the valley, but you're not sure you love the woman who lives on the other side of that village. This is not a good sign. Sometimes we love a place for its restaurants, or the beauty of its women, but we don't want to live there. The bouillabaisse is intoxicating, but the congestion on the streets is overwhelming. Here is my advice, just go to her because the sex is scrumptious."

I can see Max almost pouting when he admitted to Robert that his advice had merit. According to Robert Max replied, "Maybe you're right. Just for the pussy, no obligations, as you say."

Robert said he put his hand on Max's shoulder and told him, "*La femme est un mystère mon ami.*"

I think Robert was shocked when Max said, "Damn right, she is one hell of a mystery isn't she?"

Apparently Max's French has gotten better. I was impressed.

The two proceeded to get drunk and at three in the morning the waitress threw them out. The next day, still three sheets to the wind, Robert managed to take the bus to Avignon, and from there he caught the train back to Marseille.

Robert called me a few days after he retuned to Marseille. He apologized for not stopping by the gallery; he said he was too busy. Fuck him, I don't believe it. In spite of the fact he is married, he was probably shacked up with some woman in Pigalle.

I asked Robert how he was coming with his negotiations for the next restoration project at the Louvre. He said that he was confident the contract would come through soon. I had connections at the Louvre; I volunteered to help him. He declined.

I also asked how things were in Marseille.

"Everything down here is good. I'm happy with my newest sculptures; the weather is fantastic, and the bouillabaisse superb. I'll call Max next week and suggest we drive up to Paris so he can see what I did for the Louvre a few years ago. Maybe we can take a side trip to go to Normandy. The long ride will give me time to talk some sense into our friend. Don't worry; I won't let Max get caught between Françoise's legs."

I liked Robert because he reminded me of the old guy Willy Smoot who lived above Max and me in New York.

Robert could be crude with me, but often I found his directness refreshing and even funny. After all, he was an artist, and the good ones are always honest. Picasso, Lautrec, Rodin, they all were seekers of truth.

Over the next month Robert called Max two or three times. I asked him if he was making progress to disentangle Max and Françoise. He said he was working on it. I was disappointed. Robert promised me that he would intercede; I was beginning to learn that I could not rely on Robert's word.

I had reason's to believe Robert was not the man he purported to be. My source of apprehension was my friend HP. He had called to say that his informant in Marseille asked him to inquire of me how well I knew Robert Chéron. HP was puzzled by the question, so he asked me to give him some background on Robert. I explained to HP that I have represented Robert's work for years and that it has been a profitable business relationship for both of us. I consider him a friend and we occasionally have lunch together in Paris, but in reality I rarely socialize with him, and have never met his wife or family. So, in fact, my relationship with him is primarily business. I asked HP if he knew why his informant inquired about Robert and if he felt there was a connection between Robert and the criminal element of Marseille.

HP replied, "The man did not explain why he asked about Robert, but he also wanted me to ask you if you knew anything about Robert's relationship with the curators, and especially the conservators, at the Louvre. He was particularly interested to know if you have any relationship with a woman by the name of Dominique Dubois."

I told him the name sounded vaguely familiar and asked, "Who is she?" HP said he didn't know and was unsure why his informant asked, but he thought his snitch was implying that there was a connection between this woman, Dominique, and Robert.

I replied that I vaguely remembered Robert, or someone else, mentioning the name once, "The name rings a bell," I said. "But I don't remember the connection."

Another question that seemed odd was that the stoolie wanted to know if I was aware of the head wound that Robert had sustained in Marseille. I told HP that Max had mentioned it.

HP said the conversation ended suddenly when the informant hung up the phone. HP speculated that there must be some shadowy reason for the contact to have asked these questions. "My conclusion is that there is something going on between criminal elements in Marseille, this woman from the Louvre and your friend Robert Chéron."

HP promised to get back to me once he knew more.

As if he didn't want anyone to overhear him, he said in a hushed voice, "Something is brewing and I suspect it is huge."

I began to worry. I decided not to alert Max. God forbid that, unbeknownst to Max, he might be involved in something nefarious. HP told me not to tip off Robert or Max as to our conversations. I promised to seal my lips.

****

A few days after my conversation with HP, Max called and sheepishly informed me that Françoise had returned. Max was apprehensive. On the other hand he enjoyed being seduced. Needlessly to say, he had to tell me all the details, which of course I found to be upsetting.

It started when she came over to draw in his studio. They were both working together. Max was copying one of his sketches onto watercolor paper. This was his normal approach to doing complex watercolors. Often when he was in nature, he worked directly with the medium, but this was another methodical approach to his more detailed "WC's", as he called them.

Françoise raided his kitchen, taking a hand-made ceramic bowl with a yellow and blue Provencal placemat and a bunch of grapes bought from the local grower, and carefully arranged them on his studio table to draw. Max could tell from her cursing that her still life drawing was not going well. When she threw her eraser across the room it was abundantly clear she was not having a good day.

Out of the corner of his eye he noticed she was removing her blouse, bra, blue jeans and panties. He figured sex was in the offing. She walked over to the open window of his studio and sat on the deep-set stone sill. He told me the Provencal sun was pouring in behind her. She was in silhouette.

The sun was so bright that looking into the scene, he could not make out the features of her face. He said he watched the swallows, darting back and forth as they crisscrossed the valley behind her. A few tourists walked by and saw her; they whistled and she was pleased. He began drawing her.

They were back together again.

In August, at Françoise's suggestion, she and Max drove south to St. Maries de la Mer on the Mediterranean. It was a typical seaside town not far from Marseille. A tourist trap, filled with cheap shops selling post cards, trinkets, swimsuits and t-shirts. They stayed the night at the Hotel La Dauphin Bleu and made love across the road on the beach. Things between them were good again. Max was grateful, but cautious. Over the course of their relationship, he had discovered much about her that worried him and gave him cause to be wary.

The following morning while they were sitting together on a seaside bench drinking coffee, she said she had to meet someone. Max asked whom. She told him a friend. He thought it odd; she hadn't mentioned needing to see someone on the drive down. She suggested he enjoy the sand and water while she had lunch with her friend.

Max was suspicious, and as far as I was concerned,

he had every right to be. He asked her. "Who is this person?"

"An old acquaintance from Paris; she moved to Ste-Maries- de-la-Mer many years ago. I miss her, Valerie and her husband Pierre lived near the Opera Garnier and we would attend ballets and operas together. We once saw Rudolf Nureyev perform in *Sleeping Beauty*. Russian men are so handsome."

"Her husband died a few years ago, and she moved here to Southern France to take care of her aging mother. I have not seen her for almost two years. I spend so much time with you that I neglect my friends."

Before he could reply she stood up, grabbed her shopping bag and kissed him on the cheek. He watched her walk across the wide road heading for the narrow paved village lanes. Her blonde hair dancing in the breeze made her stand out from among all the black-haired Gypsy ladies. As she walked farther into the distance, he watched until she was almost gone. Then he rose from the bench and started walking leisurely in the same direction. She never looked back; he quickened his pace so as not to lose her.

The streets were crowded with gypsies who had come for the annual pilgrimage. Max hid in the crowd. He stayed several yards behind her. She walked towards the Church of the Three Marys', the place that marked where Mary Magdalene, Mary Salome and Mary Jacobe landed in France along with Joseph of Arimathea. She walked inside. The Church was filled with pilgrims. Max slipped in and hid behind one of the large columns. He saw Françoise approach a large man. He was fit and looked like a military officer or mercenary. She handed him a package from her bag. He untied the jute twine that held the cream colored wrapping paper concealing whatever was inside. He did not remove it's contents, simply parted the wrapping far enough to be satisfied by what was inside. He never spoke to Françoise. He handed her an envelope, which she put into her bag, and they both turned away from each other. He walked to a side door and joined a woman who was wearing a veil and they left together. Françoise sat in a pew appearing to pray and a few minutes later rose and walked down the center aisle. The clicking sound of her high heels echoed and bounced off the ancient stone walls and high vaulted ceiling. She turned and genuflected, then exited through the massive wooden doors.

Max stepped from behind the huge stone column and fast- walked to the street. He spotted her; she was heading back the same way she had come. He trailed her at a safe distance and watched her cross the two-lane road towards the beach. He ducked into a pharmacy and saw she was heading to the bench overlooking the shoreline. She looked up and down the beach for Max and then sat down to wait.

Max also waited. After a while he headed towards her. She recognized his whistling. She turned. He smiled. They kissed.

"Where have you been? I didn't see you on the beach?"

Max was not a great liar, but he could weave a decent tale when needed. "I went to the place where van Gogh painted the fishing boats."

"Oh oui, the one that hangs in the Hermitage in Russia." "That's the one. A beautiful oil painting," Max said. "But it is not an oil, it's a watercolor on paper," she stated. Max knew his art history, he had taught 19th and 20th century art survey courses at the school in San Francisco. "I was certain it was an oil."

"Well you are wrong, Max. I have seen it in person."

"You've been to Russia?" She had never mentioned she had traveled to Russia. He wondered why.

"I went there several times with my husband." "You told me he detested travel." "No, I never said that." She did, but Max did not dispute her words. At this point in

their relationship he knew she was a pathological liar. He decided it was a good time to catch her in a lie. He wondered if in some other life she had been a fiction writer, after all, she could make up stories that were flawless and so believable. "How was your lunch with your friend?"

She launched into a tale as if she were an actor who knew her lines without thinking. "We had a lovely time. I miss her. We went to a restaurant named Table du 9 and had eel and mussels in a cream sauce with carrots, green onions and a pretzel. She was happy to have a break from her mother. We promised to meet more often. I invited her to come to Les Baux. I hope she can get away. She needs a vacation."

"That would be nice. I'd like to meet your friend. Does she like old churches? We could take her to the beautiful church in Aix or the small one with the cobalt blue ceiling in St. Remy."

Max said he almost smiled at how believable she sounded and if he hadn't seen what had happened, he'd fall hook, line and sinker for her story. Even though he knew the truth he felt that, while she was talking, he was listening to a nice story of two girls having a great lunch together. Damn she was good. To be lying to someone who knows you're lying, and they still believe your lie, well that's a real talent.

Max said that they walked back to the hotel to retrieve their car, and then began the long drive to Lacoste. Evidently Françoise fell asleep. Even a beautiful woman can snore. Her bag was leaning against her knee. It was open. He leaned to the side, and saw the envelope was still there. Max had already decided not to confront her about the truth. But, it was now clear to him, she was a liar who could never to be trusted. He quietly pulled the envelope from her bag. It was not sealed; he folded back the flap and looked inside. It was filled with small diamonds. For an instant he stared at what must have been a small fortune. Then a car horn screamed and Max saw he had drifted into the oncoming lane. He quickly pulled the car back onto its proper side of the road. A truck driver shouted an obscenity, but in spite of Max's slowly increasing understanding of French, he was probably unaware he was being called an "asshole." Paralyzed by surprise, the diamond filled envelope still in his hand, the sounds of screeching brakes and the swerving of the car awoke Françoise and brought Max back to his senses. He quickly shoved the envelope between his legs just under his crotch.

Groggy, and still half asleep, Françoise asked, "What happened?"

As he looked at her, he saw three diamonds lying on the center console near his coffee cup. Max lied, "That fucking truck diver almost plowed into us!"

He reached for his coffee and was able to swipe the three stones so that they fell into the space between his seat and the console. He took a long gulp of the lukewarm caffeine. He told her to go back to sleep. When he heard her snore, he pushed himself up and retrieved the envelope. He leaned over, put the envelope back into her bag, and breathed a sigh of relief. But all the way home he worried about those loose diamonds.

As they approached Les Beax, Françoise awoke to the sounds of tourist busses coming down the mountain road. The noise acted as her alarm clock. Max said, "We're here." She smiled, stretched her arms and then yawned. "It's good to be back home."

Lucky for Max there was no parking allowed on the narrow streets of the village. He was able to drive to the door of her apartment where she grabbed her bag and got out saying, "It looks like the carpark didn't have many vehicles in it, so you should be able to find a good space. See you in a few minutes."

Max told me he thanked God for small villages and their parking lots. As he continued his story, he told me that he drove the car to the top of the steep hill where the turnaround was located, shifted into first gear and slowly navigated his way down through the village to the parking area. He looked around to see if anyone was nearby. Seeing there was no one, he opened the door, planted one foot outside and placed his hand on top of the door. He then carefully rose from his seat, twisted his body to exit the car. Standing alone on the pavement, he peered intently at his vacated seat. His eyes focused on the floor and around the console. The three loose diamonds were nowhere to be seen. He reached under the driver side seat, pulled up the thin bar to release the seat from its locked position and slid it back as far as he could. He still was unable to find the diamonds. They were hiding somewhere amid the mess of candy bar wrappers, two pencils, some sticky M&Ms, a bank deposit slip and the key to his studio that he had lost several months back.

He had two choices. One was to take the flashlight

out of the glove box and shine its light into the area in hopes that the precious stones would reflect the light back to him or the second approach, which was to take the small battery powered vacuum from his trunk and suck everything into it. Later he could empty the vacuum bag and sift through the debris. He realized the vacuum idea was fraught with possibilities for catastrophe; what if the tiny stones somehow got caught up in the internal mechanisms of the machine. He quickly decided his first idea was the best. He was right, the heavy-duty emergency flashlight was powerful and it quickly caused the diamonds to sparkle. One at a time, he pinched each diamond between his thumb and finger and placed it into his sunglass case. He then put the case into his glove compartment, set the car alarm to the armed position and locked the automobile. He hurried up the asphalt walkway leading to the village and Françoise's apartment. When he reached her door his heart was racing, but it was not because of panic. It was simply because of his fast pace and the steep walk up the hill through the village, and his agitated pounding on her door.

When she opened the door and smiled, he felt relief. She was obviously oblivious to his discoveries. He now understood she was more than just an irrational lover. He was armed with evidence that her strange behavior was grounded in criminal activities. Her secrets and strange conduct were now exposed as nefarious; she was a criminal. The behavior she had used to torment him had nothing to do with him. He felt exonerated, free of guilt, released from remorse, but more importantly, he was now armed with a sense of revenge.

Later, after revealing this event to me, he told me he was confused, uncertain as to what was going on and didn't know what to do. He knew he absolutely could not confront Françoise. He said that he thought about calling Robert; thank goodness he didn't. He remembered a line from one of Bob Dylan's songs, *"Something is happening here, but you don't know what it is, do you Mr. Jones."*

He told me this story the day after they returned, but since then he's not said a word about anything regarding the strange incident. I wondered what he did with the three diamonds. I thought that odd. Was he hiding something from me?

After the trip to Saintes-Maries-de-la-Mer, Françoise stayed away from Lacoste. She told Max she was working on a special project. That was fine with my friend; he too had several paintings in progress and wanted to finish them. A week turned into a month and they were again estranged. I was foolishly hopeful that she would disappear from his life.

Not long after that, Robert called Max to invite him to join him on a trip to Paris. I guess Robert knew better than to contact me about accommodations. Max telephoned, asking if I would be in town. I told him no, I was going to New York City. I was shocked, when he asked me, "Do you have any lady friends who might like to spend time with a handsome, sexy, witty, talented, respectful, no, not always respectful, artist?"

I told him he was the last person I'd recommend to one of my girlfriends.

Before leaving for the States, I called Robert to tell him what Max had asked regarding my girlfriends, and also to encourage him to keep trying to convince Max to get rid of Françoise. I also called HP.

****

HP told me more about Robert. His spy in Marseille told him that Robert's wife, Olga, was from Latvia. She was blonde, beautiful and mysterious. In all the years I've known Robert I have never met her. You would think she would have attended his openings at my gallery or been at one of his Louvre events.

What HP told me next was surprising. At birth Olga was given up for adoption and raised in an orphanage. Olga's father was a Soviet intelligence officer posted in Latvia. HP said the French National Police had accumulated a lengthy dossier on him. HP was certain that his informant knew much more than he was telling. HP thought this man was giving him just enough information so that HP would dig deeper.

The informer said that when Olga was 16 she disappeared from the orphanage. Somehow she turned up in Sweden. Robert had met her in Stockholm; that I knew from Max. After studying sculpture at the Royal Institute of Art, Robert was, for a few years, employed as a conservator by the Modern Musée on Skeppsholmen Island near Stockholm. This was where Robert perfected his talent to restore sculptures.

What HP told me next was startling. Olga's father was now living in Marseille under an assumed name and working at the Musée d'Art Contemporain in Marseille.

****

Max told Robert they could stay at my place in Paris while I was away. Robert replied, "Great I shall come up from Marseille and drive us to Paris."

Max thought about Robert's old truck and what a terrible ride it would be. The truck was rusted, its mainsprings shot, there was no air-conditioning and the passenger seat was as uncomfortable as a saddle. There was no way he would ride all the way to Paris in such a vehicle. Hell, it was plain dangerous.

"Are you planning on driving your truck?"Robert said, "You'll see."Robert ordered, "Pack light, no art work for this trip. I have a meeting at the Louvre and I thought afterward we'd visit the d'Orsay museum and some sites around Paris."

Three days later, Max heard the rumbling of a revved up car approaching the hill. When it reached the Goats Gate and entered the village the sound echoed off the 500-year-old stone buildings, scattering crows and cats alike and exciting the boys who were at recess in the schoolyard below. Max opened his front door and there was Robert sitting in a candy-apple red Lamborghini surrounded by several of Max's neighbors. Someone yelled out, "You're lucky you're not a German driving a kraut car."

Robert looked at the men and tried to ask 'why' in Provencal. A few laughed, but several were impressed with his botched attempt to speak the old French dialect, the language of the troubadours.

A local farmhand shouted, "Because, if you were a Kraut visiting our village, you'd quickly find our ancient lanes are far to narrow for your car to navigate. A Frenchmen knows how to maneuver in such terrains, but a German would panic and put his transmission into reverse and get the hell out of here. But, being the kind helpful Frenchmen we are, we'd assure them that there is just enough room to pass. We would, of course, assist the German by directing him ever so slowly to nudge forward. We'd tell Fritz to turn your wheels a centimètre here or a few centimètre there, we would promise him there would be no problem. One of us would assure the Hun that this happens all the time and we know how to guide his automobile safely to the wider part of the street."

"But, unfortunately...well, really not unfortunately. The man's car would wedge itself between the pigeon keeper's house and Marie's bakery building and as we run off laughing, he would be hollering, 'God damn sie mutter fuckers'. Then a couple of our friends would come along and apologize for the village ruffians who tricked him. They'd offer to help the German fellow move his car back far enough so it could put it in reverse. Of course he'd say yes, maybe even offer a few Francs for the kindness of their offer. They'd say, "No no Monsieur, we cannot accept your money. We just want to atone for the mean trick played on you. Then they would magically produce crowbars from a rusty Renault parked nearby. They'd jam the steel leavers between the hard rock walls and the car's thin metal fenders, sidewalls, doors, hubcaps and tires. Of course the damage to the vehicle would be considerable, but the car would be unstuck and the German fellow would be on his way."

Robert Laughed as Max's neighbor ended the conversation saying, "You can never fool a Frenchmen, but a stupid sausage necked German can be had over and over again. And the amazing thing is they think they are the superior race."

Another local said. "We've been doing this for years. It's sport to us, especially during the tourist season. We only do it to Krauts. You could say we are the French Resistance."

Walking by, carrying her laundry, Marie, the owner of the Lacoste boulangerie shouted. "Vive la France, Vive la France." Everybody cheered!

****

It was Robert who told me the following story. Max later gave me his input. You see, Robert is the one who embellishes, Max can be counted on to be more precise.

Max squeezed his overnight bag into the trunk between Robert's sculpture tools and jackhammer. "Are you planning to repair the Louvre while you're in Paris?"

"Maybe yes, maybe no. We will see." "Where did you get this car? Did you steal it?" "No, our friend Michelin lent it to me."

They left Lacoste taking the high road towards Avignon. Max pleaded with Robert to slow down. "This road is dangerous, if we go over the side we're doomed!"

Robert scoffed, "This car was made for these kinds of roads."

He pushed the accelerator and Max fastened his seatbelt. "Shit," he screamed as Robert laughed. They took the Luberon mountain curves at speeds in excess of 130 km/h. They drove the A7 towards Lyon, where they had lunch and then drove another four hours to Paris.

During the seven-hour drive, Robert broached the topic of Françoise. He said he agreed Françoise was indeed beautiful, but she was like the female creatures who devour their male partners. Max scoffed, "So I am just prey to her, is that what you think?"

"Maybe yes, maybe no." "Bunk!" was Max's reaction.

"Well my friend, just remember, Gauguin couldn't keep his zipper shut and it cost him dearly. His wife appropriated all his Degas and Monet paintings, and then sold them for a fortune. Gauguin caught the clap from whores in Arles and syphilis from teenage girls in Tahiti only to die penniless on an island in the middle of nowhere."

Max snickered. "Oh, so that's what you think my fate will be if I continue seeing Françoise?"

Robert feels, as I do, that Max is crazy to stay with Françoise. He told me that during their ride he felt that he had been successful in dissuading our friend from committing himself to her. He thought Max was ready to give her the boot.

Robert suggested to Max another option regarding amour. He told Max that Olga's sister was coming to Marseille for a three- month stay. He showed

Max a picture of her. She was tall, thin and buxom. Her jaw line was perfectly sculpted and her figure was as nicely proportioned as the statue of Aphrodite in the Louvre. Robert told our friend that being with his sister-in-law could sooth his wounds and would also be a huge relief to him because being in his house with a wife and her sister was a nightmare. Robert told me that Max seemed amenable to such an arrangement. He also felt certain that Max would be ridding himself of Françoise shortly. I was overjoyed. However when I spoke to Max a few days later, he told me a different story.

When they arrived in Paris, they quickly dropped off their bags at my apartment and headed for the Champs-Elysées for dinner at Le Café Kolomnikov. According to Max that was Robert's idea. Max said he wasn't happy with our friend's choice. "After all, how can you get a decent French wine in a Russian cafe? The Provencal salad that I had tasted odd, it must have been the dressing." Robert drank vodka, had Kholodets and a Russian meat Jelly.

Robert winkled his nose at the French cuisine saying, "Don't you get enough of that stuff in Lacoste?"

Max replied, "I have become accustomed to

Southern French cooking. But you, how can you eat that Bolshevik crap?

"I've acquired a taste for Russian food and especially vodka."

"What about Russian Women?"

"Nice, big boobs! But don't ever touch them! In Marseille, the Russian Mafia cuts off the pricks of any French philander caught with one of their women. If an Arab so much as flirts with a Russian woman, his head will be chopped off and his cock jammed into his dead mouth."

"What about Germans?"

"They hate Germans even more than we French do. So, if a Kraut messes with Tatyana, God help him, he will beg for death!"

It's disgusting the way men talk. I would expect it at a bathhouse or sporting event, but not over dinner. Knowing those two, they were probably talking loud and offended the other patrons.

They came back to my apartment. Max slept on my couch and Robert took my bed. The next morning they were standing in the courtyard of the Louvre. Half way up the facade was the row of statues of noted French scholars and other academics who played a part in the history of France. Robert pointed out the sculptures he had been restoring. "There, that's Sébastien Vauban, he was a military engineer. He designed over 120 fortresses that protected France's borders, kept the God damned Krauts out of France. Over there is Moliere, known for his comedies, but he was nowhere as funny as your Richard Pryor. Pryor was a genius. You know, we French love comedy, and that man was funnier than anyone who ever lived on this earth, funnier than Charlie Chaplin, Jerry Lewis or even Chuck de Gaulle."

The two friends continued to walk in the huge open plaza. I am sure Robert was happy to point out his accomplishments. Several years ago when I received the call from the Minister of Culture, Jack Lang, that Robert was selected to restore the sculptures, I was ecstatic. Not just any sculptor could win such a coveted commission. We French only entrust such tasks to the most skilled artisans. After all, this was the Louvre.

Robert pointed towards Montaigne, the 16th Century French essayist saying, "I liked him because he was skeptical of Christianity. Now, look to your right and the one with the palette in his hand is François Clouet; he painted ostentatious portraits of the royal family in the 16th century."

"Are you sure that's who he is?" Max said. "According to me, that's who it is." "The guide book says otherwise." Robert pretended to be indignant, "Who do you want to believe, me the artist, or some architectural historian? Truth is an illusion. I make my own truth, therefore it is true."

They walked into the gallery viewing area. Max had been there many times before, but still he couldn't get over the interior architecture with its incredible carvings, frescos, ceiling paintings, gold, gilt and marble. The vast wealth of the French monarchs was displayed in all its splendor. It is now the people's palace and it houses much of humankind's important works of art.

After several hours of looking at the world's great paintings, sculptures and artifacts, they felt their eyes couldn't consume another Michelangelo, Rembrandt, Monet or Cézanne. Max refused to stand in line to look at the Mona Lisa. "How can I see the painting behind such thick glass? Let's leave."

That afternoon they visited the Jardin d' Plantes. Not only was it bursting with a thousand of varieties of medicinal plants, but also there was a greenhouse teeming with orchids from all over the world. They bought ham sandwiches and coffee from a small snack bar and, on a shady walkway;

they found a bench where they sat and watched children ride the antique merry-go-round. They then strolled through the streets of St. Germaine d'pre. From a Left Bank book dealer, Max bought an old manuscript written by Jean-Paul Sartre. Leaning over a guardrail, smoking a cigarette, Robert patiently waited for him and watched the tourist boats moving up and down the Seine.

They continued on to my favorite museum, the Musée d'Orsay. The building was originally a railway station and hotel. Built in 1900, the structure was restored a few years ago and re-opened as an art museum. It was Thursday, the one night during the week when the museum stays open until 9:30pm.

Of special interest to Max was the collection of paintings by the Post Impressionists. For Robert, his interest was obviously sculpture. Max said Robert was intrigued by the Camille Claudel piece entitled, *Maturity.* While looking at the piece, he became angry. Max said our friend muttered under his breath several expletives. Finally, a guard approached him. An argument ensued; the guard told Robert if he didn't stop cursing he would have to leave.

Robert replied, "Everyone thinks Rodin was so great, when he was young he did some good work of his own. But he became a bandit, a thief with no vision of his own. The fucker stole Camille's ideas. Bastard, that's what he was, a fucking bastard, a Judas who sold his soul for public acclaim and the bullshit reviews of art critics."

The guard took Robert's arm to escort him out of the museum. Max interceded, "This is the famous artist Robert Chéron, he's the man who restored the sculptures at the Louvre. He's a passionate artist, you know how that is. Give him a break, and let me take care of him. I assure you, he will behave."

The guard bowed to Robert saying, "Désolé, (sorry) monsieur; please enjoy your visit."

Side by side, in the great hall of the museum were three beautiful heads sculpted by Charles Cordier. Robert was an admirer the French sculptor. He wanted to see, (probably for the 50th time), Cordier's *Negro from the Sudan*. In the mid 1800's, the beauty of this African model inspired him to chisel the black man's face. That led Cordier to develop a genre of work glorifying the physical characteristics of different races. That may have been the inspiration for Robert to restore the figures around the exterior of the Louvre

The other piece Robert had to see was Degas's *Little Dancer Aged Fourteen*. The torso was sculpted in flesh colored translucent beeswax with actual blonde coiffed hair meticulously woven into the wax. Degas dressed her in a tutu and dancing slippers. For effect, or maybe some other unknown reason, Degas had exhibited her in a glass case. The piece was the only figurative sculpture the master had exhibited in his lifetime. This was remarkable because after his death, hundreds of wax figures were discovered in his studio and at a local foundry.

On a plaque affixed to the wall across from the sculpture was a description of the famous piece. Max read it out loud, "Most art critics of the time were critical of the piece; the most derogatory review compared the work to something one would find in Tussaud's tourist attraction in London. Another wrote, the dancer in the glass case reminds me of a stuffed monkey. The sculpture should not be in an art gallery; it's nothing more than a tableau one would find in a natural history museum."

Robert spat on the floor and yelled. "The only monkeys were the goddamned art critics!"

A number of people who were following a tour guide suddenly began to clap and cheer. Obviously they were pleased with Robert's blunt assessment. Despite the tour group's approval, a museum guard approached Robert. Max put out his hand saying to the guard, "It's okay. I'll clean it up."

The guard shook his finger at Robert saying, "Monsieur, if you misbehave again I will be forced to remove you from the museum."

Max assured him that there would be no more outbursts and begged forgiveness. "My friend is an artist, an admirer of Degas, and he was only commenting on the outrageousness of art critics."

The guard replied, "While I agree that critics are the bloodsuckers of the art world, please tell your friend to express his disdain with quiet words and no saliva."

Max got down on one knee, pulled a handkerchief from his pocket and began wiping up the spittle. The uniformed security man returned to his station by the door leading into an adjoining gallery. He winked at Robert.

Max was interested in seeing Cézanne and van Gogh, mostly because they worked in Provence and he wanted to compare their interpretation of the landscape to what he was seeing in Provence. He was drawn to Cézanne's *Rocks near the caves above Château Noir*. It reminded him of the Cézanne in Françoise's Les Baux apartment. Sometimes when he and Françoise went to draw in the countryside she would insist that they work near Mont Sainte- Victoire and the Biremes quarries. She said she liked to work near Aix because she felt a kind of lyricism in the blues, greens, browns and mauve colors of the mountains.

But of course there were other wonderful van Goghs painted in and around Paris, as well as Arles and further south in the Camargue region. One of his favorites in the d'Orsay was "*Thatched Cottages at Corneille, Auvers-sur-Oise.*" The painting was done during Vincent's most mad and yet most productive period when he lived outside of Paris in the small village of Auvers. During Vincent's three-month stay there he painted 70 paintings, all considered to be masterpieces. The painting of the thatched cottages was done a few weeks before the Dutchman's tragic death.

While Robert was more engaged with the sculptures in the museum, Max was intrigued with Monet's water lily garden and pond at Giverny. In the last years of Monet's life the pond became the artist's singular source of inspiration. Eliminating the horizon and the sky, Monet was fixed upon painting the pond. He didn't paint details, only the impression of the reflected garden on the surface of the water. For him, the pond and its mirror–like reflections was a metaphor for the eternal.

Sometimes Monet would see his own likeness looking back at himself from the pond.

As the two modern artists stood in front of the Monet, Max said, "This is where abstraction began."

Robert said, "Let's go to Giverny, I think we should, after all it's a short ride in Monsieur Michelin's fancy fast car."

Max reminded him, "But you said you have an appointment tomorrow?"

"We could go this evening.""They're not open at night.""Let's see if we can find a back way to sneak in?"Robert was always one to take risks. Rules never detained him. I was not surprised when he told me this story.At first Max thought he was joking, but then realized he wasn't. "I'm not so sure that would be a good idea. After all, you almost got arrested downstairs."

"Ah, come on. It'll be an adventure."

Max thought his friend would forget the idea. After all he thought, he might still be a little drunk from last night and will realize it's a hair-brained scheme later. Max replied, "We'll see."

Robert and Max took the Metro back to my

apartment. Robert changed clothes, put on a leather Jacket and said he'd see my friend the next day. Max asked where he was going and he shrugged saying, "A business matter with one of the conservators from the Louvre. Don't wait up for me."

That evening, Max called me in New York to thank me for the use of my apartment. He told me about their day and how Robert was almost removed from the Musée d'Orsay by Gendarmes. We laughed. It was nice to chat, but I knew the real purpose of his call was to ask me where the key to my wine cellar was. Just what I needed, two artists rummaging through my most precious possessions. Max said it was just himself, that Robert had some kind of secret get-together and would not be back until morning. He promised not to drink anything exorbitant. Good, I thought, the Rothschild, first growth Bordeaux would be safe and the Chateau Lafite and the Leroy Corton Charlemagne were also out of danger. I suggested a Provence Rosé; the Chateau Risqué Rosé was technically average, but tasty. He was delighted and hung up the phone.

The next day Max slept late. He left my apartment and walked to a nearby cafe. The Americano coffee was strong enough to clear away his headache. The bastard had drunk two bottles of my Dom

Pérignon. Later he walked to the Jardin des Tuileries, put his feet in the water and watched tourists at the Bassin Octogonal. After an hour or so of people gazing, he returned to my place to take a long nap. Robert had returned earlier and was snoozing on my sofa.

That night, Max and Robert took a private tour to Giverny.

It was Robert's idea. And no, he was not drunk or high. At least that's what I was told by Max. Robert was supposedly inspired by our friend's love of Monet's paintings.

He told Max. "I hate to admit it, but I have never been to Monsieur Monet's place and I'm getting tired of explaining why to people. I usually say I'm a sculptor and only attracted to carvers and cutting stone myself. Beyond that, I don't go out of my way to look at paintings."

Max tried to talk him out of the excursion but when Robert gets something stuck in his craw you can't dissuade him. It would be hopeless for me to try to stop the insanity, so off they went.

****

Robert parked the Lamborghini behind an old mill about a mile from Monet's Giverny home. The moon that night was full, and as if they were shadows on the dimly lit road, they walked towards the home of France's greatest impressionist. When they reached the gate, two slobbering Newfoundland giants ran to the entrance. They barked and Robert threw several slabs of meat over the fence. The dogs disappeared and Robert took a set of keys from his jacket pocket. The gate swung open. Max waited for the alarm to go off, but apparently there wasn't one. Once inside, Robert closed the gate. Max asked where he got the keys and Robert smiled saying, "You know my friend from the Louvre, the one who is a conservator? I was with her last night; she was kind enough to give me the key."

"Have I met her?"

"No, not that I know of. Remind me to tell you later about a project she is working on. There might be an opportunity in it for you."

Max was beginning to sweat. "If we get arrested this will turn into a huge scandal! Our pictures, and your girlfriend's too, will be plastered all over the front page of the every Paris newspaper!"

"You worry too much. We are protected.""What do

you mean, 'protected'?" "I have credentials." Robert took two badges from his pocket and handed one to Max. Max turned his flashlight on what appeared to be an official document. "Clip it to your jacket," Robert ordered. "Where did you get these?" "Friends." "You mean fucks, not friends."

The two walked along a path surrounded by iris and peony beds, down a footpath through the rose trellises and approached the Japanese bridge that curved over Monet's pond. Max pulled a camera out of his pocket and took several pictures of the garden. Robert offered to take a snap shot of Max standing on the green Japanese walking bridge, Max agreed and posed with his hands on the railing looking into the pond. Robert took two pictures. One, he took from the bank below the bridge pointing the camera up to show Max looking down towards the water lilies. The other, a side view from the bridge capturing Max's profile and hands on the rail. Max reached out and took the camera back.

Max told me he thought it odd that Robert became nervous. One moment he was taking pictures and then all of a sudden he said, "We shouldn't take pictures, it's not a good idea. I don't want any evidence that we were here. You make sure you destroy that roll of film. Better yet, when we get back to the car, give the film to me."

For Max, it seemed out of character for Robert to react so strangely. Max took the film from his camera and put it back into its canister and threw it into his knapsack. Using a black gel pen, he wrote on the gray plastic canister cap, "*GIVERNY.*"

Under the light of the moon they walked to the bend at the top of the red wooden bridge and looked at their reflections in the water. Robert put his arm around Max's shoulder, pulled a pint of Vodka from the inside pocket of his leather jacket, took a long gulp and handed it to Max saying, "Well that was easy, let's return to Paris."

"We just got here, let's look around a bit.""No, I'm worried about the dogs."When they returned to the car, Robert neglected to ask Max for the film. Maybe it was the vodka, or the fear of the dogs that had begun to howl strangely, that caused Robert to forget.

****

When they got back to Paris, Robert dropped Max at my door saying he was staying the night with a friend. Max figured the "friend" was a woman.

The next morning, Robert showed up at my place. Max was ready and waiting for him. Max grabbed his bag, jumped on the small elevator and then walked trois pâtés de maisons, (three blocks for you Americans), to the bistro down the street for coffee. Robert tried to read the morning paper, but his head was throbbing. Too much vodka of course. Max drank his new French favorite, *café noisette*, and chewed on a raisin bagel smothered in cream cheese. He watched Parisians coming up or going down into the *Métro*. He was impressed with how fashionable the women, and even the men, looked as they were going to work. The schoolchildren were also stylish. Even the dogs in their sweaters looked impeccable.

Finally, Robert felt well enough to travel. They went to my garage, the valet brought their car up and Max jumped into the driver's seat. He wanted the thrill of driving a racecar. Robert was hungover; he had stayed up all night drinking with an exotic dancer in Pigalle.

On the long drive back to the Luberon Valley, Robert and Max chatted about their future projects. Robert said his meeting with the conservator at the Louvre had gone well. She told him that another major project would be coming his way, but warned him to keep it quiet until the official announcement became public.

Robert also told Max an interesting story regarding three small Monet drawings that were found in an old mill near Monet's estate. As he explained to Max, the mill had long ago been transformed into restaurant and hotel. The owners were expanding the place by converting the attic into more guest rooms. During the renovation, a worker found three signed Monet drawings stuffed in the ceiling insulation. Dampness and roosting pigeons had scratched and stained the drawings. Two of the works had faint signatures and the other one was so badly damaged that not only Monet's signature was obliterated, but so was a third of the image. Robert told Max that if he were interested, he would speak to his friend at the Louvre about having Max work on the restoration of the sketches. Robert made a point to emphasize that there would be considerable compensation paid for the work to be flawlessly conserved. Max was interested, but he reminded Robert that he had never done conservation work. Robert told him one Dominique Dubois would assist.

Max was curious. "Who is this woman? How did you meet her?"

"Mademoiselle Dubois is a remarkably talented woman of Algerian descent. Her grandfather was an early French settler in Algeria. In 1954, during the Algerian War for independence, her parents fled the country and settled in Paris. She was raised in the largely Muslim neighborhood of Clos Saint-Lazare in Paris. It is a rough area that is fast becoming a separate Islamic society. More and more, it seems to be cutting itself off from the French state, to the point where Islamic Sharia law is displacing French civil law. French values have all but disappeared in that section of Paris."

"When she was a teenager, a local cleric saw she had immense talent and he did not want her to stay in Saint-Lazare. He knew if she did, she would be doomed. This cleric had a rabbi friend who helped him to get her into the École des Beaux-Arts across the Seine from the Louvre where she studied painting. She lived with a Russian orthodox family during the four years she studied at the famous school. She received an internship to work at the Louvre and has never left."

"I find her exotic and rather mysterious. I love fucking her."

Max doubted his friend's veracity and his capabilities. "But you're twice her age and you're also married!" Max apparently does not understand we French.

Max told Robert that he was becoming complacent with his work and needed to push himself in another direction and that maybe this kind of project might inspire him in someway.

He also told Robert that he could use the money. "Most of what I sold from my recent show at Céline's has run out and I'm getting worried about my ability to meet my expenses."

He told Robert he was going to see if Michelin might consider commissioning him once again to do some small sketches or paintings of the rich man's gardens.

Robert smiled knowingly, "What to create, how to survive, that is the question for most artists, but not for me. I just copy what others have done. That is the sad truth of where my talent lies. I don't have original ideas anymore. I don't starve, my talent provides a good living, and I am content not being the next Michelangelo."

Max shook his head saying, "I have no illusions about fame, I don't paint for fame. I paint to discover. I have been painting since I was small child; it is what I do and who I am. I don't do it for money, but I need money to do it."

"Max Connor, you are a romantic and this is why I

like you so much. Now, as for your driving, it stinks. Pull over and let me get us back to Lacoste before dark."

They didn't stop for dinner, just gasoline, coffee and a MacDonald's hamburger outside of Avignon. When Robert pulled up to Max's studio they embraced. Max suggested Robert spend the night, but he begged off saying he had to get back to Marseille. Like a true Frenchman, Robert kissed each side of Max's face. "One last thing I need to say to you about Françoise. I will support whatever you decide to do about her. Protect your heart, but let your manhood enjoy the sex. After all, she is perverted in ways that most men would die for. And don't tell Céline what I have just said to you. (Eventually Max told me, he had no other choice.)

I heard both sides of the story of their trip to Paris. Max's interpretation and Robert's report of the trip were somewhat different.

After he got back to Marseilles, Robert phoned to thank me. "Why are you thanking me?""For agreeing to let me stay at your apartment in Paris." "You shit, you didn't stay at my apartment; you were fucking some bitch and staying at her place."There was a pause, finally he confessed. "Guilty.""Why do you lie to me? You know I have sources that report to me on your whereabouts."

"*Qui, ce putain de Max est un mouchard,* (fucking Max is a snitch)."The fool thinks it's only Max who spies on him.During the conversation he mentioned something odd. He said Françoise was working on a series of Chagall-like watercolors. I thought it strange that Robert would know what she was doing and Max was completely in the dark. After all, Robert rarely saw Françoise, and as far as I knew, he had never been in her studio or apartment in Les Beax.

Later, during one of my weekly conversations with Max I asked him about Françoise's Chagall style paintings, he said, "I don't know what you're talking about. I've never seen her doing anything that looks remotely like Chagall. Robert must have been drunk when you talked to him."

Perhaps I shouldn't have replied, but I couldn't help saying, "No, I don't think so, he wasn't slurring his words or saying stupid shit like he usually does when he's blitzed."

****

A few days after my conversation with Robert, Françoise returned from Paris. Max went to Les Baux to visit, or should I say to fuck, Françoise.

Anyway, he got what he wanted I'm sure.

Max told me the disturbing story of how he was almost killed. Maybe it was because of his Lamborghini experience, or the libido pulsating in his loins that he drove faster than he would normally drive. He took the steep climb toward the peaks of the Alpilles, but while snaking along the treacherous curved road, his back wheel separated from the axle and disappeared over the edge of a cliff. Sparks from the Peugeot's undercarriage threatened to ignite the gas tank. The shaking of the automobile made it difficult to keep the automobile under control. Finally he was able to stop it. He quickly got out of the car and, as he approached the rear end of his vehicle, the earth and rocks beneath its axle began to crumble. Seconds before the entire automobile plunged over the edge of the cliff, Max was able to grab the handle of the rear door, snatch his knapsack and save his drawing supplies and his camera case. He watched the car tumble into the famous Valley of Hell, where it exploded.

At first, several locals ran down from the village, and then a tourist bus stopped in the middle of the road blocking traffic. The police finally showed up, made a report and checked to make sure Max had not been drinking. Thankfully, all they got was a whiff of the cheap cigar he was smoking. One of the villagers must have recognized Max and alerted Françoise. She held Max just as the SMUR, *Service d'Aide Médicale Urgente,* arrived. After being cleared by police and medics, Max was allowed to leave the scene. Shaken, but happy to be alive, he and Françoise walked back up the incline to the village. They hadn't been in the apartment but a minute when the phone rang. It was Robert. Françoise answered and handed the phone to Max. Max began telling him he had just been in an accident. It was as if Robert didn't hear words like crash, fire, bottom of the mountain, police, firemen, lucky to be alive.

The first thing out of his mouth was, "Do you have the roll of film from Giverny?" Robert seemed fixated on the camera. Max went to his knapsack, opened it and took out the camera saying, "It's here. I'll take care of it."

Robert was relieved. Our friend from Marseilles was then able to inquire as to Max's condition. Max told him about the accident and Robert was thankful to know his friend was unhurt and the only thing injured was the Peugeot. Totaled. Burned to a crisp. Dead. Thank goodness Max was not.

After the conversation Max wondered how Robert knew her phone number. Françoise had a private unlisted telephone. He asked Françoise how Robert got her number. She brushed him off saying; "You must have given it to him." He thought for a moment, but couldn't recall doing so. However he thought he probably did, just couldn't remember. After all, he thought, I spend a lot of time at her place, so it would make sense that I gave him her number. Françoise poured him a glass of wine, took him into her bedroom, messaged his body, and then, as you can imagine, they visited kinkytown.

The next morning, after breakfast and several calls to his insurance agent and a rental car company, the two went to the Roman aqueduct at Pont du Gard to draw. Max completed an image in sepia ink of the high ancient stone waterway with two large poplar trees in the foreground. The results were pleasing. However, Max's vision had become blurred. At first he was concerned it had something to do with the accident. But, he reminded himself, after several hours of staring towards the direction of the midday sun it was the intense glaring light on his corneas that was causing the blurring and pain.

Françoise was not pleased with her drawing and threw it into the river. She was frustrated. She suggested they climb down to the shoreline of the river and have sex. "I want the boy scouts standing on the top of the aqueduct to watch us."

Max was uncomfortable, but being of an erotic

nature, he agreed. Françoise stripped off her sundress, left her sandals on and waded into the water where she pulled herself up onto a large flat rock and laid naked for all to see. The boys cheered as Max joined her. She performed oral sex on Max in front of the scouts. An angry scoutmaster shooed his troop off the slate rooftop of the historic Roman monument. As he led his boys away he picked up a rock and threw it at the couple. It fell far short of its target and splashed harmlessly into the river. One of the young men waved goodbye to Max and Françoise; the scout leader cuffed him on the back of his head. The boys disappeared. I wonder if the Boy Scouts give a badge for blowjobs?

****

Françoise drove them back to Lacoste. They unpacked the gear from their knapsacks. Max said he noticed his camera, plus the canister containing the Giverny pictures were missing. He asked Françoise if she had them.

She said, "No, they probably slipped out of your pack when we were jumping the boulders in the river. I suppose they are now scraping their way along the river bottom towards Nimes."

That evening she drove Max back to Lacoste. They sat on the wall of the overlook drawing the swallows that flew from Lacoste towards Bonnieux and back again as they caught their dinner of insects. Every so often a bat would fly from the bell tower of the old church. The dark yellow sun was sinking below the horizon near Mont Ventoux. Max ran down the street to the Café de Sade for a bottle of wine and stopped at his studio and brought two wine glasses back to the overlook and filled them with the wine. Françoise drank quickly and asked Max to get another bottle. As he was returning he saw she was talking on the pay phone. He leaned near the wall of the Mairie building trying to listen to her conversation, but she was speaking French. He came around the corner and she hung up. He asked her who she was talking to and she said her girl friend Valerie in to Saints-Maries-de-la-Mer. A red flag went up in his mind. "She wants me to come tomorrow for a visit and I was wondering if you wouldn't mind if I take a few of your drawings to show her? She loves my work, so I am sure she will be enthralled with yours."

Max told her she could have a few drawings and that he would accompany her on the trip to Saints-Maries-de-la-Mer. At first she pretended it would be nice if he could join her. But Max knew she was mulling through her mind a scenario she could use to go by herself.

A half hour later she found her lie, "Max, we are going to the beauty salon and not only having our hair done, but also our nails. It will take hours and afterward we are going to the opera. You hate Opera. Stay home and paint." Max planned to follow her, but he remembered he didn't have a car.

That night the two crawled into bed. Max thought there might be some lovemaking, but within minutes Françoise fell into a deep sleep. Max lay on bed, tortured with thoughts of betrayal and jealousy.

Finally he realized that his mind was fixated on treachery and sleep was impossible. He gently lifted her arm from his chest, slid off the bed and quietly walked from the bedroom to his studio. He sat in his paint-spattered chair studying a painting in progress. He thought about her supposed friend. Max had no idea if there really was a friend named Valerie. He did know there was a man she met in Saints-Maries-de-la-Mer who was a Vladimir, not a Valerie.

By his side was a bottle of liquor; in his hand a tall glass of cognac and between his fingers a dying cigar. Françoise was sound asleep. He was out of smokes. He went into her purse to find cigarettes.

He was fishing for her pack of Gitanes, when he found the canister marked Giverny.

He threw back his head, swallowed the rest of the glass filled with cognac and said out loud, "SHIT."

Max told me that at that point he wasn't sure what to do. He opened the plastic container. The film was gone. What did she want with it? Was she thinking it might be evidence that Max was having a romantic affair during his weekend in Paris? He put the canister back into her purse.

He saw her address book, pulled it out, and began going through the pages. There were names, addresses and phone numbers of men, woman, museums, public officials, stores, restaurants and even a few newspaper reporters. He knew none of the friends or associates who were listed in the book. He was relieved to see a number for a Valerie. Her address was in Saints- Maries-de-la-Mer. So she did exist.

What did it all mean? There was also Robert's telephone number. How could this be? Françoise had never met Robert, she was only aware of him through Max. So again, here was another deception. Nothing added up, but something was going on. There were the diamonds, the camera, the man in the church in Saints- Maries-de-la-Mer, and now the phone number mystery. Something foreboding was going on and the strange connections between events were leading both him and me into a dark and dangerous place.

Most men would confront her, but my friend Maxfield Connor had come under her spell. When it came to the bitch, he was often oblivious, sometimes blind, and simply in denial. Just like the time he followed her into the Maries-de-la-Mer church, he couldn't or wouldn't confront her. He knew that if he told her that he had tailed her, she would have made up some sort of story about the man and the envelope and, with self-righteous indignation, declare her innocence. That episode was a conundrum, but now he faced a new challenge, if he told her he had gone through her purse, she would be furious. In her twisted mind, the fact that she lied about the film would not come close to what she would perceive as the greater betrayal of going through her purse. After all, foraging through a woman's purse was like reading her diary. Max had a conscience; Françoise was a fraud.

****

In the morning they both got up early. Max made

coffee for her. He said nothing about the missing film or the camera. She took the drawings he had given her to show to Valerie and laid them out on the kitchen table, quickly rolled them in butcher paper to protect them from fingerprints and then grabbed her purse and keys. She kissed him and off she went for Maries-de-la-Mer. He told me he went back inside to the bedroom and stood sipping his coffee and looking at the unmade bed. The impression of her head on the pillow was still visible. He noticed the notecard on the sheet. With a quick flourish of her pen she had written, "I won't be back tonight. I don't know when I'll return."

He wasn't sure how to interpret her words. Her writing in English was poor and maybe she meant to say, or if I'll return soon. He wondered if she was telling him it was over? Or, that it simply meant see you at the end of the week. By nature Max was an optimist. However, he was upset enough to call Robert for advice. Robert didn't answer, however, the next day he returned Max's call. It was a huge mistake on Robert's part.

HP shared a conversation caught on a telephone tap. When I asked whose phone, he said he couldn't reveal the owner's identity. It was not Robert's phone but the phone of someone important in Marseilles. The conversation between Max and Robert was disturbing to hear, but answered some questions and brought clarity to my relationship with the two.

Sometimes in life you have a friend, maybe from childhood, or a college mate that you think you know, but you find out things about them that make it clear they are not the person you thought they were. That's what happened here.

Robert's conversation with my old boyfriend was disturbing. I learned things that I didn't know about and attitudes that depressed me.

Max told his friend some of what had taken place on the last trip he took with Françoise to Maries-de-la-Mer. Apparently, Robert listened intently and waited for the story to unfold. Wisely, Max decided not to mention the diamonds.

Robert seemed irritated. "Max, I told you to keep her around for fucking, but not for fucking your mind."

"I know...I know what you said is probably right. Last week we went to draw at Pont du Gard. She wanted to have sex with me in front of group of boy scouts. She is insatiable, exciting, the most erotic woman I have ever known."

"Listen to me Max, here is what I propose. I will ask my friend, Michael Corleone, to make her disappear. Send me her picture. I'll give it to him. If he is not busy making *Godfather 4 or 5 or 6* he'll come up to Les Baux and wrap a wire around her throat!"

Max interrupted his friend's comedic response. "Fuck I need to buy a car, I have no money. Maybe I can get a car loan."

Robert kept up his joking manor. "Who's going to give an artist credit?"

Max came up with an alternative. "Maybe I can rent one." "I don't think so, who is going to risk renting a car to a person who drove off the side of a mountain? Your vehicle was a piece of shit anyway. No loss, I'll get our friend Michelin to loan you his Lamborghini. By the way, are you okay?"

"Yes, thank goodness I didn't roll down the cliff with it. I hate to lose Françoise, but she's fucking me up. I love her; I hate her. I don't know what to do. Help me here."

Robert offered his advice. He had some good points, but he's a sexist pig and a traitor.

Robert said, "I have never met the woman, all I

know about her comes from you and Céline. Like most of us men, you are confused and conflicted by females. Women love to fuck with us. You probably should have stayed with Céline. She's a woman, but thinks like a man. If you find you don't love Françoise, then leave her. There are lots of fish in the sea, another woman will come along. Look, you are my best friend. You are a great artist, a kind man with a big heart. We have known one another for a long time. All I want for you is happiness. We have talked many times over the last year about Françoise. I go back and forth on the issue of you and her being together. Our friend Céline does not like her, and maybe she is jealous. You and Celine have a special relationship. In the past, you shared her bed. You also are in business together. Being lovers and doing business together is not a good combination. So when you found Françoise, I was supportive."

"Celine believes you need to rid yourself of Françoise. I am less sure. She gives you great pleasure. She is an artist and, by the way, I would like to see her art work someday."

"This Françoise woman is obviously complicated, maybe there is more to her than you know. From what you say, she has connections in high places. Céline tells me Françoise claims to sell her work for considerable money and we know she is divorcing a very powerful politician, so there will be a big payoff in her future. I guess when all is taken into account; it might be best if you hang on to her for a while longer. I am sure that some of her mysterious behaviors can be explained; after all, she is not a criminal. Stay with her, that's my advice. But do me a favor; do not tell Céline what I think. She is also my dealer; I am her friend. We don't always see eye to eye and I don't want to cross her. As far as she is concerned, I am on her side. Let's keep the deception going. I don't need her to be pissed off with me."

Although he never intended to honor his commitment, Max agreed. He called me the next day and repeated word for word the conversation. You see Max is loyal to me.

Apparently, Robert suddenly changed the topic and his voice sounded tense to Max. "Now, on to other important things. Did you destroy the film?"

"I seem to have misplaced it." "Damn it Max, find it and burn the damn thing. I should have taken the film from you that night in the garden. I am deadly serious about this. We both could get into a shit load of trouble. We can't afford to be indicted for trespassing on Monsieur Monet's property."

I haven't told you because I knew it would worry you, but I have a friend who read something in the *La Provence de Marseille* about the two dogs being found dead at Giverny from food poisoning. I played dumb, but after he told me the story I ran to the *tabac* for the paper. Dog stories in the newspaper will always draw readers. So this thing might not blow over for a while. Dog lovers are like pit bulls with a bone. They don't let go. Next thing that could happen is the Société protectrice des animaux will launch an investigation."

Max was beginning to become paranoid about his role in the fiasco of the break-in. "You gave those dogs poison meat? How could you do that?"

Our sculptor friend pleaded innocent. "Max, of course not, you know me better than that. I couldn't hurt a fly, well maybe a fly. But to poison a dog, come on, I am incapable of something like that. It's just a coincidence. They probably ate a dead duck from the pond or a sick koi fish. You know those Newfoundlands love water; they certainly were in and out of Monet's pond all the time. But the thing here is, coincidence or not, we broke the law. Sure, we were a bit drunk, but we are famous artists and the public outcry could ruin our reputation and livelihood. So please, find that damn film."

Max said, "I think you're overreacting. No one saw

us; you told me your friend from the Louvre said there were no cameras or alarms at Giverny. You made us wear gloves, so no fingerprints. This is not the crime of the century."

"That's what you think. You're an American. We French adore Monet; the man is a national treasure. Get the film and burn the Kodachrome today. Also, when Françoise returns tomorrow, don't ask her any questions about her friend down there in Saintes- Maries-de-la-Mer. I'll do some checking around, I have a few friends living in the Camargue. They'll get us all the answers we need."

Max promised, Robert hung up the phone. I remember HP saying, "The crew from the Camargue are Corsicans." I knew the implication of what he was saying. It was code for Mafia and murderous cutthroats.

I suppose my friend looked all through his studio, into closets, under furniture and in every place he could think where Françoise might have hidden the film. Nowhere to be found, he probably figured she must have taken it with her.

HP asked me why would they be so reckless to break into Giverny. I had no idea. Sometimes men act like boys. I was more upset with the duplicitous nature of Robert than I was with the childish prank.

HP said he thought there was something more sinister behind the break-in. I thought he was way off base. Max didn't have a mean bone in his body. And as far as I was concerned, Robert was just dumb, drunk and stupid.

****

Sometimes life is mysterious. When you need something, which is not the same as wanting something, then the need will manifest itself.

The roar of Maurice Michelin's Lamborghini engine driving through the Goats Gate announced his coming. The familiar rumbling of Michelin's toy brought Max down the stairs and out onto the street.

Michelin is a diminutive portly man in his mid 60's. He has thin graying hair and a white goatee. According to Max he was wearing a touring cap turned backwards, a Ralph Lauren blue blazer and an out of fashion pair of corduroy pants. Max watched as the collector twisted his tubby body between the steering wheel and the leather seat to get out of his racecar. The two embraced. Maurice reached into his jacket pocket and handed Max a Havana cigar. He turned back, leaned into the car and stretched his short right arm down into the space behind the driver's seat and the small cargo area behind it. He pulled out a bottle of wine. Not just any wine, it was a special reserve bottle of Rosé from the Château Sainte Roseline.

Max asked Maurice, "To what good fortune do I owe this visit? Has Castro died?

Michelin laughed, "Not that I know of. As long as Monsieur Fidel has good rum to drink and fine cigars to smoke, he will outlive all the Kennedy's. I have tried to call you several times, but you do not answer your phone. I was worried you may have been overtaken by paint fumes and might be lying dead on your studio floor. Your space is far too small and congested. I am concerned about your health and the danger that someday your studio will explode. You know, the painter Françoise Bacon once told me that was his greatest fear."

"You saw the painting of Pope Innocent at my home. That, and the Cézanne your friend Françoise helped me purchase, are my most prized possessions. She was able to find the Bacon in Monte Carlo just after he died a few years ago. Its value will increase exponentially."

"As to the real reason I'm here, it is to determine if you have a large painting that I might purchase for my collection. But I fear the size of your studio may be too constricted for a painting of the measurements I require."

Max said he thanked God for bringing Maurice to him. "What size are you looking for?"

"I need something measuring 152cm by about 244cm. I need the painting to be predominantly green, but no reds. I'm not interested in looking at something Christmassy. So, blues, blacks, yellows, anything but red. I don't care if it is completely abstract or slightly based upon our local landscape. It must be recent, fit with the furnishing in the room, go with the colors of my Afghan carpet and be sufficiently eye catching."

Max told me he was concerned about, "sufficiently eye catching." As a painter Max found this kind of language repugnant and demeaning. It also brought into question the veracity of the collector. However, when he called to tell me about the transaction, my thought was, who cares. It's a sale.

As Max thought about the aesthetics of his work versus how his painting would go with carpets and curtains, it was offensive to him. But paying his bills and having a roof over his head would allow him to continue living the life of an artist. No matter what Michelin picked from Max's inventory, it was going to be a good painting.

Max told Michelin that he had rented a larger space for painting. It was an old barn where he had been storing his paintings. Recently he cleared out the pigeon poop and cobwebs and had begun doing large oil paintings. He invited Maurice to take a look. They walked down the hill to the outskirts of the village and next to the road that curved its way towards Bonnieux was the barn. It was more like a big garage; but then barns in that area were never meant for herd animals, they usually served more as a place to house tractors and cultivators, spare parts and as a domicile for the farm dog.

Max told me that when he threw open the double doors, Michelin's jaw dropped. Max had restored the 100-year-old oak beams and boards. It was immaculate inside. He had built storage bins for his paintings. Each piece of artwork fit between sheets of plywood so the canvasses would not touch one another, therefore no scrapes or scratch marks marred the surface of any painting. He had built a staircase leading up into the loft that was now his working area. He had hung tools such as trowels, palette knives, hammers, scissors, T-squares, canvas cutters and yardsticks on pegboards attached to the side walls of the loft area. There were several long folding tables on which he laid his tubes of colors. Max was organized. Standard blues together, reds down to oranges, oranges to yellows, Prussian Blues and Phthalo Greens in one place, and cads were in another. Seven whites, like seven dwarfs, each with different complexions and consistencies lay side by side. Underneath the tables were gallon containers of linseed oil, turpentine and at least a hundred cheap housepainters brushes from half inch to 6 inches wide, some with black plastic bristles, some golden hogs hair and many white latex. Max rarely used sable or squirrel hair for his oil paintings, but for watercolors they were precious. In the corner were two large garbage cans. He had brackets on the wall holding up bolts of canvas, linen, and rolls of watercolor paper. He had found and installed a cement washtub and put in a bathroom himself. He traded an electrician a watercolor in return for putting in outlets and lights. The space was perfect for him.

Max had hung some new work on the walls; the pieces were still wet, but finished. Maurice was impressed with the fresh paintings, but he wanted to see more. Max pulled three pieces from the racks that were the size Michelin was interested in. He pointed to one and said, "That's it! But can you take the red flicks of color out?"

Max agreed. The collector reached into his jacket pocket and pulled out a manila bank envelope. Inside was an American Express cashiers check made out to Max for thirty thousand US dollars.

"Tell Céline I will send her a commission check when you deliver the painting.

When Max called and told me the amount, I was stunned. Including the 50% commission that Maurice would send me, sixty thousand dollars was twice the amount that was ever paid for a Maxfield Connor painting.

Max could buy a car. He thought a Citroën or another Peugeot would be good. He needed a small automobile that could squeeze through the narrow streets in the villages and towns of Provence. When Françoise returned, he would have her take him to the dealership in Apt.

****

When Max called me, astounded by the sale, I too was happy. Happy for both of us.

I asked him if he had talked with Robert in the last few days. He lied; I wasn't surprised. I decided it was best to not let on I knew differently. For one thing, I didn't want him to know about the wiretap. Plus, I sure wasn't going to compromise the fact that I knew what he was saying about me, or the visit to Monet's gardens. I have my own secrets to keep, so playing dumb or unaware is an advantage for me.

He told me about his recent drawing excursion and then followed it up with something disturbing.

He had gone to an abbey close to Lacoste to do watercolors. I knew he'd been there before. It was too far to walk in the Luberon heat. He exited the Goat Gate, walked down to the crossroad, put his thumb out and quickly got a ride.

Max says the 12th century Carmelite abbey is beautiful. There is an old chapel and a high stone terrace overlooking gardens of iris, roses, and other flowers. Just outside the gated wall is an olive orchard. Max spent the afternoon doing a small watercolor sketch of roses against a tall stone wall. When the sun started to drop from the sky he returned to Lacoste in the same fashion that he had taken in the morning. Hitchhiking was a young man's game. He was middle age and enjoying an experience he long ago had forgotten.

He got home and showered. There was a small black scorpion on the floor tile. With his sandaled foot, he nudged the creature towards the drain. Like the water that swirled down the hole, it too disappeared. He did not dress, he ran around in his undershorts. That was typical; summer heat in Provence feels much the same as the temperatures in the Sahara. He made his own dinner, Salad Niçoise. It was Max's favorite dish, simple to make and refreshing. Max preferred canned tuna to tuna steaks. He didn't use capers or anchovies. He was a fan of potatoes, green beans, egg, onion and olives. He felt strongly that the dressing was the key factor to making the perfect Niçoise. He used the traditional ingredients of basil, thyme and oregano leaves, sometimes a bit of mint, but instead of lemon, he liked lime. The mustard and oil were critical. It didn't have to be Dijon, sometimes good English mustard worked well for his palate.

He slept soundly that night. He said that as he was lying in bed he thought of Robert. This was interesting. He said he treasured Robert; he had always been a true friend. Although his language could be crusty at times, he spoke directly and didn't mince his words. His advice was almost always correct. I could have spit up when I heard this bullshit. But then he went further and I thought, yes, you might be getting wise.

Max told me he needed to be cautious with their

friendship. "Sometimes in life a feeling of doom can be a warning sign. It has nothing to do with insecurity or fear. Your gut tells you not to go down a certain street. It looks safe but your mind tells you that your feeling is unjustified. I've learned to trust my gut."

Early the next day, Max was awakened by the sound of someone's fist pounding on his door. Max was not an early riser. Most of the people in the village, with the exception of Marie, from the boulangerie, took their time getting up in the morning. Max picked up his sandals and carefully looked them over to make sure there wasn't a scorpion hiding inside. One always has to be careful of scorpions. The black one's sting is very much like an American yellow jacket sting, it hurts like hell, but if you're not allergic to bee stings, you will be fine. Not so with the sting of a white scorpion, it can kill a human.

He slid his feet into the safety of his sandals. He went down the stairs and opened the door. Two national policemen asked if they could come inside. Max's first thought was of Françoise in a car accident and then he thought of Giverny. The bigger of the two burly men dressed in military style uniforms said, "You are Monsieur Maxfield Connor?"

Max replied with a yes. "What can I help you with?"

You are the leaseholder of the Peugeot that went off the road near Les Baux?"

Max thought it best to reply in French, "Oui""We have some questions we need to ask you." "*Excusez-moi*. Would you mind if I change into a pair of pantaloons?""*Oui, s'il vous plaît faire* (Yes, please do)." The officer spoke simply and to the point. That was a bit disconcerting to Max."Feel free to go into the kitchen and pour yourselves café, the crème is in the réfrigérateur, cups in the cabinet on the right and the sugar is in le bol sur la table de cuisine." Max ran up the stairs to get dressed. He returned wearing his jeans and a paint splattered t-shirt. The two officers where standing in the living room looking at Max's paintings. Putty Tat came into the room and jumped up onto the deep window ledge and stared at the intruders.

"Monsieur, your French is awful. We speak English, so please, do not attempt to speak our language. Is your shirt going to be in one of your paintings?" Max awkwardly laughed. "Are you nervous Monsieur? I did not mean to offend you with my small jest."

The fact was Max was worried with the police

being in his house and where the questions might go. "No, I am used to such jokes. But should I be nervous?"

"Maybe. On the day you drove to Les Baux, had you noticed anything odd about the way your car was operating?"

"No, I don't recall anything, why? " Max noticed the other officer was writing notes.

"No feeling of instability? Did your automobile feel bumpy?" "I don't recall anything like that.""Humm...had anyone else been in possession of your car?" "No, of course not."

"When was the last time you had maintenance done on the vehicle?"

"I think maybe three months ago.""Did you lend the car to anyone?""No. Why are you asking these questions"?"Are their any ruffians here in Lacoste who might have tampered with your car?" "Of course not."

"You are not French. Sometimes people in our villages play jokes on foreigners."

"I get along well with my neighbors."

"Monsieur, I understand you have girlfriend who lives in Les Baux, yes?"

"That's correct." "Would you have lent her your car recently?" "No. She has her own. What do all these questions have to do with the accident?" "One more question please. Do you know of anyone who would want to see you dead?"

Max was stunned. In a shaky voice he replied, "Of course not. Why are you asking me this?"

"Monsieur Connor, during the examination of your car by your insurer he found something out of place and called our office. Someone had removed all but two lug nuts from your back tire making the wheel unstable. You are lucky to be alive. You could have gone over the edge with the car. Now I ask you again, do you have any enemies who might have done this or paid someone to cause your death?"

Max said, "I have no enemies, I'm just an artist. Why would anyone want to kill me?" Max told me he excused himself and went to the bathroom and vomited several times. He took a washcloth and wiped his face. He said he was sweating when he returned to the room. The officer handed him his card. He told Max that if he thought of anything that might shed light on what happened, or who might have a grudge or reason to see Max dead, he should call him. "Au revoir Monsieur Connor, if we need anything more we will be in touch." They shook hands. The police left.

Max immediately called and told me about the unexpected visit by the gendarmes. This event obviously added to his paranoia. I was shocked. I confessed some of what I had learned from HP but not everything. Max was not surprised that I was suspicious of Françoise and as a result had gone so far as to make secret inquiries. He was relieved to hear what I had done and what I had learned. It brought clarity to the strange happenings that had been occurring.

Thank God he was not angry with me. I treasured his reply. "Céline, you have continuously looked out for me. I know I've not always valued you as I should have, and for that, I am embarrassed. Thank you for being my friend. You have been the most important woman in my life."

For a moment my heart went soft, but my self-control prevailed. I tried to hide my concern, but the truth is I felt anxious. Even though we didn't realize it at that time, Max and myself were being pulled into a dangerous conspiracy. We both agreed that I would inform my government friend, HP, about the details of the events Max had shared with me. I told Max to continue his relationship with Françoise until HP advised otherwise. He agreed. I knew he was capable of fucking a woman without remorse. This time he'd fuck Françoise Gemmer for revenge.

****

What happened next was to be expected. I should have warned Max; he is weak sometimes. Françoise is a seductress, as slick as Mata Hari or Delilah. After being gone for three days, she returned from the Camargue and the historic city of Maries-de-la- Mer. Max played it cool. He asked if she had a good time and inquired as to how her friend was. Before she answered, she threw her arms around his neck and her tongue, almost like a snake, twirled between his lips and the roof of his mouth. Françoise noticed a change in his demeanor. For a moment she pulled away and stared into his eyes. He grabbed her, cupped both hands around the cheeks of her ass and pulled her back into him. He could feel his cock beginning to harden; so did she.

His tongue was on her neck and moving slowly towards lobe of her ear where it gently and wetly circled the inside. She could hear his breathing; at first it was like the whispering of the Rhône River delta winds, but soon changed to something more animalistic. She pushed him back, smiled, then reached for his crotch and unzipped his pants. His khakis' fell to the floor. She unbuttoned his shirt and bent down to lick his nipple. She went lower. He felt her mouth on his stomach and her almost erect tongue slid into the opening in his navel. She dropped to her knees, pulled his cock through the slit of his boxer shorts. He began to breath like a bull. It was all over in a moment.

She licked her lips, stood up and said. "I had a wonderful time with Valerie." She then stuck her hands out, palms down to show her finely manicured nails to Max. They were pink and matched her lips and toenails. She turned and went to her suitcase, then pulled out an envelope and handed it to Max. "What's this?" he asked.

She smiled, "Open it."

The envelope was stuffed to the point that it bulged. Someone had licked the inside of the flap, sealed it and intentionally left a lipstick imprint on the fold. It was not a color that Françoise would wear. He tore the envelope open.

"Holy Shit." Max howled.

He was surprised by the amount of cash inside. Forty 500F notes fell out of the envelope onto the floor. He bent down and scooped up the money. He admired the image of Marie and Pierre Curie on each bill. There was also a folded note card.

"Max I love the three drawings Françoise brought to show me. If you require more money I will gladly send a check to you. I want to commission a few more pen and ink drawings. Françoise will fill you in on what I am looking for. I am excited with the prospect of becoming a collector of your work." The card was signed: Valerie.

Françoise smiled, saying, "Well, Mister Important Artist, isn't today a nice payday for you? Are you going to give me a commission? No, I'm just kidding. Congratulations."

Max took in a deep breath of air and then blew it from his lungs saying, "This couldn't have come at a better time. I really need money. Thank you for your help."

She curtsied and said, "Well there's more where that came from."

Max put out his hand, she took it and they walked into the kitchen. He placed the envelope on the table, pulled out two glasses and uncorked the bottle of wine he had been saving for a special occasion. "So what else is Valerie looking for? Do you think we should go through my portfolio and send her a few more pen and inks?"

Pulling her lips together, Françoise shook her head and then said, "No, she wants something particular. She would like you to do three or four drawings in the style of Cézanne and she wants them done somewhere near Aix-en-Provence. She also wants them executed on a cream colored paper that she apparently loves. She gave me several sheets for your use."

He frowned, "Hell, you could do the drawings for her, why me?"

She smiled, "Yes, I could, but I am not the famous American artist Maxfield Connor."

He shook his head and agreed to take the assignment. "Call her, let her know I will do them soon."

Max then told her of Michelin's purchase. She smiled. "Good you can buy a car now, no more rental and you can get something more appropriate. Maybe a Jaguar or a used Mercedes."

"No, I don't want to spend all the money; I need a cushion."

The next day Max called me about the sale and proposed commission by the woman in Saintes-Maries-de-la-Mer. I was happy for him. It was a good payday, not as good as the day before when

Michelin bought the big painting, but all in all, combined, he could buy a new car, and order art supplies from America.

I called HP to tell him about Max's good fortune and let him know that Françoise had returned. He asked if I knew the name of the woman commissioning the drawings. I told him that Max said her name was Valerie Bonnaire.

HP said, "We know her. Her real name was Valeriya Kurochkin.

HP's reaction to Max's good fortune was to say, "Could be a payoff, maybe a bribe. I don't believe in this kind of luck. In my experience coincidence and corruption often go hand in hand."

****

Max made lunch and afterward they gathered their watercolors and paper and walked to a nearby vineyard.

Side by side Max and Françoise painted. She faced west, towards the valley, and Max east, to the mountains. He finished two watercolor sketches. The first was of newly planted grape vines; the second, a view of a farmer harvesting sunflowers.

The sun was beginning to disappear so they decided to return to the village where Françoise prepared a light meal for them.

I spoke with him a few days later and he painted a verbal depiction of what happened next. I could have done without it, but I didn't stop him.

"After dinner Françoise told me she was very tired from our jaunt. We left the dishes in the sink and grabbed our backpacks and took them upstairs to the studio. She closed the shuttered windows tight so that, in the morning, light would not wake us. Surrounded by my paintings we made love on the carpet of my studio. Colors swirled around us and Edith Piaf sang on the radio. The smell of her perfume and my perspiration mingled with the scent of oil paint. We drifted off into our dreams; she talked in her sleep; I woke for a moment and heard her say a name of someone I didn't know; I tried to stumble back into my own dream of President Regan placing the National Medal of Arts around my neck. There was a part of my dream where I was pissing beside Willem de Kooning in the White House toilet and then the dream disappeared."

"When I woke in the morning I found myself lying in the studio on the paint splattered oriental carpet next to Françoise. The empty bottle of wine was on its side a few inches from her face. That, and the sex, probably accounted for why my arm was smeared with paint and my neck ached. I stood up and stretched, looked down at her naked body and thought she actually might be, *The Most Beautiful Woman In Provence*."

He also realized he was like a sailor worn out by the incessant winds of a terrible typhoon. Over the last year, through lies and manipulation, Françoise had exhausted him. His emotional pain was like fog on a window. It was now clear to him that she was not the woman of his dreams. She was despicable, a cunning bitch. He wanted to run away from her, to disappear like Gauguin into the jungles of some far away exotic island.

Max dreaded playing a role in the nightmare that was unfolding. He just wanted to paint, intrigue was not part of his palette. He wanted to vanish, but he couldn't escape. There was too much at stake. We both had to endure, there were no other choices for us.

I was less queasy about my role in what was happening than Max was.

HP asked me if I had ever heard of Han van Meegeren. I vaguely knew of him. He added, "Françoise Gemmer is a very talented artist, as was her father."

I went to the library and found that van Meegeren was the most clever art forger of the 20th century.

HP was being very careful, but as a skillful politician he was giving me clues as to what was going on. He needed me to expose an even greater and more extensive web of intrigue. This time it was not one lone gifted technician who was out to fool the art world; instead it was a conglomerate of individuals inside and outside the arts. It included artists who knowingly, and others who were being duped, into making fake works attributed to important French artists. They were not copies of famous paintings or drawings, but facsimiles in the style of the impressionists and the early 20th century masters. There were professional appraisers, collectors, curators and conservators; some even employed by the Louvre and other prestigious art organizations, involved. HP hinted that some of his colleagues, public officials and even a foreign nation were playing a role in the conspiracy. He implied some were in it for money, but others wanted more. Uncertainty, disruption of the art market and public confidence as well as the honor of the French people could cause doubt in the Republic's financial markets. The goal of the conspiracy leaders was to upset world markets.

The Japanese were collecting van Gogh, China was beginning to seek Western Art, and Sheiks and potentates from around the world were already heavily invested. The auction houses in London were in control of the European market and the American market was still dominant.

Millions in different currencies were being stolen from collectors. Collections, once thought priceless, were unknowingly being undermined. Extortion, corruption and even murders were taking place to protect the lords of the hoax. Neither side was aware that they were being undermined.

Perverting the art market and stealing the integrity of the works of the great French painters was unthinkable to me. As a French woman, and dealer of art, I was not going to shy away from exposing the deception that was infecting the Art. I knew I was in danger. The easy way out for me would be to leave the scandal for others to unravel. I couldn't do that. Besides, I was on a quest to destroy Françoise Gemmer.

Robert called Max to say he was in Paris and wondered if, on his way home to Marseille, he could stop and stay for a few days. Max replied. "Yes, of course, it will be great to see you. You can meet Françoise. And in that regard, I have some things to share with you about her."

"I hope that you are not going to tell me that you're planning to ask her to marry you."

Max replied, "That's the last thing I'd do."

"Good, so you finally realize that fucking can be a benefit without obligations?"

Max didn't elaborate. "See you when you get here."

Max was glad his friend was coming to visit. He mentioned to me that it would be the first time Robert and Françoise would meet. I reminded him to be careful not to tell Robert what was going on with HP, the police investigation, or the strange behavior of his Madamé Gemmer. I warned him about drinking and loose lips.

He condescendingly remarked, "Yes Céline, I hear you. I know, I know, I know. Okay?"

I only had HP and Max to confide in. I wanted to talk to my shrink or my sister, but it was too dangerous to bring them into the situation. I was so worried about Max. Hell, when somebody tries to kill the one you love, you're bound to be paranoid. So there, I've said it, I am in love with Maxfield Conner.

****

The day before Robert arrived, Françoise drove to Lacoste. Early in the morning she was banging on Max's door. He had only been awake for an hour and was still in his boxer shorts with a toothbrush in his mouth when he opened the door.

I'm sure, because the door was locked, she must have thought it odd. She asked him. "Max, why is your door locked?"

If you live in a Provencal village, as opposed to the city, you will find that most inhabitants only keep their doors latched in the winter when the unmerciful Mistral winds are blowing.

"Sorry, I must have accidently bumped against the latch with my knapsack when I came in last night."

After the police visit, Max had taken to locking his door at night. He had every reason to believe that whoever was out to kill him would make another attempt. Françoise knew nothing about the police visit. With all that HP had discovered it was best to not tell her anything.

Max and Françoise decided to work in the afternoon. That was unusual for them; normally, when they painted together, they worked only in the morning and evenings. Normally in Southern France, the afternoon sun is too hot to be outside working. But on that day, according the weather report from the Aix radio station, it was going to be unusually cool. Françoise suggested having morning sex, and then later, after lunch, they could spend the afternoon making art.

Max told me it was his duty to go along with her plan because, as he said, "After all, I'm a detective now."

Smart aleck!

That afternoon they decided to work in the village. They set themselves up not far from the crumbling walls of the castle of the Marquis de Sade. They both opened their plastic toolboxes. Françoise only intended to draw so there was not much inside her box other than a package of six assorted graphite pencils, a small jar filled with various sized pen nibs, two pen nib holders, a bamboo pen, a roll of paper towels, a pair of pliers and a few small brushes.

Max described her drawing method. "She starts with a pencil sketch, and in the beginning phase of drawing she isn't concerned with detail; that comes later. She just wants to get the proper perspective before applying permanent black ink. The drawing she did was complex; she wanted to capture the swallows in the sky flying over the church at the bottom of the village that was below us. The church was in the foreground, and then far away, off in the distance, the farm fields were laid out at the horizon line. It required a difficult three-point perspective challenge. Perspective is not her forte. The most useful tool she employed for getting the perspective right was her eraser."

She laid all her tools on an old discarded blue and yellow Provencal scarf. She had three jars of the antique ink she had purchased from her friend, Antoine, in Apt. She took her pliers and slowly twisted the cap until it loosened enough that she could hold it between her thumb and forefinger and remove the stopper. I am sure the jar of ink hadn't been opened since the early 1800s. She sniffed the ink to make sure it had not gone rancid, then, inserted the tip of the bamboo pen into the container and quickly removed it. She breathed in a sigh of relief. I was surprised that after almost 200 years it was still liquid."

"She then reached into her carrying bag to retrieve a cassette player, a bottle of burgundy wine, two water glasses and the latest album of her favorite recording artist, Françoise Hardy. We both like to paint to music as it stimulates the creative right hemisphere of our brains. Françoise began to sketch to the song, *La Pleine Lune* (The Full Moon). She has good taste in music."

"I was looking out over the valley in the opposite direction and had started to work on a watercolor of a distant view of a farm below Bonnieux. I mixed Winsor Newton sap green with burnt sienna. I started off rendering the shadows of a grassy field bathed in strong sunlight. I painted the tiled roofs of the farmhouse reflecting the sulfur sun with cadmium orange mixed with a touch of alizarin crimson, sepia and yellow ochre. My brush moved fast, filling the watercolor paper with a view that magically appeared within minutes. For effect, I dipped a toothbrush into my paints, pulled my thumb across the bristles splattering complementary colors on to the already dried surfaces representing trees, fields, buildings, mountains and sky. I was pleased with the intensity and excitement that I created in less than hour. It was effortless. Learning to see is the key to being a successful artist. To start on an empty blank white surface can be intimidating. To know when a work is finished is vital. It's taken me a long time to reach this point were I no longer have to struggle."

Max told me that when the sun dropped low to the horizon they stopped painting. He said the moon was full that night. "So bright, so beautiful" is how he described it. Max admitted to me that he felt conflicted. He knew he shouldn't feel guilty about the possibility that he was about to destroy her. The problem with Max is that sometimes he seems to care too much. I guess that's typical of artists. In spite of all the shit she was doing to him, he didn't want to hurt her. He told me that sitting next to Françoise that day made him happy. I figured he still had romantic feelings for her.

But that ended quickly. As he started packing up his painting gear, he knocked over her bottle of precious ink. She was furious; she gathered all her supplies, put them in her toolbox, then stood up and slapped him. Not once, but twice.

He was stunned. As she pulled her arm back to deliver another blow he grabbed her wrist screaming, "If you do that again I will knock you on your ass."

Still holding her wrist tightly, and with his other hand free, he reached into his pocket and threw two 100 Franc notes at her. He let go of her. She turned, and like a fast moving marching band member, she rushed towards her car. Max watched her as she tossed her bag onto the back seat, sat down behind the steering wheel, turned on the ignition, and thundered down the road. He bent down, picked up his money and began walking home. As he headed back to his studio, he could hear her car roaring down the winding road that led away from Lacoste. The echo of her shifting gears on the curvy valley road below told him she was heading in the direction of Les Beax.

This was not the first time she had struck him. In the past, Max always let it go, thinking it was just part of her passionate nature. Now he worried she might be capable of even greater violence.

That night Max couldn't sleep. He had every reason to be restless AND paranoid. When he got back to his place, he took the money he had thrown at Françoise and went to put it in the envelope that Valerie had given him. It was in the sock drawer of his dresser, along with the other envelope Maurice had given him. Since he had no car, Max was unable to deposit the cash or the cashiers check. Max noticed something odd; maybe it was just a coincidence, but both manila envelopes were stamped on the front with the same Marseille bank name and address on them.

****

Early the next morning Max called me. After

several minutes trying to clear my sleepy head I was able to understand what he was telling me. I told him the envelope thing had to be nothing more than a coincidence. As for attacking him I wasn't completely surprised. I realized she was an ugly conniving bitch. But I also knew she was incapable of murder.

"Calm down Max, we know she's involved in something suspicious and HP is gathering more information about her and her associates. You need to keep your cool. I suspect she is dangerous, but not to the point of taking your life. You need to keep stringing her on, remember what you said to me about being a detective?"

"Maybe you should go back to bed. Take some soothing tea, that will help you sleep."

"No, I think Pernod straight from the bottle will be much better!"

I laughed, that was a typical Maxfield Connor reply. "Tomorrow Robert will be there. Isn't he supposed to meet Françoise for the first time?"

Max's voice was hard to hear, there was a kind of hollow sound on the line. "Not sure that'll happen now. She'll be pouting over the spilled ink for days. To be honest, I'd just as soon have a nice, peaceful visit with my friend. I thought we'd go drawing at the old monastery near Lacoste."

I suggested to Max he call Françoise to see if he could patch things up. "I'll try to get a hold of my HP; perhaps he's picked up more information that will be useful to us.

I went on to say, "I will be sending you a card tomorrow." Max asked, "A card, why are you sending me a card?""I forgot to send one on your birthday. It's been sitting on my desk. I keep telling myself to put it in *la poste*. I'll send it tomorrow. Keep an eye out for it. Let me know when you get it, it's kind of funny."

Max could care less about birthdays and I knew that. Once past 40, who wants to remember?

He said, "My birthday was eight months ago, why not keep it and send it next year?"

There was no birthday card. My phone had been compromised. Even though the public postal service was in flux, it was still reliable. I wrote the following and sent it out first thing in the morning.

Max, HP has told me that from this point on we should not be talking on our home phones, or, for that matter, my gallery phone.

He believes someone is listening. He gave me a new kind of telephone; it's called a GMS mobile phone. The damn thing is hefty and large. Some of my business friends keep them in their cars. These phones are not connected to a hard-wired line like the ones we use in our homes. I can use this new fangled thing anywhere I go, even outside. However, it's heavy and bulky, so I'll probably keep it in the car and we'll talk from there. Here is the number, 33 (0) 1 40 20 53, and then use the last two numbers of my home phone. HP assures me that these new phones are safe from eavesdropping. On your side, call me from different public phones; they are unlikely to be tapped. If we need a covert conversation, you or I can call each other on our home phones and say a few sentences, then stop mid sentence and say: I have to go, the kitty has just caught a mouse. That will be our signal to expect a conversation via my mobile and a payphone near you. Don't use the one in Lacoste. Find one in Oppède and another in Ménerbes. Once you've done so, let me know the numbers.

After he hung up, Max called Françoise. He told her he was sorry for what happened and she apologized profusely.

Max repeated their conversation to me. "Max, you have nothing to apologize for, you were just being a klutz. Antoine can replace the ink. I know it wasn't intentional. I over reacted. I can be a hothead sometimes. I wish that wasn't part of my character; it embarrasses me and seems to always cause trouble in my life. I'm embarrassed that I slapped you. If I ever do it again, hit me back, BUT NOT IN THE FACE!"

"I was up all night thinking about how I wronged you. If it is okay, I still want to come over to meet your friend. I really want to join the painting outing with the two of you."

Max was happy he didn't need to grovel and try to convince her to tag along. "Great, let's put the incident behind us and have a nice time this afternoon. Robert should be here in another hour or so. How soon can you get here?"

"I'll quickly throw an outfit together. Do you want me to dress a little sexy or should I calm it down a bit?"

"Well since we'll be outside drawing, a white blouse and a pair of shorts would be more appropriate. But I'd enjoy seeing you in the wedged platform shoes with the bow on the sides. You look both sexy and cute in them."

"Is this for you Max, or is it for your friend

Robert?" Max responded, "BOTH!" She giggled and said she'd be in Lacoste soon. Max once told me. "With Françoise, soon usually means two hours or more." Within a few minutes of hanging up the phone, Max heard the familiar growl of the Lamborghini. Obviously, Michelin lent it to Robert again. Max opened his door and walked out into the street to greet him. They hugged. Robert leaned over the side of the car and reached behind the drivers seat to pull out his overnight bag. They went inside.

Max had just made coffee and he had recently stocked his small refrigerator with fresh eggs, milk and butter from a local farmer, plus chives pulled from his neighbor's garden. Max had become proficient in the art of omelet making. Robert sat on a wooden kitchen chair while his friend turned on one of the two burners atop of the small electric range. Max threw a sizable wedge of unsalted butter into his only frying pan. The recently made fresh butter began to slowly melt. Max cut up an onion, chopped the chives and threw them in the pan. He turned down the heat, spun to the sink and proceeded to crack six eggs into a glass bowl. He added a splash of water and a small amount of cream. Going to the refrigerator, he pulled out a roll of goat cheese.

He reached into the cabinet above the stove and took down a lidded glass jar containing truffles. The earthy truffles were a gift from his new-found poet friend who lived in the next village over. With his sharpest knife, Max thinly sliced the delicate, pungent, earthy tasting mushrooms and added them to the butter and onions in the pan. Then he turned the pan over and poured its contents into a small white porcelain bowl and set it aside. He whisked the eggs and when they were the right consistency, poured half of them into the frying pan. Turning the heat up just a bit higher, the eggs began to cook. He was careful not to allow them to become overcooked. He checked to make sure the eggs were soft, not runny. He wanted his omelets to stay moist and retain the yellow color throughout the eggs. He did not want them to fry to the point where they might become crispy and brown on the bottom. As it cooked and became firmer he sprinkled the goats cheese, onions, chives and the sliced truffles on one side of the nearly cooked eggs. He waited a few seconds and, using the palette knife that was in his back pocket, he folded the opposite plain side of the egg over so it lay gently upon the bed of cheese, truffle, chives and onion.

When finished, Max slid the omelet out of the pan and onto a plate, then covered it with another dish and proceeded to do the same procedure over again with the remaining eggs. When both omelets were finished, he garnished them with the chives, sea salt and black pepper. From out of the oven he took four pieces of toasted French bread and lathered them with butter.

He poured more coffee into Robert's cup and did the same for himself. Placing the omelets on the table along with the toast and some homemade peach marmalade, Max, in his best Carolina accent, said, "This will be a lip-smacking good breakfast."

In between talking and stuffing their faces with food, Max noticed that the scar on top of his friend's head had healed. The hair was growing back. Max said. "You never told me just what the circumstances were regarding your split head."

Robert reached up and ran his hand through his hair. "True. It wasn't a big deal, just got into a scrape with a couple of ruffians in a part of town where I shouldn't have been. I'd like to forget it, but I can still feel the scar. I suppose it'll be with me until my dying day."

Max pushed his friend a little more. "Did they rob you?" Robert shook his head. "No, it was just stupid stuff." Max kept pressing, "You weren't in a whore house were you?"Robert was starting to get pissed off. "Come on Max, just drop it." He asked how things were going with Françoise. Max was honest, "We fight often, she has a difficult nature, but the sex is worth the grief I have to endure."

Just then, Max's front door opened and Françoise walked in. She went up to Max, and after a long slow kiss, turned and put her hand out to Robert saying, "You must be the famous Robert Chéron."

****

Françoise was a good actress. Like a black widow spider, she could trick any male. She was a temptress for sure; the devil in disguise.

Robert stood up, took her hand into his and then kissed both sides of her cheeks. "Well," he said, "you are as beautiful as my friend has told me. As a matter fact, you're the most beautiful woman I've seen in Provence."

She smiled coquettishly. "Yes, so I have been told many times over by men and by women. You are quite handsome yourself. I bet the women of Marseille proclaim you the most handsome man in Provence-Alpes-Côte d'Azur."

Robert pulled out one of the chairs for her to sit on.

While the two of them talked, Max began to clean the dishes. As he expected, she was flirtatious. However, unlike in the past, Max was neither aroused nor jealous. He excused himself and left the two to get acquainted. When he went into the living area, he saw Françoise's purse laying on the floor next to her toolbox filled with art supplies and her other bag where she usually kept her drawing tablets and watercolor block, as well as the cassette player, sunscreen lotion and bottled water. He peeked back into the kitchen and saw they were deeply engaged in conversation. He looked into her bag of art materials; he wasn't searching for anything in particular, he was just curious and playing detective. He opened her purse and was shocked to find the film canister. He snapped open the plastic top and inside was the missing roll of undeveloped film from the fiasco at Monet's Gardens. He wasn't sure what to do with it. It was evidence, but at this point risky evidence. He decided to put the film back into Françoise's purse. He needed to find out how she intended to use it.

He then went upstairs to the studio to get his own art supplies.

He gathered up his papers, inks, watercolors and essential tools. When he came back downstairs he placed his equipment next to hers and rejoined the two in his kitchen.

He asked them if they were ready to go to the Abbey. Robert spoke first. "Why do I want to go to some ancient Catholic monastery when I can sit here all day long talking to the most beautiful woman in Provence?"

Françoise laughed, "I am flattered, but Max is a serious artist who works almost every day. You, on the other hand, appear to be a flirt."

Robert replied, "Who would you rather be with, a serious hard-working artist or a fellow who appreciates spending his day with a beautiful woman?"

Max waited for her reply. He was anxious to hear what she would say.

"I am drawn to those who have exceptional talent. Sitting next to Max while he's drawing is erotic."

Robert snorted, "I can't compete with that. Okay, let me get my pencils and pad of paper out of the car and we'll go drawing."

Robert suggested it would be nice for Françoise to ride in the Lamborghini. She agreed. That meant Max would have to drive to the abbey in her car.

Robert added, "The abbey is too short a ride. Why

don't I take her for a longer drive? She'll really enjoy it; there's nothing like a fast drive on these twisting narrow roads around here. We'll meet you up at the abbey when we're done." Max agreed.

Robert eased out though the Goat Gate and then tore off with Françoise. He took the road that led past Peter Mayle's house heading for Menerbes. They must have been a mile away, and yet Max could still hear the Lamborghini screeching around turns, accelerating and braking.

Max got into Françoise's car and drove to the abbey. He did not want her Mercedes coup to get dirty by driving down the dirt lane that led to the abbey, so he parked the car on the side of the main road. He walked the quarter mile to the old stone buildings. Upon arrival at the historic site, he spent a half hour reconnoitering for just the right spot to sit and draw the best scene. He settled on a place near the vineyard. The grass was soft and the ground flat. He sat down and took his box of drawing pencils out of the knapsack and laid them by his side. He unrolled a sheet of Coventry rag paper from its plastic wrapping case and clipped it to a Masonite board. He surveyed the scene before his eyes trying to figure out what composition would be best. He held out his hand, and with his forefinger and thumb clinched together, he created a hole that acted as a window or viewfinder for him to look through. It was a technique he used to determine composition. Framing the scene was vital to making a good drawing. He also held a pencil horizontally to denote the horizon. He then placed a line on the paper. Everything on the land needed to move into the distance. Fields, orchards and vineyards would recede towards that first line he had drawn. Structure and perspective were vital to a successful composition, but the style of line and the marks of his pen would be his signature. Max was recognized as a draftsman. Rembrandt, Dürer and van Gogh were his teachers and Maxfield Connor was every bit as good as they were.

He never looked at his watch to see how long he had been sitting, but the soreness in his back told him he had been sitting in the same position for far too long. He got up and stretched, then looked at his watch and saw that he had been there for almost 2 hours. He wondered what was taking Robert and Françoise so long to get to be abbey. As he sat down on the ground to continue drawing, he heard the unique honking sound of the Lamborghini's horn. He looked towards the cloister building. There, on the high walled patio, stood Robert and Françoise waving to him. He gestured for them to come down. Carrying her bag and toolbox of art supplies, Françoise was the first to reach him. She plopped down beside him and started to chatter.

"Sorry we took so long; there was an accident on the road and traffic was stopped for over a mile for the SAMU to extract the victims. Wow, I like this scene you're drawing. Do you mind if I sit beside you? I'd like to do it in watercolor."

Just as Max was about to say it would be fine, Robert fell onto the soft grass beside them. "This would be a nice place for a long nap," he said.

Max looked at him. "No way, I could never concentrate on drawing listening to you grunt and snort." Françoise laughed.

"Okay, I'm going to leave you two love birds alone. I'll be on the other side of the cloister building, either sleeping or drawing." He picked himself up off of the ground, walked back up the hill, and disappeared.

Françoise began to rummage through her supplies. She stopped. "Would you like to fuck me?"

Max wasn't sure what to say. As he told me a few days later in one of our clandestine phone conversations, he wanted to say yes, but he also wanted to complete the drawing. Apparently he didn't answer quickly enough, so she began sketching the scene on watercolor paper. She became distant, pissed because he didn't fuck her.

I hated to tell him, but I did. "In the future, you have to play along with her and that includes sexually. If you don't, she will undoubtedly become suspicious. We need her to think that you are the same damn fool you used to be. Do you understand?" He assured me he did.

The sun was sinking low in the sky. Max was surprised when he looked at his watch; it was almost 8pm. No wonder he felt hungry. They gathered their supplies and set off to find Robert. They walked all around the buildings and grounds of the abbey calling his name. He didn't answer. Max said he would keep looking and told Françoise to take their materials to the car. The interesting thing I noted in Max's telling of this story was that without saying it to me, Max's behavior towards Françoise had changed. He apparently was no longer chivalrous towards her.

He went inside the ruins of the chapel but no Robert. He walked towards the grove of dwarf apple trees and just as he was about to enter the path between the first and second rows he heard the horn of the Lamborghini blast three times.

As he rounded the corner of the small chapel he

heard three more blasts of the horn. He saw the car and the two of them off in the distance. They saw him and began waving. By the time he reached them it was getting dark and he was pissed. Robert said he had fallen asleep under an oak tree. He apologized. Max told the two of them to return to Lacoste. He would follow in Françoise's car. When he reached the main road, Max gunned the engine and roared down the lane.

He parked her car near the school at the bottom of the village. His back was sore, his legs tired. By the time he reached his place, all he wanted to do was to take a quick nap, clean up and go to dinner at the Café de Sade. He was hungry for their pork in caramel sauce and a bottle of their local Luberon wine. The problem was, it was late and the last customers would soon be finishing their meals. He said he would just sleep for a half hour.

Françoise told him she was going to head back to her apartment in Les Beax, but planned to return in the morning so that she could finish her watercolor. Robert was sitting in the kitchen drinking Max's Pernod. Françoise left and Max went upstairs and crawled into bed. He didn't wake until morning. When he came downstairs, he found Robert asleep on the couch. He was snoring and his hand was lying across the empty bottle of Pernod.

Max walked into the kitchen to make a pot of coffee. He was still sleepy. He went back into the front room, sat in his big chair sipping coffee and watched Robert who occasionally twitched and then would stop snoring for a few seconds. Max looked at his watch and it was 10am. He swallowed the last few sips of the cooling coffee in his cup, set it on the side table, got up and walked back upstairs to dress. He was in the bathroom shaving when he heard Françoise enter the house. He wasn't anxious to go downstairs quite yet. He heard her talking to his friend, but didn't hear Robert responding. I'm sure he was still drunk and undoubtedly passed out. Max told me that Françoise came upstairs, entered the bathroom and kissed him.

She stood beside him and reapplied her lipstick. She went back downstairs. Max heard pots and pans being slammed, the refrigerator door opening and closing and could smell the scent of toast coming from the kitchen. He finished dressing, came down and found Françoise making eggs benedict. According to Max she was a "good cook and a fine cock sucker." He poured coffee into a mug, walked into his living room and shook his friend until he woke. After they ate, Max suggested that it would be a good idea for Robert to take the steep walk to the top of the village and then come back down. Apparently that's what old-timers in

Lacoste say you should do to avoid a hangover.

Françoise volunteered to be a Sherpa and make sure he survived the climb. While they were gone Max rifled through her purse, but was unable to find the undeveloped roll of film.

Max was sitting in the kitchen waiting for them to return. When the door swung open, there was Françoise and the drunkard, arm in arm, laughing hysterically. Robert stumbled and almost fell to the floor.

Slurring his words, Robert asked, "When are we going back up to be abbey? I saw something up there that intrigued me, good subject matter to draw. Let's go now."

With Max on one side and Françoise on the other, they led Robert to the sofa where he fell into the worn out cushions. He vomited on the floor. Max turned and held his nose while *"The Most Beautiful Woman In Provence"* ran to the kitchen to get a bucket. Just in time, she was able to shove the bucket between his legs and he threw up again. Max felt sick; if he didn't get out of the room, he too would start throwing up. He remembered how it was as a child in kindergarten; when one kid threw up, so did a bunch of others.

Max went into the kitchen, bent his head over the sink and gagged. He grabbed the towel stuffed on the handle of the scratched and rusted refrigerator door, turned on the water, dampened the cloth, and proceeded to wipe his face. In anger, he threw the towel across the room where it hit, and knocked over, the peppershaker. Françoise heard him yell "Son of a bitch!!!"

He lifted a coffee mug from the drying rack, filled it with hot black coffee and carried it back into the room, handing it to Robert.

When it touched the sculptor's lip he quickly pulled it away, spilling the scalding coffee on his pants and dropping the cup into the bucket of vomit. As he did so, Françoise jumped backward and screamed at Max. "He is your friend, you can clean him and this fucking shit up!"

She turned and walked away. Max could hear her footsteps as she walked up stairs to the bathroom. He heard the water running and figured she was washing her hands. Francesca was a hypochondriac. She was obsessed with her heath, and more so, her looks. She always had to look perfect. It must be agonizing to always look beautiful. Did she do it for others, or was it for herself? A therapist could make a fortune off of her!

When she came downstairs Max noticed that she had changed her clothes. When she first came through the door she was wearing a short sundress and heels. It was unusual to see her in long khaki pants and tennis shoes. She could tell Max noticed. "Since we are going back to the abbey today, I need to wear long pants. Yesterday the ants bit my legs and fanny. How could you not notice that I spent half of last night lathering myself in cortisone? My legs are riddled in red welts. You should be grateful the cream is working. As you often say, Max, my legs are my greatest assets. I always want them to look good for you."

All of a sudden Robert yelled out. "It's what's between your legs that is your greatest asset!"

Max couldn't help himself, he started laughing. "He's drunk, I'm sorry."

Françoise put her hands on her hips and glared at Max. She left the room and went into the kitchen to fill Max's canteen with water. When she came back she said to both of them. "I'm going down to the boulangerie. When you finally have yourselves together meet me there. If you're not there in half an hour, I'm going to the abbey by myself."

She walked out the door and slammed it shut. Max put his hand out to help Robert get up from the sofa. Robert's breath reeked of alcohol and vomit. He managed to climb the stairs on his own. He went into the bathroom and took a shower and, of course, brushed his teeth. Max gathered his painting and drawing gear and also Robert's small satchel containing his meager drawing tools.

Robert came downstairs. As Max told me, "He cleaned up nicely." Apparently, Robert felt guilty. That was very much unlike him. He hung his head and told Max he was sorry for his behavior. In earlier times, Max would have laughed it off, but not now. Max was unsure that he really knew his old friend from San Francisco.

They walked down the narrow stone street. Robert smoked a joint and shared it with Max. Françoise was sitting outside at a small round café table reading Mademoiselle. She took one last sip of coffee, then rolled the slick publication and jammed it into her art material bag. The three hiked silently down the hill towards the schoolhouse where Max had parked her car the night before. Robert opened the passenger side door, folded the backrest of the passenger seat forward so that Françoise could slide her slim body into the storage space behind him. She sat sideways with her legs stretched out and Robert placed her the bag of art supplies on her lap.

Max opened the diver side door. Robert was sitting uncomfortably in his seat. Max handed his knapsack to Robert who struggled to put it on the floor between his legs. He hugged his own backpack tightly. Max put the car in reverse and off they went. Françoise pulled knees up and shifted her position so that she was more comfortable.

Robert turned his head to the side and said to Francoise. "I'm sorry, I should have taken the Lamborghini."

"That would not be a good idea. I think you are sill too hung over to drive."

It was only a short drive and when they arrived Max noticed that someone had replaced the old damaged sign. The new one identified the historic place as Saint Hilaire Abbey.

This time Max drove down the dirt road and parked his car close to the cloister building. Robert headed up the hillside that led to the grove of oak trees. Gathering their art materials and the canteen of water, Max and Françoise walked towards the vineyard. Françoise lagged several yards behind.

When Max describe to me that days happenings, he told me the tension between the three was palpable. The grass was still matted down from where Max and Françoise had sat the day before. In silence, the two artists renewed their acquaintance with the vineyard.

Max leaned over and said to Françoise. "Do you see how different the scene looks under this light? I like what I'm seeing today, it's much better than what I saw yesterday. The grapes are a deeper purple which makes the contrast between the sky and the fruit juicier."

She smiled and replied. "You should be a poet."

They both worked and talked together for over an hour. The tension between them dissolved.

Françoise stood up and stretched. She reached down and unclasped her khakis. She kicked off her shoes then rolled her tight pants past her slim thighs. She smiled at him. "It's too damn hot out here."

Max agreed. While she was taking off her panties she added, "You could do the same."

He took off his boots, unzipped his jeans and slid them off. She took hold of his hand and pulled him into her. She told him. "I want you to lick the part of me that Robert says is my greatest asset."

Max complied. Françoise Gemmer may have

thought she had Max by the balls, but it was she who was being set up.

****

Robert drew a decaying carcass of a large hare. The hare's ears had been ripped apart by crows; a dog or a cat had torn the creature open, exposing its bone and sinew. For a sculptor this was a far more picturesque image than any painting of a farmhouse or lavender field.

I suppose all three of them were tired. When Françoise and Max packed up their things and walked up the hill towards the oak grove in search of Robert, they found him under the largest and oldest tree on the property. He was just putting some final marks on his drawing. Max leaned over to look at what Robert had created; he was impressed. Françoise said the piece reminded her of Albrecht Dürer, the German artist who often depicted animals and one of them, she pointed out, was of a hare, and was quite famous. Robert seemed pleased.

They came back to Lacoste and all three took a nap.

That night during dinner, Françoise leaned back in her chair and put her hand on the stone wall. In Provence, you never touch the stone without looking first, maybe it was the wine that dulled her caution, but whatever caused the mistake in judgment, it resulted in a painful and frightening experience. A scorpion stung her. As the small black creature scurried away, she screamed. Max managed to calm her fear. One of the local patrons told the waitress to put a raw onion on Françoise's arm. The onion drew out the poison. Robert asked for ice and proceeded to wrap it in a cotton table napkin, placing the cloth and ice over the sting on her arm. Soon the swelling disappeared. Max felt it best that she stay the night in Lacoste.

During the night, Max awoke several times to check on Françoise. Sometimes he would put his hand on her head to see if she was running a fever. By morning she was fine. She and Max came down from the bedroom to find Robert had gotten up early and set the table for breakfast. He probably was feeling a bit guilty about how he had acted the night before. Robert had made coffee, and because the pastries were still warm inside the bag, he must have just returned from the boulangerie. There was also a box that filled the small kitchen area with the aroma of chocolate. He hugged Françoise and Max and pulled out two chairs for them to sit at the table.

He took three chocolate-topped choux à la crème from the pastry box and put them on plates. The delicate rounds of hollow pastry were filled with cream and covered in gooey chocolate. He tore open the bag filled with cinnamon rolls, and croissants and laid it out on the table beside the dish of farmers' butter. He pulled the small stepstool that was in the corner and sat down. He and Max gobbled down the treats as fast as they could. Typical of Françoise, she ate only half a croissant.

Max was convinced his girlfriend starved herself to stay slim. She was fixated by how her body looked. It was an obsession. She needed to constantly be on the move. She walked twice a day; they weren't short walks either. Hilltop villages are steep climbs and her stride was so fast that no one could keep up with her. The other thing she did almost every day was exercise and dance. Max felt her fixation on fitness had nothing to do with health and was possibly a symptom of some emotional trauma.

After the meal Robert announced his leaving. He planned to return the racecar to Michelin. Françoise offered to follow him in her Mercedes and then take him on to Avignon to catch the train to Marseilles. Because her car was small, there was little room behind the two seats for more than his suitcase plus the backpack of art supplies. She told Max she'd come back to pick up her stuff before returning to Les Beaux. Max was happy to stay behind and fine- tune his latest drawing. Françoise thought it would be nice for her to visit with Maurice. She called him, but he said he was on his way out and wouldn't be back until after dark. He had planned to take Robert to Avignon then, but this arrangement would work nicely for him,.

"Wonderful, this allows me to stay in Saint-Rémy longer for the wine tasting party hosted by the Coca-Cola heiress. By the way, has Max bought his new car?"

How did he know that Max needed a new car, Max hadn't told him of the accident.

Françoise said, "Not yet."

Max expected she'd return to Lacoste that evening, but she didn't.

****

The next morning she appeared at his door. "Let's go car shopping."

Max told her he had to deposit the check first.

She said, "I am here, I have my car, Let's go. We will deposit your check in Avignon and then go to Auchan to buy a car."

Max had never been inside an Auchan store. When they pulled into the parking lot he thought he was at a supermarket. Why, he thought, would they find a car there?

When they walked in, he was shocked. Everything a person could use was under one roof; groceries, appliances, furniture, and yes, even cars. It was the easiest transaction he ever had. In the US, he would have had to haggle with a salesman. Not so in Auchan Mistral, within an hour he was driving back to Lacoste in a Citroën Xantia wagon. It was perfect; there was plenty of room for his art supplies and would even hold a small easel.

I congratulated him. He said the next time he was in Paris he'd buy me dinner at La Tour d'Argent with the best bottle of wine that Claude Terrail had in his cellar.

I asked him how things were going with Françoise and her upcoming divorce and how her family was reacting.

Max said she rarely spoke about her family. She made it clear to him that under no condition was he to ask any questions about her husband. Every once in a while she would mention her mother. All that Max knew about the woman was that she came from a small town in Normandy and was a good cook. Françoise credited her mother with teaching her how to be, as she saw herself, "An excellent chef." She told Max that she could have been a professional, but her father pushed her to follow in his line of work.

"And how did she explain him?" I asked. "Well, according to Françoise, he was an extremely talented painter of portraits and a restorer of antique furniture. One night, after she had too much to drink, she revealed her brother had committed suicide. When I asked what happened, she became angry and screamed at me to never ask questions about her family or her life. She said that if she wanted me to know something, she would tell me. She threatened to end our relationship if I ever brought it up again."

So, that explained why Max never asked questions about her personal life. Things are different now. We needed all the information we could get on Ms. Gemmer.

****

I haven't heard anything from HP in almost a month, so I assume there isn't anything new to report. I did let him know about the commission from the Valerie woman and the big check from Michelin. He had seen the police report regarding the demise of Max's Peugeot, so obviously he is up to speed on everything. I'm a little concerned that he hasn't called, but I know he has many other important problems to deal with. The world is a fucked up mess. 2,000 people were just massacred in Rwanda and here in Paris there are protests everywhere because we conducted a test of a nuclear weapon somewhere in the Pacific Ocean. Strikes throughout my country are paralyzing our transportation infrastructure. I had hoped to get down to see Max, but under the circumstances, the trains only runs sometimes, but more often than not, the union that represents the rail workers sabotage the tracks or the engineers are overcome with flu. A bomb blew up a government building in some city in America. We live in scary times.

After a month's absence from Lacoste, Robert returned to visit Max. He was on his way to Paris to meet Mademoiselle Dubois and he thought a few days with Max would be good.

On the second day of Robert's visit, Françoise came by for breakfast. Afterwards they sat around the table talking about what they were going to do for the day. Max mentioned going to Saint-Rémy to draw, Robert said he was planning on leaving in the evening to head up to Paris and his meeting at the Louvre. Françoise suggested they stay in the village. She suggested that maybe Bernard, the surrealist painter in the village, and head of the little art school there, would let her use the schools photo studio. "I shot some nice images of Michelin's gardens that I would love to print."

Robert nodded his head in agreement. "Yeah, that's a good idea. The old man and I are good friends. I'll go along with you. He may be in his 70's, but he can't resist a beautiful woman. I'd say your chances are pretty close to 100% that he'll give you the key."

Max realized this might give him an opportunity to sneak away so he could call me. First, he'd go to the post office to mail his bills. He didn't have many, just car insurance and the telephone bill, and also a letter to Clifford Ragnetti. After the weird event at the arrogant Russian's Chateau in Avignon, Max had tracked Cliff down to verify that he was right regarding Naum Gabo. Since then, the two old acquaintances had begun corresponding.

Max noticed that a new person was behind the post office counter. Her nameplate identified her as

Gabrielle LeBlanc. Max felt lucky she was there, while the post office had prescribed hours of operation, the former postal worker seemed to come and go on her own schedule. That is pretty typical of most of the locals working for our government in the villages throughout the Luberon.

The new clerk and Max chatted for a moment. He was surprised that she spoke fluent English. Because her accent was definitely not Provencal, he asked her if she was from Paris. "*Qui*, but I am only here as a fill-in until a permanent person can be found." The previous postmistress couldn't, or wouldn't, speak English,. Max's French was horrid. Most of the locals laughed when he tried to speak their language. But they seemed to appreciate his attempt, and for the most part, they would let him muddle through pigeon French for a few minutes and then shake their heads and begin to speak English to him. He found that to be the French way. They were proud of their language and even had laws to protect it. He was glad that, with this new woman, he wouldn't have to go through the dance of language.

He paid her, she gave him change and he thanked her. He walked back up the hill to his house. He passed a few of the art students who were on their way to the printmaking studio. He could tell from their accents that two of them were American and the other sounded Scandinavian. Max detected a Southern drawl coming from the tall young man carrying a large copper etching plate in one hand, while using the other to pet Jezebel, the shaggy collie, that belonged to Marie from the Boulangerie.

At some point he'd be introduced to them. His lease agreement with Bernard had a stipulation that required him to give a lecture once a year to the students of the art school. Max hated having to get his slides organized and he was uncomfortable talking about himself. He was basically a modest man who simply wanted to make good paintings. Notoriety was not something he sought. I can't tell you how many times he purposely sabotaged my efforts to arrange meetings with the art critics or magazine editors who wanted to interview him. It was frustrating, that's for sure. After all, public relations are a vital component to the success of my gallery. Unlike so many of my other artists, he wasn't inarticulate. Once he got going, his passion and honesty was compelling. I always thought he should write a book outlining his approach to painting. He was convinced Muses brought great art into the world. He believed that by silencing his conscious thoughts a channel was opened for him to receive inspiration, giving him the ability to bring something new into the world. When he began talking about this subject, it was as though he transcended being the artist and became a maharishi.

After walking up the steep hill, Max reached his house and opened his unlocked door. He was over the paranoia of locking it. Françoise and Robert were not there. He supposed they were at the photo studio. Robert's satchel was not in the house. He decided he'd walk to the photo studio. When he got there the door was locked. He banged on the door and a student opened it. Max asked the girl if any one else was there.

"Not now, but when I came up earlier, there was an older couple here, they left when I started using the enlarger." Max asked her if could come in and look around.

"Sure come on in. Aren't you the artist who lives down near the old bakery/dormitory building?"

He shook his head yes. "How long ago was it that they left?"

She wasn't sure,. "Maybe a half hour or so ago. I'm not really certain; I get pretty engrossed when I'm working.

'Do you mind if I look around for a few minutes?"

He asked.

"Naw, go ahead. Just make sure you don't turn on the overhead florescent light. The photo light is on so let your eyes adjust and then you'll be able to see."

Max knew the drill. Long ago in New York, he had experimented with photography, but it was too technical for a man who cherished the immediacy of creativity.

The photo studio had been converted from an old stone garage. What quickly caught his attention was the falling dust from the aging mortar. All he could think about was how the grit must scratch the student's negatives. The space smelled of chemicals and mold. He thought it best to leave, but maybe he'd find some of Françoise' unsuccessful images in the black trashcan. There was nothing there. He began to walk away when something pulled him back. He leaned over for a second glance, and in the dim red light of the darkroom, he saw several gray plastic film canisters. He reached in and pulled them up. They were empty.

The young student came in. She said, "I have more. Do you want them?"

He replied, "Sure, I'll take them, they are great containers to store my pen nibs in."

She leaned into the trashcan and felt around for the tops. Handing them to Max she said. "Here they are."

He thanked her; they walked out of the darkroom together. He left the photo building and began walking nonchalantly down the lane. He was putting the lids on the canisters. He stopped, vomited, and his heart began to pound. Scribbled in gel ink was the word "*GIVERNY*." And it was in his handwriting.

****

He called me an hour after finding the canister cap. The two were still in his midst, down the road, near his house, sitting near the boule park drawing.

I heard panic and fear, before he asked the *'what to do'* question. Trust had exploded; it was fragile before, but now the situation had completely disintegrated. Max said he was cold, shaky and scarred.

"Where are you calling from?" I asked."The pay phone near the Café de Sade."I reminded him that he was out in the open. "Calm down

Max, talk slower and more quietly." I heard him taking deep breaths. Max said he went back to his place. Françoise had piled her art supplies and overnight bag by the door. Robert's bag of clothes and his satchel were nowhere to be found. Most likely they were locked in the trunk of the Lamborghini. Max said he went through Françoise's belongings and didn't find any photographs of Giverny. What he did find was an old Polaroid with Françoise and Robert in a group of people. It had been taken when they were young, maybe in their early 20's. They were standing on the steps of the Louvre Museum. In the photograph, standing next to them, was the girlish young Domino, the tattooed bitch from the Russian's party in Avignon. There was also a much older man, and a slim middle-aged fellow, both of whom Max didn't recognize.

For what seemed a long time, but in reality was probably not more than a few seconds, we said nothing to each other.

I was stunned. I knew what I was going to tell Max next was going to be equally confounding.

HP had called the night before. He wanted me to know that no divorce papers have ever been filed, not by Françoise, or her husband.

He said, "There is more to their situation. I'll get to that later, but right now, I have something even more stunning to tell you."

"Madame Gemmer's father was known as an art restorer, however Jean-Philippe Gaillard was much more than that. A highly placed intelligence officer in the DCPJ has told me her father was one of the most gifted forgers in French history. The officer revealed an astonishing tale regarding her father. He had made a painting that fooled the experts."

"During the Nazi occupation of Paris, it came on the market mysteriously. One day an elderly man walked into a small art gallery/antique shop on the Rue de Rivoli. Under his arm, wrapped in brown paper, was a painting. This kind of occurrence was not unusual during the war. Money and food were scarce; the people of Paris desperate. To survive often meant selling precious heirlooms."

"The shopkeeper was polite; he was used to people bringing him their treasures to sell. He took the package, placed it on the counter and respectfully untied the twine binding. Slowly he folded back the butcher paper to look at the man's treasure. The frame was cracked in several places and specks of gold leaf danced through the air and fell on the shopkeeper's glass countertop. The landscape portrayed by the artist was familiar to him. He took a sable haired artist brush from the drawer behind him and whisked the dust off the surface of the painting. Then, reaching into a nearby cabinet, he withdrew a magnifying glass. He looked intently at the angle of the brushstrokes. He held the painting up to catch the natural light shining through the stores window. The sunlit surface of the painting revealed a unique application of paint, one that he recognized. He carefully examined the signature; it appeared to be authentic. The shopkeeper quickly came to the opinion that it was an original."

"When asked how he had come by the painting, the old man replied, "After my Papa died, I cleaned out his house. It was just one of lots of old stuff that I had to remove. I suppose it is a view of the area near Aix in Provence where he grew up. It's been up in my attic for years."

"Monsieur," the shopkeeper replied. "Do you know anything about the artist who might have painted this?"

"No, I'm a chimney sweep. I don't know anything about art. I don't think it's very good. It doesn't look like whomever was painting it was finished. Could you give me a few francs for it?"

"This may be worth far more than a few francs. I need to show it to some of my colleagues to verify its authenticity. Would you mind if I keep it for a day or two?"

Apparently, the old man agreed and said he'd return in a week, but he never did.

After the man left and the shopkeeper had another chance to further examine the picture, he found, tucked between the linen painting surface and one of the stretcher bars, an old yellowed sticker. He was stunned; it was an Ambroise Vollard Gallery label on which was written the painting's title, *Vallée de la rivière de l'Arc* and the artist was Paul Cézanne.

"Word that the shopkeeper was in possession of a newly discovered Cézanne painting reached the ear of Alfred Rosenberg, the notorious looter of artwork for the Nazis. HP went on to explain that the Nazis realized there was a market for what they described as "*degenerate art*". Impressionism and modern art fell into that category. The painting was confiscated and fell into the hands of Hitler's infamous gallery dealer, Hildebrand Gurlitt. Gurlitt orchestrated most of the sales of looted art for Hitler. But this painting was handled differently. Joseph Goebbels himself took personal ownership of it."

"Unbeknownst to Gurlitt and his Nazi cohorts the painting was a fake. Goebbels had no idea nor did anyone else. He ordered Gurlitt to sell the painting, for a hundred thousand Swiss Francs. Goebbels used the money to purchase Rembrandt's, *Portrait of the Father* for himself. Hitler personally approved the transaction."

"After the war, Gurlitt was exonerated for his participation with the Nazi's. The official reason given by our government was that because of his Jewish heritage, he had been forced to work for the Nazis. That was the official lie."

HP went on to explain to me that he had learned of a rumor regarding Gurlitt and Françoise's father. "I have been told that the fake Cézanne was done to trick the Nazis. According to the story, the painting sold for much more money than Goebbels received, and the extra money ended up in the hands of the French Resistance. After the war, authorities uncovered several more forgeries done by Monsieur Gaillard but, strangely, there were never any consequences for him."

"Over the years Françoise's father was allowed to continue fooling collectors and museums. Apparently some powerful individuals in the government, (my source believes it was both Emmanuel d'Astier and Charles de Gaulle), turned a blind eye, not only because of the Cézanne forgery, but because Françoise's father worked to fool the Nazis several more times. In 1956 Gurlitt died in a mysterious car crash. In 1975, Françoise's father went to a quaint village near Bristol England to visit a former student and protégé. Gaillard's disciple's body was found floating in the river beneath a famous suspension bridge. He either committed suicide or was pushed. The cause of death was listed as accidental."

Max interjected. "Françoise has never mentioned her father. I asked once or twice about her family and she got upset and angry. Obviously there are family secrets to hide."

I told him there was more to the story. According to HP, Françoise's father taught her everything she knows about making art. He was her teacher, kind of like Andrew Wyeth's father, N. C Wyeth. HP is certain that her father taught her more than just how to draw and paint, but also chemistry. He showed her how the old masters painted and schooled her in the techniques of the Impressionists and Modernists. HP is 90% certain that she may have even worked on some of the forgeries her father created. Not the ones from the war years, after all she wasn't born until 1945, but the ones he made in the 1960s. I could hear Max moan on the other end of the phone line.

I told my friend that I would call HP to tell him about the film canister and the old Polaroid. It was now clear Robert and Françoise we're not strangers to one another, but in fact, had known each other for a very long time.

Max asked me how he should proceed. I told him he had to keep up the charade, although I knew it would be extremely difficult for him. I reiterated how important it was to not let on that anything was different. I hope Max is capable of doing so.

I remember reminding him, "You're a detective now."

"Okay, okay. You don't have to keep reminding me about the detective stuff. It's not so funny anymore."

Before I hung up the phone I reminded him about our secret phrase. I told him, "Remember, when we need to talk we say the phrase and then you go to the pay phone."

Max retorted with an uneasy laugh, "Putty Tat might like the part about getting off the phone, but she's going to be really pissed when she finds out there's no mouse.

****

Right after talking with Max, I called HP to tell him the details of what Max had told me. I was unable to reach him, one of his staffers said he was in an Internal Affairs Committee meeting of the Sénat at Luxembourg Palace. He assured me HP would call back.

Max walked up the hill to his place.

Françoise was sitting in his rocking chair with a glass of wine in her hand and Robert was on the couch petting the cat. Max told me his first thought was that Putty Tat was also a traitor.

Françoise walked over to Max and kissed him. "Can I pour you a glass of wine? Where have you been?" she asked.

Robert said, "We looked for you everywhere."

"I'm sure you did." Max said. He caught himself from being more sarcastic. "I was absorbed in a long conversation with the postmistress. She was talking about some of the students at the art school. She said one of the girls has shaved her head. Probably she couldn't bare the heat. She was also telling me about the poetry teacher, Gustaf Sorbin.

She said he had just returned from Harvard University where he had presented a seminar on his poetry."

Françoise handed him a cabernet she had bought from a winery situated on the Bages Plateau not far from the village. It was a very good red. Max needed a drink. He gulped it down in front of his horrified French friends. He pointed his empty wine glass towards Françoise, she was reluctant to pour him another.

"Max," she chided, "Sometimes you are a typical American jerk."

Robert laughed, "Qui, but the jerk is my friend!" Later, Max told me he pretended to smile.

They finished the bottle and then Robert gently lifted the cat off his lap and stood up. "Okay it's time to go. I want to get to Paris before midnight. I am staying with a friend. It's been a great visit. I like some of the drawings I did today here in the village. Thank you, Françoise, for your help; you're critiques are better than Max's here."

She raised her glass to him. "I'm just more honest."

"Max, you are a lucky man to have such a beautiful girlfriend as Françoise."

After Robert left, instead of going back to Les Beaux, Francoise decided to stay the night. I suppose she and Max went upstairs and fucked their brains out. Bastard!

The next morning they slept in. Evidently it was a non- productive day. They stayed in bed till noon, had lunch at the Café de Sade and took a walk. Keeping stride with her was difficult for Max. After all, he was older, heavier, and didn't dance or exercise everyday. On their walk, Max asked her if she had been able to get into the photo studio the day before. Like a sailor, worn out by the incessant winds of a typhoon, Max was exhausted from three days of charades and drama.

****

HP finally called me. He asked, "Are you on your mobile phone?" I was filling him in on the latest drama and lies. I told him what had transpired; he was not surprised. What he said next was confusing.

"I want you to attend the reception of the annual meeting of the French Conservators Association, scheduled to be held at the Pompidou Center at the end of next month."

I told him I was not a member.

"I know you're not. I will make sure you receive an invitation that identifies you as representing the Russian Cultural Attaché, Vladimir Bogdanov. Of course you will be recognized by many of the people attending the reception as the owner of the leading independent gallery in Paris. If someone asks about your affiliation with the Russian attaché, just tell whoever asks that you have recently been employed as a consultant to assess the Russian embassy's collection of artwork."

"What if someone checks on my supposed relationship?"

"Any queries to the Russian Embassy regarding you will be forwarded to the Attaché's office. They will substantiate your employment. Also, I want you to put this new association on all of your gallery's promotional material. You must do a news release today of your affiliation; I want it to go out to your clients and the Paris newspapers.

I asked, "Why do you want me to attend this meeting?"

He avoided an answer. That worried me. "I will have a package delivered to you tomorrow. It will contain a Gucci cocktail purse. Inside is a camera.

The micro lens is built into the handle and so is the shutter release button. I want you to take pictures of women attendees who look to be Moroccan or Arabic. If they have a name tag, write it down."

I asked. "Am I becoming a spy?" He replied, "Let's just say you're a consultant." As almost an afterthought he added. "I want you to also note the shoes of the woman you are snapping pictures of. "Why?" I asked.

"Well, you are a woman who appreciates fashion. My secretary will want to know what style ladies in the arts are currently wearing."

Doing something surreptitious like this with a camera isn't foreign to me. I have been tape recording conversation since college.

Memories are fragile, more so for me than others. I have a memory disorder. It's a disability that makes it difficult for me to process, understand and remember some of what I hear. It's strange how my memory works. It's almost like my brain chooses what to hear and what not to hear. It functions like a filter. One conversation is consumed, another thrown away. I wonder if the purpose is to protect me. Maybe this memory disorder is an offshoot of my chromosome anomalies. Perhaps I should have asked the doctors, but I gave up on them long ago.

Ever since I was a young girl I have audiotaped the things that are important to me. I have file cabinets filled with recorded teacher assignments, employer's directions and even advice that my mother and papa gave me. I still have the tapes and the transcriptions I made of them. Most of my memories are held in boxes and journals.

I learned not to tell others or ask them if I can tape our conversation. People change if they know their words are going to be recorded. They become cautious and guarded. It's true; words are powerful. Politicians have learned not to speak off the cuff, husbands lie, wives keep secrets and criminals live by a code of silence. Lawyers and reporters salivate. Priests hear confessions. A cassette doesn't give a damn as to what is true or false.

My evenings are predominantly spent transcribing the day's conversations onto paper. I am judicious to retain only the important things I need. Those are usually meeting dates, schedules and vital discussions. I'm proficient in short hand. I'm as good as any court stenographer. My apartment and the storage locker that I own are filled with conversations. Almost like wallpaper, my apartment is plastered with yellow post-it notes.

****

I phoned Max and told him about the strange assignment HP had given me. We both figured it had something to do with the investigation, but sometimes HP was not forthcoming as to reasons for some of his request. But I trusted him, and so did Max.

Max told me that Françoise reminded him about the drawings her friend in Saintes-Maries-de-la-Mer had commissioned him to do. She gave him a box of drawing paper that Valerie wanted him to work on.

Max informed Françoise that he planned to begin working on her friend's project once the Mistral winds had stopped. That meant in another month or so. He told me he asked Françoise if she wanted to join him.

"I think I'll stay in a hotel in Aix. It will be easier on me. I can get up early in the morning before it becomes too hot, then I can finish them in a nice air-conditioned hotel room."

"Not this time Max. I need to go to Paris to meet with my attorney and finish up the details of my divorce. The court day has been set and we need to prepare for the proceedings."

"Françoise, when this divorce is finally over, I'll

take you to the United Sates. We can go to Carolina for a vacation."

"Qui, that will be delicious, I have never been to Carolina." She began humming a James Taylor song.

As Max was telling me about this conversation, I could just see him smiling as he said over the phone, "She may be the '*The Most Beautiful Woman In Provence*', but she sure as hell can't carry a tune."

A month later Max called me from Goult, telling me he was ready to begin the project. I immediately called HP to let him know. HP told me to have Max take the box of papers to the Lacoste post office. "Tell Max to bring the postmistress everything he receives from Françoise. If its just paper in sheets, or the paper is in an envelope, a box, or some sort of case, he needs to give her all of what Françoise gives him. We will return the papers to him within a few days. Once Max begins the drawings he will have to wear gloves whenever he handles the paper.

"He's not going to want to draw with gloves on." I said.

"Tell him it's vital. There will come a time when

we will hopefully retrieve the drawings; someone, or maybe several people, may leave fingerprints. If so, that will help us to identify the people involved with the cartel. It will also be important for Max to make sure he signs the drawings."

"I don't understand, if Max signs the work it's not a forgery?"

"We believe Max's signature will be erased and Cézanne's replaced. When we locate Max's augmented drawings we will be closer to apprehending the players involved with defrauding collectors and museums around the world. Max must take the materials that Françoise has given him to Gabrielle at the poste. As soon as she gets them I'll have one of our agents pick them up and deliver them to me in Paris.

"Why?"HP began, "We are going to....."I quickly stopped him mid sentence, "Who is we?" "Best you not know!"My thought at that moment was, fuck! What have I got myself into? But I just said. "Okay." Another thought came to me. How did HP know the name of the new postmistress?

A few days later Françoise delivered the materials to Max.

I called HP and he asked, "Do you know if the

paper Françoise gave him is in a box?"

"I don't know. I'd have to ask him."

"Call Max back, I want to know if the paper is in a box or rolled up between tissue or laying flat between pieces of cardboard. If it's in a box, ask him if the box is corrugated."

"What does it matter?" I inquired.

"If the paper came in a box, and if that box is corrugated, we are in luck."

"What makes a corrugated box lucky?"

"We will be able to slip a micro chip tracking device between the folds of corrugated cardboard. When Max returns the box with the finished drawings, we can track it by satellite. My hunch is the box and the drawings will show up in Marseille. If all falls into place, we will know the address and maybe even the person who accepts it. We are also going to print an invisible watermark into each sheet of the paper. Tell Max that he will receive a message from Gabby as soon as the materials have been impregnated. It should only take a few days for us to do what we have to do on our end. When Max is finished with the drawings, call me. Make sure he knows not to give them to Françoise, there are other things my colleagues will need to do before Max can hand over his commission to Madamé Gemmer.

"Call Max now. As soon as you know what he has been given, call me back."

I did as told. The box was just what HP hoped for.

"Return Max's call. Remember; use the phone method that we agreed to. I can't have your conversations compromised. Tell him that under no circumstance is he to touch the paper with his bare hands. I need him to deliver the box to Poste within the next two hours. He should hide the box in his knapsack; calmly walk from his studio to the poste. Tell him to carry an envelope in his hand so it appears he is simply going there to mail a letter."

Max did as told. When he handed the woman behind the counter the box containing the drawing paper she asked. "Have you touched the paper?"

"No, only the box and I didn't open it."

"*Bon. Excusez-moi.*" She walked to the back of the small building. He could hear her talking on the phone, but of course it was in French. He couldn't understand what was being said. When she returned he asked if he should have a receipt.

"No, that would be foolish."

She put cotton gloves on and then placed the box into a metal container. She pulled a key from her pocket and locked the container.

"You must leave now," she said. "Someone will be here soon to pick up the package."

Max was perplexed. "Why do I have to leave now?

"Monsieur, we don't know who may be watching you, or, for that matter, watching me."

As he went out the door she said. "Monsieur Connor, I will be in touch with you soon. In the meantime, I suggest you practice drawing.

****

Max was uncomfortable with the pressure he felt coming from HP to do "the best possible drawings." Also he was not happy about having to draw wearing gloves. Max had planned to leave Lacoste the following day, but now he had to wait until the paper was returned from Paris. So he decided to draw something for himself nearby. He made a sketch of a view he saw below the Goat Gate. It was of a small cherry orchard nestled around a very old farmhouse. After working all day under a pulsating the sun, he was ready for a meal

317

with a glass of wine and bed.

As Max told me, he awoke early in the morning to pounding on his door. When he opened it, he found Gabrielle standing there with the box that contained the papers. He described her as tall and thin, maybe Arlesian or Spanish. He said that, in spite of all the intrigue in which he found himself, he couldn't help but think she was attractive. As she handed him the box, he noticed there was no wedding ring on her finger. It flashed through his mind that she might be someone he'd like to become acquainted with. I don't know why Max was compelled to share this with me, but fuck him, he did.

She gave Max a message. "You are to proceed tomorrow morning to Aix; a room has been arranged for you at a very nice hotel not far from where Cézanne's restored studio is located. Not only is the paper in the box, there are some very old looking pencils and a plastic food bag that contains a bottle of ink and a note for you from Madamé Gemmer."

As Max opened the package, the postmistress turned and walked down steps away from his house. She turned and said, "Don't forget, we need you to be in Aix at the hotel by tomorrow noon. After you check in, you are to go to the Cézanne Studio Museum. Take a walk along path and sit on the wooden bench under the sycamore tree near the croquet hoops. Be there at 2:15. Someone will meet you there with further instructions."

He opened the plastic bag and removed the note from Françoise. "Max, use these old graphite pencils and the ink for your drawings. They come from Antoine Arseneault's shop in Apt. The ink is made the old fashion way, by hand. It contains iron salts and tannic acids from the gals that form on the oak leaves here in Provence."

The next morning he loaded up his drawing supplies and placed them in the trunk of his car. He took the road to Bonnieux and then headed south on the D36 towards Aix. It took him about an hour to reach the city suburbs.

The hotel was once a chateau, but now it was divided into rooms for tourists and vacationing Parisians. They even welcomed Germans. The hotel was filled with truffle experts attending a convention of mushroom hunters. There was a swimming pool, tennis courts and formal manicured gardens. The rooms were air-conditioned and that was a treat for Max. He couldn't see Mont Sainte-Victoire from his window, but there was a print of it over his bed.

He drove into the city for lunch, parked his car and

strolled along the avenue of the Cours Mirabeau. As usual, Aix was bustling with tourists, university students, musicians, artists, and street performers. However, this time it was busier than he had ever seen before. The reason for the congestion became evident when he saw a banner hung across the avenue announcing the annual truffle competition.

The outdoor cafes were all filled. There was no place to sit, and there wouldn't be for several hours. Since coming to Provence, Max had learned that unlike, in his country where people eat and run, we French are civilized. To truly enjoy a meal takes two, maybe three hours at a leisurely relaxing pace. In France, patrons, restaurateurs and waiters expect such culinary refinement. Americans and Germans have no patience and I'm sure that is just one of the reasons for their poor health.

Max searched for a boulangerie and a cheese shop. He found a small fromagerie on the Mirabeau. After looking at all the options Max picked goat cheese.

As the owner placed the creamy, mild flavored Florette in a brown paper bag, he signed his name on the sack and said, "You buy the best fromage de chèvre from me, but now you must spread it upon the most delicious bread in all of France." The Fromâger then directed Max to *La fabrique à pain*,

Cézanne had been outside sketching his mountain when a heavy storm came up that caught him far away from his studio. He walked in the pouring rain towards the atelier. It was October; the chill of the cold rain and the long walk caused him to collapse on the road. A local laundryman found him, placed him in his a horse drawn cart and brought the painter home to his flat on the Rue Boulegon. He died there of pneumonia.

The group of Japanese art lovers left the studio. They were anxious to see the artist's gardens. Max was alone in what he believed to be a holy shrine. By himself in the studio Max heard Cézanne say, "Where in the hell have you been?"

Picasso was sitting in a chair to the right of Cézanne. He was silent and marveling at each stroke of Paul's brush on the canvas. Max heard the click on the floor as Cézanne dropped his palette knife.

My friend walked over, picked up the tool and handed it back to the master who said, "*Merci, Je l'espère, je ne vous ai pas sursauter.*" (I hope I didn't startle you.)

Max told me Cézanne's voice was raspy, almost as if his words were encased in phlegm.

suppose the paint splattered clogs and his shirt of many colors was like Jacob's coat of old. It was disturbing to her clean, neat and tidy self.

When the bus arrived at the atelier Max waited for the tour group to disembark. He followed them through the narrow entrance gate and down the path to the small building that had been Cézanne's studio.

Cézanne bought the land in 1901 and sited the studio on the crest of a hill. He was 72 years old when it was built. A year later his boyhood friend Émile Zola died, without ever seeing the studio. According to letters published after Cézanne's death, he regretted the falling out between them and felt betrayed when Zola wrote the novel, *L'Œuvre*. It was published in 1886 and the main character appeared to be based on Paul. I'd like to think that Cézanne started a few reconciliatory letters to his friend, but like two old lovers, who part and can't forgive, he was unable to finish them. Who knows, maybe he regretted never reaching out to his old friend. As it does for most of us, death came unexpectedly to Cézanne. The opportunity for Zola to ask his friend to forgive the indiscretion, coupled with Paul's own long held bitterness, spoiled the opportunity for the two artistic giants to reunite their companionship.

be a good idea. Then he looked at the advertisements in the windows of a real estate office, saw the rental rates and that ended his fantasy.

He had one of his episodes. He told me that while he was sitting on the bench sipping coke, Paul Cézanne walked up the street carrying a small easel under his arm. Next to Cézanne was his young friend, Émile Zola, shouting about Napoleon. Coming from the opposite direction was Ernest Hemingway and in his hand was the manuscript for his novel, *The Garden of Eden.*

Max told me the three artists vanished onto a side street. Good thing they did, because he needed to be at Cézanne's studio by 3pm. He asked a nearby shopkeeper how to get to there, she told him it would be too long a walk in the heat for him to get from the Cours Mirabeau to in Cité du Livre where the studio was located. She advised him to take the No. 5 bus from la Rotonde Victor Hugo. When he got on the bus it was filled with Japanese tourists. Like him, they had come to Aix to see the studio of the "*Father of Modern Art.*" There was one empty seat. He sat down next to a young woman who had her face buried in a picture book about Cézanne. She looked up and bowed her head to him. She pushed herself as close to the window as possible. I located on the Rue Pierre de Coubertin in Aix.

Max returned to the Cours Mirabeau, sat on a bench and made himself a sandwich. He watched the crowds and chewed. A boy offered to fetch him a soda. When he returned my friend gave him a tip that was twice the cost of a Coca-Cola.

Max was impressed with the rows of plane trees growing on each side of the broad thoroughfare. He contrasted the cool and comfortable atmosphere of Aix to the arid sun drenched feel of Lacoste. At home the heat in his village drained him. Usually from about noon on, it was best to stay in his house. By 6pm he'd return to the fields and orchards to draw or paint. Once the sun disappeared, it cooled down enough to sit in the café or go home to fry a chicken and make a salad. There was plenty of fresh fruit to be had around Lacoste. Apples, cherries, peaches, and melons, you name it, one fruit was disappearing just as another was coming in. He had a fan in his bedroom. It helped a little, but sleep was difficult when the temperatures hover at night in the 80's.

It seldom rains in Provence, and when there is a breeze, it just pushes hot air from one place to another. It seemed to him that Aix might be more livable in the summer. He told me the thought crossed his mind that maybe moving there would

In Spanish, Picasso asked Max. *"¿Estás aquí para acero sus secretos?"* (Are you here to steal his secrets?")

"No, I am here simply to pay homage to the man who set us free to make paintings that don't look like photographs. Maybe it is you who come to steal."

Picasso spoke in English. "I do not steal, I absorb. When we make love we absorb our lover. When I look at Monsieur Cézanne's painting, I become one with his mountain. Look at the rhythm of his arm, it's dancing in front of his canvas. He is absorbed, is he not?"

Cézanne continued to work as if both intruders were not there.

Picasso pointed at his own eye. "This is not how I see." He touched his chest. "My heart has better eyes than my head. An artist sees things that others cannot. A poet finds words that others can't speak. Watch the face when the pianist plays, then look at his audience. They are stuck in their seats and he is floating above them."

"We should live for moments of floating."

Max said someone tapped him on his shoulder. A woman said, "Monsieur, would you like to pay for your museum ticket?"

Max snapped back into reality. He was upset to lose Picasso and Cézanne.

He reached in his pocket and pulled out a few francs. The woman handed him a ticket and a little bit of change, told him he could not photograph in the studio, but that it would be fine if he wanted to take pictures in the garden. Max looked around to see if Picasso and Paul were hiding somewhere. The easel on which Cézanne had been working was there and the palette knife, with wet paint on it, was still on the floor. Cézanne was gone, so was Pablo. Next to the easel was a table displaying a white bowl filled with several apples. There was a painting, half started, on the easel. He touched it. The paint was dry. Obviously it was a prop. As Max looked at the shelves around the room he recognized several objects Cézanne had once used in his paintings. The olive pot and a plaster sculpture of cupid were sitting on a table near the easel. There was a potbellied stove, a ladder and several wooden chairs. The dark walls of the studio were painted in warm gray tones.

He asked the woman if it would be all right if he sketched in the studio. She turned her head and, like the ticking hand of a metronome, her finger wagged to reinforce her stern words, "No! It is not allowed."

Max looked at his watch and saw he had only a few minutes to get to the place where he was to meet the mysterious stranger in Cézanne's garden. He left the studio and began to jog along the narrow crushed stone walk. Monsieur Cézanne's garden was designed not as a formal site like his friend Monet's, but to be more of a natural setting. It was unkempt, unplanned and out of control. Max liked it. It was real, not like Michelin's manicured fiefdom. It was as God created the *Garden of Eden*; a wild place, with its own soul.

There were signs with photos that gave tourists a sense of how it had looked in Cézanne's time. There were birds singing in the trees and the cicadas were sawing raspy tunes in harmony with their feathered friends. The earth was mostly flat, and in some low areas it was wet which forced him to dodge puddles of mud and standing pools of water. When the path's elevation began to rise, he quickened his steps. About 20 meters in front of him he spotted the figure of a large man sitting on a bench and, as he came closer, he recognized Boris Volkov, the fat fingered Russian fromA vignon.

Volkov smiled. Max was confused, befuddled because he had no point of reference as to how, why, or what, the Russian was doing there. How could he have anything to do with HP or the new postmistress in Lacoste? Boris could see confusion written all over Max's face.

"Sit down my friend." Max nervously complied. Volkov pulled a flask and two small metal cups from the shoulder bag resting on the ground beside his knee. Smiling, the Russian slowly poured vodka into one of the cups and handed it to Max. Then he poured a drink for himself. "You appear to be surprised to see me, yes?"

"I have to admit I am. I was told to meet someone here."

"Indeed, you were directed by the postmistress in Lacoste. She did not tell you whom you were to meet, did she? And now you are surprised to see me. You are wondering why I am here. What do I have to do with the mail clerk and the package you recently received? Correct?"

Max thought about Gabrielle, what was this man's connection to her and how did he know about the box? Max was cautious, very cautious, and replied only with a nod.

Volkov continued. "How is your friend, the beautiful blond woman? You are staying at the old

Chateau up the road; it is most romantic, is it not? You must be disappointed she was unable to join you on this excursion. I am sure you will miss, while you are here,... how should I say... her charms." He smiled and then added. "How do you like your room with the print of Monsieur Cézanne's painting of Mont Sainte-Victoire?"

"How do you know about my room or where I'm staying?"

"All the rooms are the same. Same carpets, same wallpaper and the same print on the walls."

Max took a large swig of Vodka while the Russian continued.

"I remember your friend Françoise spent some time with my friend Domino while you and I were looking at my collection. They appeared to enjoy one another's company. Did you know they were associates on several levels? I suspect she never told you the truth about their relationship. Both professionally and personally."

"No, I didn't know they knew each other until recently. I saw a picture of them together, taken maybe 20 years ago."

"Both women are, as you Americans call it, *AC... DC*. They enjoy both sexes. I suspect you are not completely surprised.

I can condone such behavior. But only between women! A man, a real man, does not suck cock, Yes?" Volkov poured more Vodka into each cup.

"Do you remember the Monet drawings I showed you at my Chateau? You doubted they were real Monets. You were skeptical and said it would be difficult to verify them. I knew all along they were fakes, but I told you I was having them authenticated by someone from the Louvre. That person was your girl friend's lover, Domino."

"If you knew they were not Monet's, why did you lie to me?"

"It was a test. I knew they were forgeries, but I needed to know if you were an honest man or part of the conspiracy."

"Of course I am an honest man. I am an artist. Artists seek truth. Artistic integrity is the first rule of being an artist. Being true to one's self and the gift that the Universe has given us is essential to our souls. If we compromise this principle, we are fakes ourselves."

Volkov smiled. "Not all gifted artists are pure, some sell out and corrupt their gift for money and vanity. I know, that you know, the father of your blond friend was such a man. He was a forger who tricked many. His redemption came because he double- crossed the Nazi's. This brought him a certain reprieve from the French government. But he was a forger just the same, and many museums and collectors were swindled and ruined by him. This man taught his daughter, your beautiful friend, the techniques of forgery and she has become quite proficient. She has been setting you up to be an unsuspecting participant in a vast conspiracy in which she plays a key role."

"She has used sex to manipulate you. Don't feel bad, woman have been doing this throughout history."

Max was offended. The Russian was arrogant and his remarks sexist. But maybe Max was no better when he screamed, "Fuck you! I have been on to her for some time. Now it's my turn to manipulate her."

"Yes, I know what is going on, and at this moment it's far more than you can possibly comprehend. Let me help you to understand some of..."

Max cut him off. "Just explain why you are here. Make it simple, no twisting of words, just straight talk."

"You Americans are not good at subtlety. In Russia, it is a way of life. So, I shall explain to you, in straight talk, as you Americans like to say, the reason for my being here. You know me as a collector of art. From the work you saw at my chateau in Avignon, you think I am a collector, with a dubious compendium of Russian and French art. You have no idea as to how I obtained such a collection. Most likely you think I am a rich Russian oligarch. Is it possible, 'Monsieur... Pure Artist', that I may be something different, or maybe more? Your girlfriend Françoise Gemmer appears to most people to be one thing, yet we both know she is another. She is known as the "*Most Beautiful Woman In Provence*." But in fact my friend, she is one of the most dangerous women in France."

Max challenged Volkov's assertion. "She may be a forger, and certainly a conniving bitch, but she is far from dangerous."

"You don't know the scope of the danger she represents. You could soon be in her crosshairs. For now you are safe. She is unaware that you have uncovered her criminal identity. Your jealousy, your suspicions, and the diamonds that you discovered have opened a pathway for us to follow."

"And who is *us* and what is *it* you are looking

for?" "I can not tell you. But I have a message for you." From the pocket of his shirt, Volkov pulled a sheet of paper and handed the small hand drawn map to Max. "Go to these spots to do your drawings for Madamé Gemmer's friend. I, or one of my associates, will be in touch with you soon."

Boris stood up and looked down at Max who was examining the areas he was to draw. The Russian then handed my friend four photographs taken from the places marked on the map. "Make sure you draw the exact composition you see framed in these photos."

"I am reluctant to tell you, but it is important that you know the seriousness of your predicament." He handed Max a gun. "Do you know how to use this?"

Max nodded affirmatively and reached for the Beretta. "But why do I need a weapon?"

"The Lacoste postmistress was found this morning, dead in the ruins of the Marque de Sade's castle. She was tortured in a very cruel way. No one heard her scream. She was drugged when the killer, or killers, split her stomach open."

****

While I was getting ready to go to the reception of the French Conservators Association, Max foolishly called me on my home phone, not the mobile!

"Céline, the meeting yesterday in the garden at Cézanne's studio was with the fucking Russian I met in Avignon, Boris

Volkov. Whose side is he on? Is Volkov dangerous or is he working for HP? He told me the

postmistress in Lacoste has been murdered. I don't know what the fuck is going on!"

I was shocked, but knew enough to hang up the phone and then called Max back on my mobile. "Oh my God, what is happening? There must be some explanation as to why Volkov was the one you met. HP has never mentioned him to me. The murder is barbaric; it frightens me. As soon as I talk to HP I'll get back to you."

I frantically called HP's secure phone. His message machine answered and I blurted out the Russian's name. I probably should not have done that, but I was scared for Max's safety.

Soon afterwards HP called and confirmed the murder in Lacoste. He told me he had received a call at three in the morning from his source in

Marseille that the killing had taken place. He said none of the villagers were aware of the gruesome killing of their new postmistress.

Immediately after the call from Marseille, HP alerted the prime minister and a special unit of the National Police was dispatched to the scene. Their investigation was done so secretly that none of the villagers suspected a horrific crime had taken place in their midst. A team of special agents, disguised as construction workers, cordoned off the castle. Signs were placed around the ruins saying the castle was closed for maintenance. Forensic experts combed the area and collected evidence. Blood was cleaned from the site and a coroner removed the gruesome remains of the tortured woman. By evening the team had sanitized the tourist attraction and left. No one in the village was the wiser. No press, no panic, no questions. Life went on as usual in Provence. The only impact on Lacoste was the post office was closed for two days for what was described as, "repairs."

HP revealed the startling fact that Gabrielle was the National Police agent who was assigned to be Max's handler. He also told me that he hadn't known the identity of the person who was assigned to meet Max. He assured me he was unaware of who Volkov was. I told him the story of how Max had met him at a restored châteaux in Avignon. HP said that the man might be working with Interpol, which would be good, or God forbid, involved with the Russian mafia.

"Céline, there is a Russian connection to the conspiracy. It is possible we have been infiltrated. I will find out whether this Russian is a friend or a foe. Tell Max to be careful. He should trust no one and continue to appear as a naive artist. He must not let on to Françoise, or anyone in her circle, what he knows or what he is doing. That includes Maurice Michelin or any employee who works at the Louvre, but especially his friend Robert. Robert has loose lips, and some in his family cannot be trusted. Tell him I said not to trust gendarmes, neighbors, or local shopkeepers. Being paranoid might prove to be his lifesaver."

"You must also be discreet, Céline. We know both your home and office phones are tapped, so you must continue only to talk with Max by mobile. I think it best from here on out that you and I do the same. We have screened your apartment for listening devices; there are none. We are watching your gallery and residence. We are also taking similar precautions with Max."

I asked HP if all this was necessary. He responded, "When billions in currencies around the world are invested in art, collectors and museums must rely on authenticity. If these investments are exposed as fakes, we could find the world teetering on the brink of an economic and cultural disaster of huge proportions. Imagine if we learned that half the gold of France was nothing more than painted bricks, what do you think would be the result?"

I am a dealer in art. Art is not decoration. It is not commerce. My goal has been to provide my clientele with substance, beauty and enjoyment. This is my *raison de vivre*. Up until this conversation, I saw my role solely as bringing collectors and artists together. I wanted to help my clients see the world in new ways. I wanted the artists that I represent to be able to make a living through their art.

I have never thought about the important role art plays in market finances and national pride. I never expected to be sucked into the world of forgers and fakes but, unfortunately, it is where I have landed. This conspiracy has caught me in its web of deception and conflict. What is my responsibility in all this? To whom do I owe my allegiances?

****

It took me awhile to select the right dress to wear for the event. I was upset; nothing in my closet seemed to go with the Gucci cocktail purse that HP had sent me. Finally I put together an outfit. Always up to date, my tight black Dior dress made me look slimmer. I needed to wear my elastic girdle to hold me in place. I fussed over several earrings and finally settled on a pair my grandmother had worn at her wedding. I have no idea as to its value, but the blue sapphires complimented the expensive cocktail bag. I tried on several scarves; in that regard I was lucky. You see I love scarves so I had many to choose from. I pulled my Roberto

Cavalli hand printed scarf off of the full size reproduction sculpture that I bought years ago from a museum shop in Liverpool, England. It is a cast marble effect copy of Hermaphroditus, the son of the Greek god Hermes and the goddess Aphrodite. They were draped around his neck and over his arms. I gave him the title, *"Keeper of My Scarves."*

I turned and looked at myself in the full-length mirror that was attached to the back of my bathroom door. I looked pretty good for a woman my age. My only regret was that I wished I had more highlights in my hair. Oh well, I thought, you're the only one who's going to notice.

I was standing in my stocking feet. The dilemma of what shoes to wear was overwhelming. I asked myself, "What shoes are you going to wear, Céline? Pumps, flats, or 'fuck me heels'?" I decided on boots. I chose my most expensive pair, Nicholas Kirkwood's 'Quantum boots.' I had only worn them once and that was to Max's opening. When I got into the taxi, the driver said, "Oh là là!" When we reached the Pompidou Center I gave him a nice tip.

The Centre Pompidou is an art museum full of galleries; it is a cultural icon in Paris. Its permanent modern collection and its changing contemporary artwork exhibits are extraordinary; one can find works by Matisse, Picasso, and every major artist from the impressionists onward. The Pompidou's public library and performance spaces are magnificent. The building's design is inside out with tubes and structures color-coded by their function, red for elevators, blue for air conditioning, yellow for electricity and green for plumbing. After dark the top floor provides some of the best views of the Eiffel Tower.

The Pompidou was about to begin renovations and this event would be the last major one until the project is completed in 2000. The Centre had just installed a show of Francis Bacon's paintings. The popes, the perverts and contorted figures were, for some, troubling. But for me, they were magnificent.

The reception was on the 4ᵗʰ floor. I went to the check in area and was given a name card. *Céline Roulin, Céline Roulin Gallery Paris: Consultant to The Russian Cultural Attaché.* I was impressed with myself.

My first stop was for fortification, meaning, wine and chocolate. There were several hundred attendees. I recognized numerous gallery owners and several cultural and art institutional employees and leaders. While wandering around the galleries, it seemed that at every turn I'd meet someone I knew and then would find myself trapped in petty conversations. At the same time I was trying to smile and talk, I was looking over the crowd in search of Moroccan and dark haired Arabian women.

I had a covert job to do. I liked the idea of being a spy. I'd press the camera button on the handle and silently take a picture of my target. At first I wondered if the camera was working because I never heard the shutter click or the sound of the film advancing. I figured it was high tech James Bond equipment, so I decided to just not worry about how it functioned. I was also taking images of shoes. HP said they were for his secretary. Maybe, but who knows, men have their fetishes. Of the hundreds of women attendees, I only saw saw two women who fit HP's description. One was short and accompanied an older man who seemed to be the center of attention. I had a strong feeling she was his bored housewife.

The other was slim, attractive and wearing a pair of Jimmy Choo 'Hoop' Pumps. They were 4" heels with corset-style wraparound laces and, I must say, she looked incredibly sexy in them.

She was with a group of people all wearing nametags that identified them as employees of the Louvre. I worked my way around the circle of them until I was able to get a clear shot of the Jimmy Choo woman talking to coworkers. I was able to get close enough to her to press the button on my bag. I was not sure if I captured an adequate image of her pumps. I took several more pictures from other views. When I clicked the last picture, I noticed the tattoo on her ankle. It was partially hidden under the leather lace-up ties. At that moment I realized I was looking at the woman Max told me he had met at Volkov's châteaux in Avignon, the one with King Solomon's magical seal tattooed on her ankle.

She turned from her conversation with her

colleagues and looked at me. She smiled, excused herself from the group and walked towards me. I was nervous; maybe she was suspicious. There was no way she could know about the camera. Maybe I hung around too long. She reached out her hand and I felt her nails touch my wrist.

"Hello, my name is Dominique Dubois. We met several years ago at your inaugural opening of Robert Chéron's sculpture exhibition. It was his first Paris showing. I'll bet it was maybe 15 years ago; you had just opened your gallery. I was new to Paris and had become an intern at the Louvre. As a matter of fact, you introduced me to Robert.

Perhaps we met, but I couldn't remember her. I told her I was sorry that I didn't recognize her. "I meet so many gallery goers, artists and their friends, it's hard for me to recall everyone."

"Oh yes, I understand, it is the same for me." She pointed to her nametag. "I am now Associate Conservator of Sculpture and Drawing at the Louvre. Over the years I've worked with Robert on several restorations for the Museum. He is such a remarkable talent. He can restore just about anything. Recently we trusted him with a badly damaged Degas piece. An arm was missing as well as the lower part of the models face, but when the sculpture was finally repaired, you'd never know it had been so badly damaged."

Mademoiselle Dubois looked at my nametag. "How interesting you are working with the Russian embassy. I just met the Cultural Attaché, Vladimir Bogdanov. He is here at the reception; he is a most fascinating man. Do you enjoy working with him?"

Again, I was caught off guard. I needed to thread a fine needle. I had not met him and was unsure how to finesse her question. Thank God for the tap on my shoulder. It was HP

He kissed both sides of my cheeks, stood back and admired my outfit. "Céline, you look beautiful." Looking at Dominique Dubois he asked, "And who is this beautiful woman?"

I introduced him as my friend HP She smiled saying, "And what do your initials stand for?"

"Hot Pickles," he said. We all laughed.

"Céline, the band is about to begin playing, would you grant this old bureaucrat the first dance?"

He took my hand and I smiled. "Qui." I wanted to get away from this woman.

"Mademoiselle Dubois, I am sorry to interrupt your conversation with my very dear friend Céline. Unfortunately, I have to get back to my office tonight and holding her in my arms for one dance, will give me the fortitude to referee a fight between our Interior Minister and the American Ambassador.

We walked away, he held my hand and whispered in my ear. "Saved by the bell!"

I smiled, he didn't. He held me close to him and we began to dance.

My relationship with HP began when he served, during the Mitterrand years, with my friend, the Minister of Culture, Jack Lang. I, along with many of France's visual arts leaders, were asked by Lang to be a part one of several planning committees for the Grands Travaux restoration project and expansion to the Louvre and the new Musée d'Orsay. HP was on the government's appropriation committee for funding of the arts. Ever since, we have remained in touch. On several occasions, he has asked me to serve on visual arts panels and also requested my advice regarding his personal acquisitions of works of art. He attends almost all of my gallery exhibitions and even owns one of Max's paintings.

"I didn't expect you to be here tonight."

HP whispered into my ear. "I didn't plan to be here,

but an hour ago I was informed that Françoise Gemmer has been murdered."

My knees gave way. I dropped down. He held me up and then steadied me. As he pressed me closer, he looked over my shoulder and saw Dominique Dubois staring at us. I was crying. Not for Françoise, but for Max, and that surprised me.

****

We left together, and as he drove me home he asked, "Have you ever heard of the art dealer Joly Hartert?"

"No, who is he?" HP hesitated, "How about his son Jack?"

Again, I said no. I was in the dark as to why he was asking about these two individuals, but then I vaguely remembered Sidney Janis had once mentioned the name, but I couldn't remember the context of the conversation. Besides, it was years ago, and Sidney told me so many stories about artists, galleries and buyers that I couldn't recall the exact conversation. I waited for HP to enlighten me as to why he was asking the question.

He continued, "Hartert sold a number of paintings

to Walter Chrysler Jr., the son of the automobile manufacturer."

I recalled meeting the younger Chrysler years ago in New York. I told HP that Sidney Janis had introduced me to him at an opening in his gallery. I remember Chrysler was with Andy Warhol. Chrysler seemed a bit odd, but he certainly knew what he liked and didn't like. As I recall that night, Mr. Janis and Chrysler got into a loud argument and Andy stepped in to quiet both of them down. After they left, I remember Sidney telling me that Chrysler was stupid and had been bilked into buying dubious works of art.

HP cleared his throat. "Yes, that doesn't surprise me. Chrysler was quite opinionated. He died a few years ago and his collection went to a museum somewhere near Washington D. C. Chrysler's reputation came under a cloud some time in the early 1960's when a Canadian museum exhibited 187 works of art from his collection and the Art Dealers Association of America claimed 90 of them to be forgeries. Among the declared fakes were works purported to be by Vincent van Gogh, Matisse, Bonnard and Paul Klee. Most of the fake paintings Chrysler purchased came from two New York dealers, H. B. Yotnakparian and Joly Hartert."

"There was also another huge scandal around that time. Mr. Chrysler offered six of his Picasso paintings for the artist's 80th birthday exhibition in New York. Picasso was shown photographs of the works and, on two of the photos, he scrawled the word 'false.' In other words, fakes!"

"We believe Chrysler purchased his fraudulent paintings from the Hartert Gallery. In those days Walter junior was not the wealthy man he would become after his father's death in 1940. He was young, maybe naïve, and in his zeal to collect art he was duped, or worse, could have just turned a blind eye to many of his acquisitions. Chrysler quickly amassed well over a thousand paintings, sculptures and other works of art and stored them in a warehouse not far from his office in the Chrysler building. We don't think he purposely acquired fakes; he just never did the due diligence that someone like his friend Rockefeller or Paul Mellon did. Unfortunately, he indiscreetly bought and sold paintings, drawings and occasional pieces of sculpture. In most cases he did not have, or even seek, proof of provenance that would have warrantied his holdings. Sadly, he built a polluted collection."

"Now, here comes the shocker. Where do you think so many of the fakes in Chrysler's collection come from? Who did them?"

"Hartert's son Jack was based in Paris. His supposed assignment in the family business was to purchase Impressionist style paintings and other old works of European art and then ship them back to his father's gallery in New York City."

"Hartert junior was an extremely gifted artist himself. His work was in the style of the Old Masters. He was also proficient with pastels. One of Hartert's drawings of a nude woman had been attributed to Matisse. It was later uncovered as fraudulent and had been included in the disastrous Chrysler Collection show in Canada."

"Oddly, the young Hartert was not interested in selling his work and he only rarely exhibited his paintings. Based on passport, visa and other records, he lived in Paris from about 1938 until he moved to Clifton England in 1961, the same year Françoise's father mysteriously disappeared. It was around the time that the FBI seized more than 600 paintings from the Hartert Gallery in New York. The International Foundation for Art Research found that Hartert senior had sold 18 fraudulent works of art to another New York gallery dealer. Up until then, it was one of the few times the Americans had ever prosecuted a major gallery for fraud."

"Strangely, Hartert the younger had only a few friends and his acquaintances were unaware that he possessed any artistic abilities. He had a reputation in Clifton as being a generous man. His neighbors assumed he was a rich American who did not work for a living; they thought him to be an heir to some fabulous fortune. He was known by the locals to only dine at the finest Clifton restaurants. He was a raconteur and enjoyed smoking only the best Cuban cigars. He was also a heavy drinker and preferred the finest scotch whiskeys. He died of cancer in 1975, at least that's the official cause reported in the local paper."

"Based on top-secret files relating to Françoise's father, Jean-Philippe Gaillard, Jack Hartert and Gaillard met sometime prior to the Nazi occupation of France. Françoise's father occasionally taught at a small Atelier in Montmartre and for a nominal fee the school offered local artists space, as well as nude models to draw once a week during the evening. That's how the two met. We know Gaillard was impressed with young Hartert's talent and taught him the skills of copying paintings of the old Masters, impressionists and a few contemporary artists such as Bonnard, Duffy and Picasso. Eventually Françoise's father employed him to do several forgeries that found their way into Hitler's collection. As I told you once, the government was grateful to her father for duping the Nazis."

"We surmise that Hartert was also supplying his father's gallery in New York with many of the forgeries that found their way into the United States. Walter P. Chrysler Jr. was probably the most well-know collector that Joly Hartert conned into buying his son's, and maybe Gaillard's, fakes. After all, if they could scam the Führer and Goebbels, they certainly would have been able to fool Chrysler."

"Our theory is that Jean-Philippe Gaillard was the godfather behind the creation of the Cézanne Conspiracy. Certainly Jack Hartert was instrumental in creating hundreds of fraudulent paintings as well. According to our interviews with old comrades, Hartert was like an uncle to Françoise."

"Do you remember telling me about the old Polaroid photo Max found in Françoise's purse, the one where she, Robert and Domino are standing in front of the Louvre? We believe Hartert and Gaillard are the other two men in that photo with them. But what we really need to know is this...who...who was the person taking the photograph? Such knowledge might be the key to unlocking the identity of the kingpin behind the cartel."

I was fascinated by how much HP knew. I asked him, "Where do you go from here?"

After an uncomfortably long pause he said. "I think we are getting closer to an answer, Celine."

****

Max began his first drawing in the landscape Cézanne had loved so much. He parked his car as close as he could and walked along a path towards the Barrage Zola, (the dam was named after Emile Zola's father who had been the dam's architect). Max sat himself up on the on a corner of the eastern edge of the Bibémus Plateau known as the Les Infernets. There, in all its grandeur, stood Montagne Sainte-Victoire.

The scene in front of Max had remained untouched since Paul Cézanne was there a hundred years before. Max wondered how close he was to the places where the master had once stood with his palette and brush. Max thought he heard a grunt and looked to his left. There he saw Cézanne standing in front of his easel. He was dabbing a sandy pink color from the tip of his paintbrush onto the half finished canvas of the mountain standing in front of both of them. But, then in a blink of his eye, Max's vision disappeared.

Max used the paper, pencil and ink that François and her supposed friend, Valerie, had supplied. He worked for an hour and in the short time captured the scene with the same intensity and feeling of his predecessor. As he leaned over to put his drawing tools back into his knapsack he caught a glimpse of Cézanne looking back at him. Smiling, the great artist raised his thumb in recognition for what Max had achieved before vanishing.

****

I wanted to call Max to tell him about Françoise's father, but HP suggested waiting until my friend returned to Lacoste. I was concerned that Max might read about Françoise's demise. HP reminded me that Max couldn't read French and the local broadcasting stations were not in English.

Max continued doing the work that the so-called collector friend of Françoise had commissioned. He stuck to the places Boris Volkov had directed him to draw even though he felt uneasy about the Russian. Whose side was he on? Was Volkov dangerous or was he working for HP?

He unwisely called me from his room in Aix and left a message. "Céline, have you heard from HP about Volkov?"

I returned his call. "Yes, HP called to tell me Boris Volkov is known by the National Police. He is not in their employ, nor is he an informant. The Russian had no connection to the postmistress. The man who was originally supposed to meet you disappeared and has most likely been killed. How Volkov fits into all this is a mystery to me. I'm not sure why, but for some reason HP won't, or can't share with me, why he believes we can trust Volkov."

I hated to do it, but I knew I couldn't go along with HP's suggestion to not tell Max what happened to Françoise. It would be a betrayal of our relationship. As I remember, the conversation went like this.

"Max, last night HP told me that Françoise was murdered." There was a moment of silence that seemed like an eternity. His voice, racing like a locomotive asked,

"How...Why...Where...What happened?" I could tell from the fast and trembling cadence of his words that he was shocked. He knew, because it came from me, that her death was true and certain. I detected his attempt at courage, but when his voice creaked, my own heart jumped into my throat. I cried. He cried.

I regained my composure. "Max, are you sure you want to know now? It might be better for me to come to Lacoste?"

"She betrayed me, made a fool of me and yet I don't despise her. I know she used me; but I did love her. You know that. Don't spare the details. I need to know everything."

For a moment I hesitated telling Max the gruesome details of her death. "She was found by a gardener in the pond under the green bridge at Giverny. Her body had been there for a couple of days submerged in the reeds and roots of water lilies. Four large wooden crates filled with counterfeit Monet dinner plates weighted her down, keeping her pinned to the slimy pond bottom. There were no mortal wounds to her body. Her mouth was taped shut, and her hands and feet tied, so it was apparent she must have been dumped from the bridge alive. Tucked in a plastic bag stuffed in her blouse pocket was a note written in an ancient Canaanite language that, when painstakingly translated, read: *The most beautiful woman in Provence* isn't so beautiful now."

I could hear Max vomiting. When he got back to the phone, he said, "So it's over now, we can go back to living our lives normally."

"No Max, not yet. I am sure you may become a suspect because the plastic bag also contained a picture of you standing on the bridge at night. I know it is from the time you and Robert snuck into Giverny. Fortunately the local police have no idea who the person in the picture is. My guess is that, within a few hours, they will identify you. By tomorrow the police will be in Lacoste looking for you. It's best you stay in Aix, but you must get out of the hotel where you're staying. I wouldn't be surprised if that picture of you will appear in the newspapers and on television. I have a friend who lives in an old restored farmhouse outside of Aix; she will put you up for a few days. I know HP will want you to finish the drawings. So leave your car at my friend's house and only use hers to get to the sites Volkov told you to work in. I will try to get in touch with HP to see what he wants us to do next."

I gave Max my friend's telephone number and hung up the phone. As I was putting the receiver back on its cradle I thought I heard a click on my line. I'm just paranoid, I thought. But within a moment HP called.

"Tell Max, that for now, the press is in the dark as

to what happened at Giverny. No one, other than the two gardeners, the local police, the coroner and the Director of Monet's estate know about the body in the pond. Unfortunately, that's too many people!"

I was incensed and screamed, "Have you tapped my phone?" Frazzled by my demand, HP replied, "Sorry, I should have called you. I was stuck all night in a meeting with American CIA Station Chief and Minister Charles Pasqua. Listen to me Céline, the Ministry of the Interior has ordered your phone to be monitored. Charles is a trusted friend; he called me just a few minutes ago. You can tell Max, that for now, the incident at Giverny is a tightly controlled secret. The local police have been ordered by the government to stand down. The Prime Minister has placed the Special Forces Unit of the Gendarmerie and the National Police in charge of the investigation."

"The note found on Madamé Gemmer's body, her involvement with the forgery conspiracy and those who we suspect were involved in her death are all top secret. Giverny was not open when the body was found. The only staff present at that time was two gardeners. They called the police and Giverny was completely shut down. No one was allowed in or out until the body was removed and all the evidence collected. The gardeners are not suspects, but they are being kept in a secure location."

"A gruesome murder in one of the most important cultural icons in France can not be kept quiet for long. It will be splashed across the media within days. The world will demand answers and we don't have answers to give them. We have to manage this killing in such a way that it appears to be a crime of passion."

"Conveniently, Françoise's husband has disappeared; Interpol is looking for him."

"While we currently have custody of the evidence, it may provide us with clues as to who did this to her. But I worry that whoever the killer or killers are, they have an agenda that we don't know. It could be that her demise was an assassination by those inside the conspiracy, or possibly it is people outside of the conspiracy who killed her. Maybe even a government. I am worried about the photo of Max found on her body. There could be other incriminating photos out there similar to this one. Sooner than later, I suspect that image will surface in the media. Thanks to Max, we know Robert is probably the last person to be in possession of the film making him our primary suspect. So far, we have been unable to locate him, but we WILL find him. I am certain, that at some point, he will call you. That is, of course, if he's still alive."

"We are getting closer to unraveling the conspiracy. Madamé Gemmer's departure does not mean the end of the forgery scandal, far from it. She was a major player in the business. She was killed for a reason, but by whom and for what we don't know, not yet anyway. But we will."

"Call Max back and tell him to stay where he is and to continue going to the sites that Boris told him to. Let him know that we have assets in Aix who are watching over him."

I telephoned Max and he was relieved, but also drunk. I didn't say it to him, but I was happy that Françoise was now out of the picture. I never liked her. She knew it, and that scared her. I also let him know that he was safe for awhile staying in the hotel and he didn't need to go to my friend's home.

In spite of his hangover the following morning, he got up early and drove to the next drawing site. As he was driving along the D14 he noticed a car behind him. It was far back, but kept a steady distance. He turned on several gravel roads and the black car continued to follow him. He pulled over, the car behind passed. He saw two men inside; both wore fancy hats, which is unusual in Provence. The heat in the south of France was far too uncomfortable to be wearing the Jean-Paul Belmondo's style hats they had on. Max doubted they were movie stars. As they flew by the fellow on the passenger side flicked his cigarette towards Max. The cigarette came through Max's open window; it hit the steering wheel and then landed in his lap. He jumped an inch off his car seat. Just as the cigarette began to burn a hole in his slacks he grabbed it, tossed it out the window, and gave the bastard the finger. He watched as they disappeared on the twisting road that led to the quarry near Lumières. Max turned the car around and quickly sped to Carrières de Bibémus.

Almost hidden in a pine forest high on a sandstone plateau, the quarries were one of Cézanne's favorite places to paint. He started painting there in 1895. The Romans had quarried stone nearby and rock was being excavated at Bibémus up until the 19th Century. My friend John Rewald, the great art historian, visited the area over a hundred times. His research on Cézanne is of monumental importance. John died last year and I suspect he will always be considered the leading expert on Cézanne. John played a major role in saving Cézanne's studio and he helped create a foundation that made the studio into a unique and fascinating museum. His description of Bibémus is both poetic and absolutely precise.

"It is a vast field of seemingly accidental forms as if some prehistoric giant, constructing a fantastic playground, had piled up cubes and dug holes and then abandoned them without leaving a hint of his intricate plan."

"And nature has since spread a carpet of plants over the turrets, the square blocks, the sharp edges, the clefts, the caves, the tunnels and arches, thus reclaiming the site that had been wrested from her."

****

Max parked his car, grabbed his gear and walked up the hill to the site where he intended to make the first drawing. It was a long way up, but living in Lacoste had fortified his physical stamina for steep inclines and long jaunts.

He reached the rocky ridge above the Château Noir estate. The shape and texture of the rocks created a rhythm of light and shadows that inspired him. His pencil flowed easily across the paper's surface. One perfect sketch without the mark of an eraser captured the scene. The nib of his pen, dipped in the ink, scratched the paper leaving behind black splatters and microscopic shards of the old copper pen point. He thought of Françoise and how she treasured her pens and oak gull ink. He told me there was a moment when a tear rolled from the inside corner of his eye and slowly followed the course of the crease between his cheek and the uneven side of his nose. The nose had been broken when he was a boy playing catcher and a foul ball smashed into his face. He never had it fixed. It gave him a manly appearance, and in spite of how it affected his breathing, he wore it like a prizefighter.

Max finished the drawing quickly. As he was packing up his materials, he heard a twig snap. He looked up. Standing on the rock formation above him was one of the Jean-Paul Belmondo characters from the black car. Max sucked into his lungs a sudden short frightened breath as the man pulled a gun from behind his waist and began to jump down the slabs of rock and boulders. Max knew he was in danger. He grabbed his knapsack, thinking he'd run down the path and escape, but when he turned to run away he was startled to be face to face with Jean-Paul Belmondo's twin brother. Two shots rang out. He was confused. He had no idea where the shooting was coming from, but both of the twins collapsed. One body was wedged between two boulders and the other laid dead at Max's feet.

Max jumped over the dead man's body and ran towards the path. He stumbled twice and then fell.

The drawing board, with the Cézanne-like image, had flipped into the grassy side of the path undamaged. His knapsack tumbled over the gravel-covered trail. He crawled and reached to pick it up; the skin on the palm of his hand was deeply scratched and bleeding. He checked inside his bag to see if the ink and other materials were intact. He felt the gun handle of the pistol that Volkov had given him to protect himself. How could he have forgotten? He wouldn't have used it anyway. In the heat of battle, a man not accustomed to combat with trained killers can only think of one thing, dying or running.

A beefy hand reached out to him, Max's first thought was of the gun in pocket but then he recognized the ring on the finger of the hand reaching out to him. Boris Volkov pulled the dirt covered, limping artist to his feet. In his free hand the Russian was holding a long rifle with a scope mounted to it.

Max told me he thought Boris would kill him next. He wasn't certain if the Russian was friend or foe.

"Brush yourself off, you're a mess. We have to get out of here fast."

Boris threw the Russian carbine into a thicket, removed his gloves and stuffed them into the pocket of his thin jacket. He picked up the drawing board, removed the artwork, and rolled it tightly. He put his free arm around Max and helped him stumble down the hill. Off in the distance, Max noticed smoke rising over the pine trees.

When they reached Max's Citroën, the two sat on small boulders to catch their breaths. Boris lit a cigarette, offered the pack to Max, who shook his head no. Maxfield removed a painting rag from his knapsack, took a bottle of Evian and swallowed several huge gulps. He poured the remaining water over his hand and gently wiped the drying blood away. He bent over, spat on the ground and then removed a second bottle of water from his bag and handed it to the Russian. Perspiration ran down his forehead, he brushed his hair back, and looked at Boris, who, as you Americans like to say, was as cool as a cucumber.

Distraught, and still breathing heavily, he looked into Boris' glacial blue eyes, asking, "Did you shoot those men?"

"Yes. I had no other choice. They were going to kill you. These are the same men who sabotaged your old car, assassins from Marseille, probably employed by someone close to the Cézanne conspiracy."

"That doesn't make sense, why would the conspirators want me dead. According to Céline's friend in Parliament, no one knows that I am working with the government."

Boris shook his head, "I don't know, but I suspect there is a fracture within the cartel."

Max looked skeptical. "You're not the one I was supposed to meet in Cézanne's garden, are you?"

"No, the contact you were to meet was found in his apartment hanging in a closet. It was made to look like suicide. It seems most probable that the two communists I just delivered into hell were likely the ones who assassinated the poor fellow. The man you know as H. P asked me to meet you. By the way, have you ever met him?"

Max took a handkerchief from his pocket and blew the dust from his nose. "No, but I know he is a friend of Céline's."

"Have you ever spoken to him over the phone?""No. Why?""Just curious.""What is your relationship with the him?" Max asked. "Like you, I have never met him. He connects with me through messages composed on a very old typewriter. Cabbies, bicyclists, and pizza delivery boys deliver his communications to me. One time he sent an internationally sensitive communication to me that was delivered by a whore. I know he exists, I've seen him on television. He appears to the public to be a typical politician. I happen to know he is far more that."

Max requested a cigarette. "I can use one now. So go on, what more do you know about him?"

Boris gave him the pack. Max noticed the cigarettes were Turkish. Volkov held out a gold lighter and with a flip of his finger ignited the flame. Max saw the old hammer and sickle emblem of the once proud Soviet Union engraved on the side of it. Boris could tell Max was curious.

"It's a souvenir. After you started running down the hill I stopped for a moment to quickly search the pockets of the shit holes who tried to kill you. Nothing on them, just the lighter. Want to keep it as memento?"

"No thanks."

Boris put the dead man's lighter back into his pocket. Off in the distance they heard the wail of sirens.

"We best be going. I don't think it would be a good idea for the police to find a SRV agent here."

"What is the SRV?"

"Lets just say we are a team of experts who collect secret information and sometimes run interference on behalf of our country."

The two got into their automobiles. Boris pulled up next to Max, rolled his window down and rested his elbow on the opening in door. He told Max, "When you drive down the road a short way, you will note that the black car of the assassins is on fire. The license plates have been removed, as was the identification seal on the dashboard. Don't stop; keep going towards Aix and your hotel. Get everything out of your room and check out immediately. I'll be heading in the opposite direction."

Volkov pointed his finger at Max. "You need to get out of the area and fast! Within a day or two of finding the bodies, the police will go to every local hotel asking questions. Because your hotel is close to the crime scene, I imagine they will go there first.

The bellman, or the manager, but most likely someone on the cleaning staff, will identify you as a guest who has been drawing in the area of the murders. You see, maids know everything about the persons who stay in the rooms they clean. If you have sex they know it. When you are downstairs to have breakfast the cleaning ladies go through your bags looking for illegal contraband, even your pant pockets for change. If you happen to be missing something, and it's illegal, you're not going to file a report. If you smoked dope they know it. If a prostitute was in your bed they know it. If you piss beyond the toilet they will seek revenge. And believe me, the police will ask the desk clerks where you live, how you paid your bill and what calls you made. They will interview the guests who watched you load your art supplies into your trunk. Within days they'll be knocking at your door in Lacoste."

Volkov shook his head. "I doubt I will be on their radar screen. But if I am, I have diplomatic immunity."

Max was concerned about what was to come of the woman who commissioned the pieces. "She was part of the key to unlocking mystery of who else is involved with the conspiracy. If I have only 2 drawings, the woman may suspect something. I don't know her address or her telephone number. I don't know if the name I have for her is legitimate. If she knows what's happened to Françoise, she will probably disappear. Everything is unraveling."

The Russian shook his head. "Stop it! What

happened to your American optimism? Come on, let's go, we have to get out of here."

Boris floored the accelerator and roared off towards Mount Victoire.

Max returned to the hotel; he was nervous, but relieved to find everything was quiet. When he put his key in the door lock, he hesitated and listened for a sound that might tip him off if someone was lurking inside his room. He heard nothing. Hurriedly he threw his belongings into his suitcase. He checked to make sure everything that he had brought was in the Samsonite case. He went into the bathroom and pissed. Then exited. So that no one could hear the door close he pulled it shut slowly. He then tiptoed down the hall to the stairway. When he reached the lobby a small terrier dog barked at him. A plump woman put her cup filled with tea down on the coffee table and yanked the leash. The frou-frou dog laid down, outstretched her paws and then tucked them under its chin. The nasty, chubby, squirrel like canine kept Max under surveillance. Max told me, that in his paranoid state, the dog's squeaky bark sounded like the growl of a German Shepherd.

The desk clerk was curious as to why Max was leaving the hotel earlier than planned. Max lied. "I have to get to Nice to catch a flight. My brother has fallen ill and I must return to Switzerland right away."

The man turned and retrieved Max's info card from a drawer under the key and letterbox behind him. Before the clerk turned around, Max pulled a wad of French francs and dropped them over the edge of the small counter where they scattered around the man's shoes. The Frenchmen bent to pick them up. It was a clever maneuver to distract the fellow so Max could grab the info card and put it in his pocket. After all, it contained Max's address and phone number. While the clerk was gathering up the money Max turned and walked towards the door. The dog growled.

The clerk raised his clutched money filled hand "Sir, you have change coming."

"Keep it; enjoy a whore on me!"

The owner of the dog shouted at Max, "You're a pig, just like most Americans."

Max stopped for a moment, removed his baseball cap and bowed to the woman. Inspired by the truffle convention, he yelled at her, "Yes, and that's why I am the world champion truffle finder."

Max got into his car and headed back to Lacoste. As he was driving towards home he remembered he had pissed in the toilet before he left his room. He did flush it. But he should have returned to clean the seat. As a man, living on his own, he rarely lifted the toilet seat. It was too late to return. Drops of urine on the seat could become evidence. He should have listened to his mother. Now he might pay a price for his transgression.

When he reached Lacoste he found the village quiet. Several of the residents greeted him. Max was relieved the village was tranquil. However, it only served to give him a false sense of security. That was, until I called him.

****

"Max, I need you to deliver a few small paintings to the gallery. I have a client,... Oh shit, I have to get off the phone; the kitty has just caught a mouse."

Max said, "I'll talk to you later," hung up the phone, got in his car and drove to Oppède.

He called from the supposed safe phone. He told me all that had happened. I was shocked and frightened. Obviously HP was completely oblivious to what had transpired. That was cause for concern.

If he was on unaware, then we were in jeopardy.

"Max I don't understand, how did Volkov know you were in danger?"

"I didn't have time to ask him. Things were happening so quickly. I'm certain that HP and Volkov are working together, so they must have been in communication. At least I hope so. Is there any chance that you might be able to come visit me in Lacoste for a few days?"

"Why? What for?" "I could use your company." "Let me see what I can do, I'll have to cancel a few

appointments, but I could probably get there by Thursday." "Fantastic."

Ten minutes after our conversation I received a phone call from the HP; it was apparent the phone in the Oppède was being monitored by someone or my mobile phone had somehow been tapped.

After hanging up with HP, I called Max and told him about my conversation with HP and what he revealed to me. "We know about the two bodies that were found outside of Aix. But what we didn't know was that Volkov was the shooter. We know who the two men were and who they worked for. I suspect our Russian friend knew them as well. The two were former KGB assassins from the old

Soviet Union days. They work now for the cartel behind the Cézanne conspiracy. When Max's car was found in the Valley of Death, fingerprints were taken from inside and outside his car, not by the local police, but by the National Gendarmerie. It was done after the car had been removed from the crash site. Of course the fingerprints of Max and Françoise, as well as you and Robert were found. Others were also discovered, mostly Lacoste locals. Curiously though, Robert's wife and the two now-dead Russians also left fingerprints on the car."

"While Max was in Aix, there was a fire in Bonnieux. Françoise's apartment has been destroyed. According to the local police and fire department the café below her place was identified as the source of the blaze. Supposedly it started because of an electrical malfunction. By the time the fire brigade reached the village the whole place was ablaze."

"As you know the building is made of stone and the structure can be restored, but everything in her apartment was destroyed. All is lost; there is no evidence. I am sorry to tell you that we had not secured the place. I had issued orders to search the apartment the day after her body was found in Giverny. Unfortunately, the command was never forwarded to the Gendarmes in Nice, but we were able to secure the Gemmer's apartment in Paris. The furniture was there, but nothing of hers could be found. Their joint and individual bank accounts, credit cards and things of that sort, are still open, but no charges or withdrawals have taken place since her death. Also, there are no transactions from investment accounts or removals from safety deposit boxes. We have worked with Interpol and the same seems to be the case in all the countries or places where money and securities are usually hidden."

We did check phone records and interviewed neighbors, associates, and people who worked with Monsieur Gemmer and found nothing unusual in his behavior. The airlines and trains have no record of Françoise's husband traveling. His cars were still in the garage, his clothes in closets and the kitchen was filled with food. There was nothing of hers in the home. Samples of fingerprints and hair turned up nothing regarding Françoise. It is as if she never lived there. The only evidence that others had been there were from his cleaning lady and a man who had recently done some plumbing work. Our investigation showed they were both legitimate individuals."

"The one puzzling thing was that there was no artwork on the walls and no evidence there had been. We know Madamé Gemmer was a talented artist and her husband a supposed collector. One would assume the walls would be covered with art. The only thing we found on the walls was a framed mirror in the bedroom and it was on the ceiling over the bed. There was no trace of holes in the plaster, no spots of spackling or any shift in the color on the walls. Normally when something is attached to a wall you can detect a slight change of color after it is removed, especially when the resident smokes, as did Mousier Gemmer. He was an avid pipe smoker."

"As you probably know from what's appeared in the papers, Philippe Gemmer is an odd character. He is what the Americans call a nerd. International economics are his passion. His career has always centered on money. Supposedly his only other interest was collecting art, not because he loved art, but because he saw it as a commodity to be bought and sold for profit."

"He has been a major benefactor to the Louvre, the D'Orsay and Giverny. Not just personal gifts of art, but directing public funding and private support to them. His influence at the Louvre has been considerable. Madamé Dubois received her job due to Gemmer's influence. He planted her there. Not only has he corrupted our most important art institutions; he has done similar things in America, Spain, England and Russia. In all cases these museums, and ours, are working to discover how far and how deep the penetration of this conspiracy goes. For now, everything is Terrence James Coffman

under wraps. The other countries, their museums and governments, as well as ours, are working secretly to uncover the scope and impact these forgeries are having on currencies and national pride. Luckily, the press has not caught on to what we are doing. However, I fear we don't have much time before everything begins to unravel and becomes public

"The two former KGB operatives, coupled with the death of Françoise, tell me there is a fracture in the conspiracy. I suspect whoever is the mastermind behind this treachery is attempting to eliminate anyone and everyone involved, even those on the periphery."

****

Through surreptitious means, Boris Volkov secured the phone number of Valeriya Kurochkin, the courier who exchanged artwork and diamonds with Françoise Gemmer.

Max said that when he called Valerie, she was surprised to hear his voice and said, "I have been trying to call Françoise for over a week, but both her home phone in Paris, as well as the one at her apartment in Bonnieux are not working. I keep getting the same message that her phones are out of service. It seems unusual that both her phones, which are in two different locals, would have the same message."

Quick on his feet, Max came up with a plausible story that she swallowed. He told her a huge mistral storm had blown down the phone lines in and around Les Baux, and not expected to be restored for at least a week. He went on to tell her that Françoise's divorce proceedings were scheduled to begin at the end of the month and she had to be back in Paris to consult with her lawyers for the next four weeks.

Valerie was caught off guard; after all she had never met Max and Françoise and probably would not have given Max her phone number. But she was curious as to Françoise's allusiveness, so she agreed to meet Max in the church where the exchanges of art and diamonds took place.

Max and Volkov drove south through the Camargue to Maries-de-la-Mer to meet the woman. Max had arranged to meet her at Notre-Dame-de-la-Mer church where he had seen Françoise, not with a demur woman named Valerie but a huge, formidable looking male creature. What if the Valerie woman didn't show up and he was faced with the Giant? Max said he had to take his chance. Besides, Boris Volkov would be close at hand.

Max arrived early, cradling the box containing the Cézanne-like drawings in his gloved hands. He placed the box down, removed his gloves and sat in the third row pew to the left of the altar. He waited for what seemed like an eternity for her to arrive. My friend traded glances with his Russian counterpart. Volkov was pretending to be praying at the Stations of the Cross. He had planted himself in front of the 5th Station, the one where Simon of Cyrene helps Jesus carry the cross.

The echo of her high heels striking the marble floor announced her appearance. He turned to see a beautiful woman walking towards him. As she approached Max, she smiled. I'm not surprised, after all Max is a handsome man. Farther back behind her, near the confessional booth, Max saw the giant who Françoise had handed the diamond filled envelope to during their previous visit to the city.

Volkov saw the man too, feigning to be absorbed in prayer he moved to the next station and then the one after that bringing him closer to the giant. The man's eyes were fixed on Valerie; he didn't notice Boris edging towards him.

There were several tourists in the church, whispering in the voices of many languages. The patter of their voices bounced off the marble and stone. The smell of incense from an earlier service still lingered in the vast sanctuary and votive candles flickered in red glass jars for worshipers who prayed for cures and forgiveness. Max assumed that Françoise most likely had described him to her. He was right; when she saw him in his paint splattered denim jacket she knew she had her man.

The woman slid along the pew and sat close beside him. She smiled; her teeth were perfect. Obviously she was wealthy.

Max described the woman, telling me that her hair was blond and pulled back tightly in a ponytail. He noticed the diamonds in her ears. They were large; their facets caught the colors of the streaming light from the stained glass windows. Max recognized her perfume. It was Shalimar, the same scent Françoise wore. She was not tall, but her heels made her proportions appear to be leggy and lanky. Her skirt was tight and her rounded tummy obvious. There were several rings with an assortment of stones on her fingers. Her singsong voice was deep and she had an accent that was slightly similar to Volkov's. She extended her hand and began the conversation with an introduction. "I am Valerie and you are, of course, the handsome man my dear friend Françoise talks about all the time."

In spite of the fact that Francoise was lying in a Paris morgue with tadpoles in her lungs, Max played his assignment well.

He said. " Françoise defines handsome much differently than I do."

"You are too modest Maxfield; I agree with my friend. You are a very good-looking man and I find the accent of yellow ochre paint drops on your blue jeans to be most stylistic. I have always been attracted to artists."

Max looked at his jeans and laughed. "I'm afraid everything I own has spots of paint on them." Pointing at the splatters of colors on his jeans, he added, "This color comes from Roussillon."

She replied with a grin. "And the red on your earlobe, where does that come from?"

Her laugh sounded phony.

"Francoise has always surrounded herself with gorgeous men. My own husband, bless his soul, was attractive. But in the end, cancer made him rather ugly."

"I'm sorry. Françoise told me he died some years ago and that you came here to care for your mother. Is she doing well?"

After an awkward pause, she figured a way to avoid any discussion concerning the mother. Max told me she explained, "Mama died last week, I can't talk about it."

There was no change in her demeanor and she continued the conversation without any break or look of sadness. She smiled with anticipation. "So, I can wait no longer, let me see the drawings you have brought."

With the tip of his index finger Max pushed the box towards her. "Here they are, I hope you like them. I have to tell you, I've only completed two. I wanted to wait until I finished more, but Françoise insisted I get these to you now. I promise I will do the others for you in a few weeks."

Valeriya was obviously suspicious, but didn't want to tip her hand. "Well that's fine, Françoise must have been so impressed with what you have accomplished, she wants me to have them now." Max was relieved.

She opened the box and removed the two drawings. Max had only one interest and that was to watch her fingers touch the box and hold the drawings in her hand. Her fingerprints were secured.

"They are fantastic. I love them." She kissed his cheek.

She reached for her purse and handed Max a check. It was a huge sum, far more than Francoise had originally negotiated for four drawings. She smiled and said. "I am sure there will be more business between us. I love your work and, as Françoise and I have talked about, I look forward to having more Maxfield Connor's hanging on my walls."

She put the drawings back in the carton. Holding the box against her chest, she stood up and, leaning towards him, kissed his cheek. Before turning to leave she coquettishly smiled, saying to him, "I look forward to seeing you soon."

Max breathed a sigh of relief. Apparently Volkov did as well. The giant followed Valeriya from the church. Volkov released his grip of the handle of the pistol in his pocket.

****

I called HP and demanded to know if Volkov was acting on his own or if he and the French government were in cahoots.
HP snapped at me. This was out of character for him. I was taken aback when he sternly replied, "Cahoots! That sounds like you're suggesting a conspiracy between us and the Russian."

I was doing just that! But it was stupid of me to say it. I let my guard down. The last thing I wanted not to do with HP was to damage the rapport I had cultivated with him. The other thing was that I really didn't want to hear his answer for fear it would upset me.

A shift of HP's normally friendly mood was evident in the curtness of his reply. "What we do on our end is not your concern, and if the Russian can be of assistance, then so be it. You are an operative, not a member of the Générale de la Sécurité Extérieure, (General Directorate for External Security). You are valuable to us and your help is greatly appreciated by your county. Yes, I approved Volkov and Max's visit. I regret not being able to inform you of certain top-secret details of the operation to destroy the cartel behind the conspiracy. But, when the time is right, I promise to reveal everything we know. I can tell you this. The forgery plot is orchestrated and led by the Corsican mafia in Marseille. We are close to apprehending members of their operation."

I was most pleased when HP told me that he and the French government were pursuing Milieu Corso-Marseillais. After all, the Paris wing of the mafia was known to be involved with counterfeiting and money laundering. Therefore it was understandable that HP and the GDIS were narrowing their sights on the organization. I apologized for being pushy and thanked him for the tip about the Corsican connection and encouraged him to follow every lead regarding them.

****

A few days later, I received another call from HP. This one was very disturbing.

"We believe Monsieur Gemmer is somewhere in Marseille. There is a small museum there that employs a former KGB officer. We think he may be one of the linchpins behind the cartel. The man is Robert Chéron's father-in-law. His assumed name is Arvids Ceplis, but his real name is Anatoly Dolzhikov. He was involved with the coup d'état attempt to take control of the USSR from Soviet President Mikhail Gorbachev. A few years ago, he and a small group of KGB officers fled to Marseille. My informant there has told me that Gemmer and Ceplis secretly own a warehouse in the port of Marseille, so their names do not show up in the public land records or real estate tax roles."

"We don't have any agents with the expertise we need in art and art history, so this is where you and Max come in. You will be our covert agents. I suspect there is a large cache of forged paintings and other important evidence in that building."

"We are now putting a team together and your participation is mandatory. As civilians you will be a part of a small squad who will break into the warehouse. Some of these men have the wherewithal to dismantle alarms and the others will be there for your protection. Céline, you and Max have the ability to quickly discern if what's there is forged or real. We need you to do this."

"We know Robert and his wife, and most likely her father, know you both. I have to admit that if you're caught in that warehouse it could place you in great danger. We don't fully comprehend the role Robert and his family plays in the cartel. We speculate Françoise was simply one of several low level operatives within the organization; it's highly unlikely she knew the leadership or scope of their activities. Her motivation was that of a dedicated forger who wanted to show the world that she and her father were as gifted as Cézanne, Monet, Picasso and others. The one thing we can't figure out is why she was killed. We speculate the two dead former KGB men had something to do with her demise and also the two attempts on Max's life."

"Two possibilities are at work here. Either someone is attempting a coup or someone is trying to shut down the forgery ring for a while. My guess is that for some reason the cartel's ringleader, whoever he is, has set up the conspiracy in such way that members are unknown to one another, including the identity of the boss. Some in my group believe the cartel is Russian, but Vladimer Bogdanov, the Russian Cultural Attaché, assures me this is not so. His government has offered to fully assist us. That leaves the Corsican mafia, or some homegrown French connection."

"The other thing you should know is that while we were doing the autopsies on the two Russian assassins, we found each man had the same tattoo on their shoulders as Mademoiselle Dubois has on her ankle. Also, while the coroner was going over

Françoise's body, he found the same symbol on the back of her skull. It was hidden under her hair."

"We have contacted the leading French scholar on symbols. He told us that in the reign of King Solomon there was a demon named Ornias who harassed a young boy favored by Solomon. Over a period of time Ornias was slowly sucking the boy's soul out through the young man's thumb. Each day, as the boy became weaker, Solomon feared the young man would die. The boy's soul would then belong to Beelzebub, the angel cursed by God for his infidelity.

God favored Solomon; after all he was the son of David. God considered him to be the wisest of all the Kings of Israel.

Because of His love for Solomon, God sent his Archangel Michael to help the earthly King defeat Beelzebub, or as we know him in modern times, the devil Satan. God sent his loyal archangel Michael to deliver the Creator's ring to Solomon. Upon this ring, burnt into the gold by God's own breath, was the imprint of the Divine One's seal. The power of God's ring enabled Solomon to command demons."

"God knew of Solomon's fear for the life and soul of the young boy so he sent the Archangel Michael to bring His sacred ring to Solomon. God told the king that the ring had the power to command demons. With this ring he could defeat Ornias and also control all other demons."

"Solomon told the boy to take the ring and throw it at Ornias. When the young man did so, the seal of God was burnt into Ornias's chest and the boy received the power to bring Ornias under his control. The boy then brought Ornias to Solomon. The King then ordered Ornias to take the ring and imprint the seal upon the prince of demons, Beelzebul. This enabled Solomon to bring Beelzebul and the entire race of demons under the King's control. Solomon orders the demons to build the great temple in Jerusalem. Throughout his life, Solomon used the ring to control the demons. The ring was to be buried with Solomon but at his death it disappeared. There are many legends as to what happened to the ring. We have no idea as to why this organization has adopted the symbol. Some of our people have theories; most are ridiculous, some others implausible or just plain speculative. It makes me crazy to think so-called intelligent, rational people working in our government can sometimes be irrational and stupid to believe such nonsense. Who in the French government can be counted to safely guide our country's decisions? Who is sane, who is nuts?"

"I want you to contact Max; do not use your mobile phone. Go to the Hotel Colisée; it is a safe house near the Roosevelt Station, secure a room and call Max from there. I need to know by tonight if he is willing to take part in the break-in. I'm assuming you are willing to do it?"

For my own self-protection, I had no other choice but to say yes.

"Good. If he agrees, I will begin making arrangements for the assault on the warehouse to take place as quickly as possible." He hung up without even a goodbye. Strange.

****

I went home and packed an overnight bag, went outside and hailed a cab. The Hotel Colisée is not far from the Arc de Triomphe. It was located on a small narrow street off the Avenue des Champs-Élysées. My room was small and the contemporary decor designed by French interior architect Sylvain Proyart. I felt a bit spoiled when I pulled down the silk sheets and closed the fine linen curtains. It would be a fine mini vacation for a night. Someone knocked on the door. It was a young man, a rather handsome boy with deep-set eyes and long wavy black hair who brought me a bottle of Dom Perignon. I sat on the edge of the bed, kicked off my heels and wished the boy could have stayed. I made the call to Max. He was home; I told him about the kitty and the mouse and he hung up to get to a safe phone. While I waited for his call, I masturbated thinking about the curly headed boy licking champagne off my breast. I fell blissfully asleep.

When the phone rang, I was not sure if the boy was talking to me or if I was hearing the announcement jingle of le metro. It took me a moment to be aware of my new surroundings and sound of the telephone. Max was on the line. He asked me why I didn't call from my mobile phone. I told him it had been compromised and I was at a hotel that HP said was occasionally used by the government as a safe house. I told him HP's plan and why he felt we would be the best professionals for the job.

Max hesitated saying, "Let him find someone from the Louvre or d'Orsay."

In my groggy champagne induced voice I mumbled, " They're compromised, remember?"

He shot back. "Are you drunk?"I laughed, "No, I just fucked a bellboy!""What! Are you crazy?""Just kidding, I was asleep and dreaming when you called.

Listen, we have to do this.""Look, you're an art dealer and I'm an artist, we are not conservators. I think someone else needs to do this job. Let the French museums do it. It's too damn dangerous."

I was not in the mood to argue. I suggested we both sleep on it and talk again in he morning. He reluctantly agreed. It was of course integral to HP's plan and my country's vital interests to have Max agree. However, I also had my own welfare to protect; HP was my conduit to what the government knew about the conspiracy and who the conspirators were.

I had no real meaningful expertise on how to spot forgeries. I am a seller of art, plain and simple, not a museum expert, not an historian, and I certainly do not posses the skills to authenticate major works of art. I wondered why my presence was required in such an important undertaking. I knew I was unqualified to be part of the break-in team, however I was grateful to be part of it. It would be an honor to help protect my country's reputation.

I thought of a few people I could suggest who might help HP. I membered Max had an old friend who was a conservator. I had met him back in the days when I lived with Max in New York. I stayed up most of the night thinking about this person, what he looked like, where he was from, and I went through the alphabet over and over trying to recall first and last names of Americans who I had known in my past. I stayed up most of the night thinking about this person, what he looked like, where he was from, and I went through the alphabet over and over trying to recall first and last names of Americans who I had known in my past. I remembered he was of Italian descent and his last name sounded like a canned food Max and I used to eat when we had little money and couldn't afford to eat out. It finally came to me. Ragnetti, Clifford Ragnetti. I'd suggest to Max that he contact Ragnetti. Max would most likely feel that with his old friend's involvement, there would be a level of expertise and familiarity that would allow him to feel comfortable about going along with the break-in at the warehouse in Marseille. That was, if HP approved.

Max called in the morning and I laid out my idea to bring Clifford into the plan. He agreed, but doubted the gifted conservator would go along with the idea. After all, it was dangerous. And besides, why would his friend want to be involved with such a scheme. Cliff had a family and a good job at a prestigious university in the States, he didn't need the excitement and he certainly didn't need danger.

I suggested the scale of an international cartel defrauding the world's most important museums and collectors would horrify Cliff. I convinced Max to call his friend and let him decide. I didn't say it, but I thought, how could Cliff say no?

Max called the University in Maryland where his old friend was now Dean of the College of Art and Art History. As Max had hoped, Clifford replied, "Absolutely, count me in!"

Now it was my task to convince HP. He was not in favor of the idea, saying, "We have a large contingent of European professional conservators who will do the forensic work. We don't need the help of some non-French supposed expert!"

Max was pissed. He yelled into the phone, "You tell your fucking friend HP to screw himself. Clifford Ragnetti is one of the most prominent members of the American Institute for Conservation of Historic and Artistic Works. He is America's preeminent authority regarding materials and methods for scientific investigation of artwork. There's nobody more qualified then Cliff to determine what's fake and what's not. If there is no Cliff, then there's no me and no you! Make it clear to HP that's the only way we will participate.

Before we hung up, I told Max I'd be in Lacoste in

three days. He calmed down.

****

Just after Max spoke with me, Robert showed up at his studio. How did he know of Françoise's demise? The news of Françoise's death was still not public; there was nothing in the papers. How did Robert know to come to Lacoste to console his friend?

Max told me he played coy with Robert, acting shocked and he was even able to fake crying. (He probably shed real tears. After all, Max had been in love with Françoise).

What Robert told Max was mostly accurate, but with two exceptions. My guess was that Robert knew nothing about the details of her death, just that the hit had taken place. Could it be that he was the one who sanctioned her murder?

Max did not share the details of their conversation that night; he only said Robert was the most believable liar he had ever met. "The fucker is a better actor than he is an artist!"

The next morning Max and Robert walked to the Lacoste parking area where the bus usually stopped to pick up tourists and locals going to Avignon. Normally there were four or five people, locals, traveling back and fourth daily between the big city and the village, plus a handful of tourists returning to Avignon to catch the train to Paris, Marseille or Nice. Max thought it odd that no one was there waiting for transportation. He assumed the bus was running late, which was unusual. They sat on a bench, finished the cups of coffee they had bought from the boulangerie, and talked about the plans he and his wife had made for a vacation to Latvia. Max asked why they were going to such an uninviting place. Robert reminded Max that Olga was from Latvia and Marseilles was unbearably hot this time of the year.

Finally the bus pulled in and the door opened. The two hugged and Robert climbed aboard. Max noticed the driver; he looked familiar, but Max couldn't place him. The man was muscular, and while it was a warm day he wore a cap with flaps that covered his ears. It seemed strange that the driver never turned his head to greet his passenger. As the bus pulled away Max waved goodbye to Robert. Walking back up the steep hill to his studio

Max racked his brain trying to remember where he had seen the driver before. Later in the day, while working on a painting, it came to him that the bus driver looked very much like the Russian collector with the mutilated ear who he had met at the gallery exhibition in Gordes.

Later that night Max went for dinner at the Café du Sade. Édouard, the owner, asked him if he had heard about the accident on the highway near Avignon. Max was not surprised, after all it was a curvy scenic road on which tourists almost weekly became distracted and crashed their rental cars into on-coming traffic. But that was not the case this time.

"A bus went off the road today, jumped the guardrail and rolled over and over almost three hundred metres down the steep cliff. The gendarmes found the dead body of a passenger who lived in Marseilles, but they're still looking for the bus driver's remains." Max turned away and vomited on the stone floor of the café.

****

Looking for a kill, the murder of crows flies over the fields. The hare sees them and freezes motionless. Both the hare and the crows know what they have to do. The hare must hide in the tall grass. The crows must plunge towards the earth.

Crows are the hunters; rabbits are their marks. Those who think they are safe are the easiest to kill.

Murder and mayhem comes quickly. There's rarely torture in death. Most the time, there are no screams, just the gurgling sound of blood.

Every time I turn on the TV news, or open *Le Monde,* I see at least one dead body. Unsolvable atrocities occur in France with regularity. The public, and even law enforcement, have grown accustomed to random brutal deaths. It is good that many of us believe some deaths are unexplainable. It is easier to not know why a mangled rabbit is floating in the river.

Men have a way of delivering death. Brutality does not seem to repulse a man. Women don't have the stomach for it. This is why I admire men. For a man, death is quick, it's dirty, it's brutal, and it's over quickly. I wish the male side of me were more prevalent.

Corsican men can chop their victim into tiny pieces, dispose of their target, wash-up, go home to hug there daughters and then make love to their wives. It's all in a days work.

When I arrived in Lacoste I found Max working in his studio. He didn't hear me pounding on his front door, so I let myself in. His radio was blaring. I came up behind him wrapped my arms around his waist and kissed his neck. He turned, we embraced. It felt good to be close to him.

He told me what had happened to Robert. We were both frightened and confused, but for different reasons that I will explain later. We immediately jumped into his car and drove to the safe phone in Oppède to call HP He knew about Robert's death and told us the Russian who drove the bus would not be found.

Max yelled at HP, "Who the fuck is the Russian? Who else is he going to kill? Is he coming for us next?"

After a second or two of silence, HP replied, "You needn't worry yourself about the Russian, his body turned up in the Rhone River this morning. There is more you need to know. Yesterday the art supply shop in Apt burned to the ground. The local newspaper paper says it was old paint that caused the fire. We know differently. Professionals torched it. The owner, Antoine Arseneault, was found in the burned out basement of the building. When his body was removed the outer layers of his skin disintegrated like burnt toast."

"That's not all. Maurice Michelin was discovered

hanging from a cherry tree in his garden. His chateau was ransacked and all the artwork has disappeared. Last night, Dominique Dubio was seen getting into a van with two Algerian men. We followed them into the Muslim area of Seine-Saint-Denis, but lost them there. This morning the Russian Cultural Attaché, Vladimir Bogdanov, was found dead in Montmartre Cemetery. His body was thrown over the grave of Russian dancer, Vaslav Nijinsky. The autopsy showed he was tortured before being shot in the head. Whoever killed him carved the image of the seal of King Solomon's ring on his stomach."

"Both Robert's wife and her communist party member father were found in the museum. Their throats slit. A few hours ago Valeriya Kurochkin was found in the confessional booth of the old Catholic Church with a wire twisted around her neck."

"Céline, you and Max are in great danger. I fear both of you are in someone's crosshairs. I want you two out of the studio as quickly as possible. Tomorrow, check into the Appart'Hotel at 35 Rue Neuve Sainte Catherine in Marseille. You will be safe there. Wait for us to contact you. When you arrive at the hotel Max is to call his friend Ragnetti. Ask him to join you in Marseilles. We've checked him out and he is the expert Max said he was." My guess was that HP figured out that without Ragnetti, Max would balk at being a part of the break-in.

Max's reaction was to say, "Fuck this shit, I'm outta here!" He was ready to run. He insisted we could leave in the morning for New York. But I felt calm. I knew there was no need to be afraid. I was safe. My job was to get Max to relax and I knew just how. That night we slept together. It ha

its been too long time since Max fucked me.

****

When he first arrived in Paris, and up until the time he met Françoise, we had been together in my apartment on several occasions. The sex was always fantastic. But now he would be mine, and mine only. It was as if we were young again, and like those days when we laid all day bed in the Tribeca loft, I climaxed over and over with him. Most men bore me, but Max has always been different. His oral technique is unbelievable. Sometimes I faint while climaxing with him. I have never met another man who could do that to me. Max is usually tender and thoughtful of my needs, but he can be rough when I want him to slap me around. I love pretend rape. I like tethering him to bedposts. I am certainly a better lover than the bitch who called herself *The Most Beautiful Woman In Provence*. She didn't look so beautiful all tangled up in the weeds at the bottom of Monet's Pond. Not that I was there, but I have seen the pictures.

****

The next morning we drove to Marseille. It would soon be October and within months a new decade. Max called Cliff from the Hotel. As an artist and art historian, our old friend was outraged to learn that forgeries, in such large numbers, were being perpetrated on a worldwide scale. Max was completely transparent as to the dangers of breaking into the cartel's lair. In spite of the danger, Cliff agreed to help. The break-in was set to occur in five days. HP made travel arrangements for Max's old friend. Cliff would bring the testing kit.

We went to the Musée Cantini in Marseille to look at the Cézanne drawing that was part of an exhibition of the Michelin Collection. The sketch of Mont Victoire looked very much like something Françoise had done. Max was looking intently at every square millimeter of the pencil drawing. He seemed mesmerized and I watched as he moved into a trance. It was as if he were on LSD or some mind-altering drug. I had seen him do this before, both in Paris and several times when we lived together in New York. I wasn't frightened. First, his head and shoulders began to rock back and forth. Then he turned in circles. I saw his eyeballs rise and disappear behind his eyelids. Like a Tibetan monk, I heard him lowly humming a drone-like chant. After about five minutes, he began to speak. Not to me, but to Cézanne.

Max whispered as if he didn't want me, or anyone in the gallery, to hear him, and yet, because of the hard marble floor and the cavernous great hall where the exhibition was displayed, I could catch his conversation with Paul, as could the few others in the room. Fortunately, the other gallery viewers quickly exited. His voice carried so that every word he spoke was clear to my ear.

"Monsieur Cézanne this drawing is exquisite.......Yes, I agree. No, you're right, it is not a lyrical line like yours.......Maybe, but I would hate to think so....... As you say, it could be a woman's hand that drew it, but I don't think she was that capable.......No, I swear not mine. Not yet. I have done two, but they are meant to help you.

Who?........Did you see it?........ Volkov, are you certain? The church is always open, how could her body be carried in without being seen? Are you sure it wasn't the other Russian?........You and Vincent were in Saintes-Maries-de-la-Mer. I never knew you painted together........Doctor Gachet, yes I know who he was. I know the painting you're talking about, the one you did on the banks of the Oise River, correct? I saw it at Michelin's house........I'm not surprised, apparently Gachet's son made lots of fakes. Do you think Michelin knew......."

For almost five minutes Max said nothing, every so often he would shake his head affirmatively, grunt or sigh. From the look on his face, I had the sense he was sometimes shocked, sometimes sad, but mostly angry.

"Yes, I'll do it."

Max came out of the hallucination disturbed and, when I asked him what Cézanne had said, he replied that he didn't want to talk about it. All he said was, "I am confused. I think Paul was lying to me."

We left the museum. All the way back to the hotel Max was quiet. It was almost as though he was unaware that I was walking beside him. That night there was no sex between us. I held him in my arms until he fell asleep. Thank God, in the morning, Max returned to his old self. It was as though the dream, hallucination, or whatever you want to call it, was gone from his mind. Almost every time Max went into this other world, he could come out of the apparition with some memory of his conversations with Picasso, Vincent van Gogh and the others. But this time was different.

"I don't remember a thing, all I know is you told me that I had another vision. I wish I could remember it, but I can't."

This was good. Whatever he had been told in this most recent dream, might serve to complicate my own situation.

I was distressed, out of my mind dreading what we were about to do. We could be discovered in the warehouse. If anyone other than HP's agents were there, we could end up with our feet in cement sinking to the bottom of the Mediterranean. I made a call to my lawyer, "The Belgian", whose office was conveniently located off shore. He didn't answer the phone.

Calling him may have been a mistake. Sometimes fear can make a person stupid.

****

Cliff arrived from the United States. I hadn't seen him in almost 30 years. We met at the airport and it was nice to see that he was still the slim, dark-haired, handsome man we remembered. His beard was graying, but he still had the good looks of an Italian. We originally knew him as artist, and now he added academic to his repertoire of talents. He was creative and he was smart, as we all were. But HP and I needed Cliff for his reputation as the expert regarding art materials. His connection to a major US research university was also important. Our bureaucratic French universities would take years, and lots of controversy, to reach an opinion regarding our country's artistic treasures. That wouldn't be the case with Professor Ragnetti.

At the terminal, we met Cliff, quickly gathered his bags and left. I noticed a handsome, well-dressed man standing by the exit door. As we got closer to him he stepped outside and threw his cigarette on the ground and crushed it under his zippered boot. Something about him made me feel queasy.

The hotel bellhop took Cliff's suitcase, plus the heavy wooden box he had brought with him, from the trunk of my Venturi Coupé 260 and loaded them onto a rolling cart. The manager came out to park my car. He must either have been worried about letting the young man park it or he just wanted to drive something he could never afford down to the hotel garage. The car was the one luxury I had allowed myself to purchase. Commissions I made from the sales of artwork by such painters as Max, Robert Chéron, Willem de kooning, and yes, even Cézanne, had paid for it.

We went to Clifford's room. On the extra bed he placed the wooden crate, unlocked the latch to reveal an unusual looking microscope. He called it his organic chemistry lab in a field case.

"I'm just like an FBI agent," he chuckled.

Clifford started to explain how he would use the tools he had brought. "First, I'll remove chips of paint from any Cézanne painting we find in this warehouse we're visiting. I'm going to take varnish, paint and gesso samples that will be no greater than a pinhead by using a micro scalpel."

"We know Cézanne worked slowly and thoughtfully. Every brushstroke he made was methodical. He also reworked his paintings numerous times. I'll take the samples, put them under the microscope, and if we don't find multiple layers of thin paint, then, odds are, we've found a fake."

"With this microscope and my Blacklight I can do some rudimentary elemental tests of the particles in the pigment used to make the colors. But first I will want to find out if the primer on the canvas or linen is white lead. Max, as you know, white lead stopped being used by artists in the mid 1970's. If the primer is not white lead then we probably have a fake."

"Varnishes afford protection from scratches, dirt and dust. They also provide sheen, which some artists desire for luminosity of the pigments. Cézanne usually varnished his work. Nineteenth-century resin varnishes turn yellow in time and this aging process will be helpful to my deductions."

"Vincent van Gogh preferred dammar varnish, which is a tree resin and Paul Cézanne used the fossil resin, copal, for his varnish. Synthetic varnishes didn't exist in the middle to late 1800's. So, if we find a Cézanne in the warehouse coated with acrylic materials, most likely it's a fake, or at best, a horrible mistake by some modern day amateur restorer."

"Cézanne only signed a few of his paintings, watercolors and drawings. He didn't paint directly from nature, as did Monet, Camille Pissarro and the other impressionists. He developed his paintings from pencil sketches composed in the landscape surrounding his studio building."

"In his later years he developed a unique style where the light seemed to come out of the landscape rather than down upon it. His compositions were governed more from the simple eight colors he used and the short half-inch brushstrokes he employed.

Using low magnification in the microscope I will check to see if the structure of the brushwork is correct."

 "When I get the samples back to the States, I'll have the University perform analysis on the paint chips. Our forensic department will use infrared spectroscopic procedures and various chemical tests to examine the samples. If we find whites composed of lead, and the blues containing copper carbonate, cobalt green, zinc and chrome, then we have the '*Real McCoy.*' However, if on the opposite side of the coin, we find titanium, barium, and manganese, we know we have discovered a fake."

Clifford frowned. "Now, here is the stumbling block. I fear we could be impeded in our effort to unravel the truth. You told me the woman Françoise had a source for old artist's materials.

More than likely the entire affiliation of corrupted cartel artists have access to his inventory. If this is the case, it will make it much harder to prove the forgeries."

Max spoke up. "He's toast, and so his shop and inventory."

Ragnetti asked, "What's that mean?"

"The shop of old art materials was torched. The proprietor was burnt to death along with his inventory."

At that moment, I could tell Max's friend, Professor Clifford Ragnetti, fully comprehended the danger he was about to step into.

Max sensed his fear as well, and added, "It's been a long flight for you. You must be tired and hungry. How about we go downstairs to the hotel's restaurant for something to eat. You could probably use a drink; I know I could. Then you can come back up to your room and take a nap. A short nap though, you shouldn't sleep long. You need to get yourself acclimated to French time. I don't want you groggy. We need you alert and ready to go tomorrow night."

Max reached into his knapsack of art supplies and pulled out the pistol that Volkov had given him, handed it to Cliff, adding, "Just in case."

****

Cliff never woke up from his nap; he slept till morning. The long flight from Baltimore to Paris, then transferring to a plane to Marseille, plus meeting us to discuss art forgery, Cézanne and what he intended to do, was I'm sure, exhausting. HP called our room and told us that he wanted Cliff to meet with someone named Jacques Fils-Aime, a chemist from the French National Centre for Scientific Research, the CNRS. The organization has the reputation of using top Europe scientists, and HP said the man Jacques Fils- Aime had something important for our American expert to see.

We met Cliff for breakfast. Max told him about the afternoon meeting with the CNRS scientist. Cliff had never been to Marseille and Max was unfamiliar with the city as well, so I suggested the two of them might enjoy touring Le Panier, the oldest quarter in Marseilles. The diversion of street life might take our minds off the intrigue and danger that would soon capture us. It is a beautiful and exciting area and the distraction would allow Cliff and Max to focus on a more mundane adventure. Plus, it was close to the place we were to meet Fils-Aime. They agreed and off we went.

My stomach was a mess, not because of the huge omelet I had devoured, but because my tummy was in knots over what we were going to be doing later tonight. As we walked the cobbled streets, went in and out of churches and shops catering to sightseers, we merged with the tourists. I wore tennis shoes for comfort; all I needed was a belly pouch and I'd fit right in with the Japanese and American tourists. No one had any idea we were something else. No one could suspect we were undercover agents about to break into a mafia warehouse.

We began our walk at the Vieux Port harbor basin of the Quai du Port. I took the boys to the Cathédrale de la Major. As we headed towards the entrance, Max stopped dead in his tracks. In a despondent voice, Max said he didn't want to go inside. "Being in Cathedrals makes me sad."

Cliff looked at Max quizzically as I took our old friend by the arm, leaving Max on the street. Relieved at seeing us walk up the steps, Max called out, "Take your time, I'm going down the street for a beer."

Cliff and I strolled through the open Byzantine

door. The multicolored mosaic work at the entrance was breathtaking. **Under the** domes, we saw several apses in which I saw the faithful, fingering their rosaries. I could see the silent movement of their lips. What were they praying for? Was it money, health or forgiveness that they beseeched God to give them? I decided to kneel on the hard baked patterned tiled floor to ask the lord to keep me safe this night.

I don't know if Cliff prayed. He looked to me like a man who doesn't need absolution. After I stood up, he came over and asked me why Max hadn't wanted to come into such a beautiful place. I told him the story about the time Max watched Françoise dance in an old church near Arles.

I could tell he was moved by what I told him. He said he didn't know about Françoise. He asked me who she was, and why she seemed to have such an effect upon Max. I spent an hour telling him their story. I told it without any of my usual sarcasm. I didn't mention my distain for her; I felt I owed it to Max. I didn't talk about how she died, but I was candid regarding her probable participation in the Cézanne Conspiracy.

We walked a short way up the hill to the nearest cafe and found Max sitting on a plastic chair with his feet propped on top of a planter containing an artificial fig tree. In his hand he held a cold American Miller Highlife beer, brewed in Milwaukee. He asked what took us so long and pointed to the four empty bottles of beer he had consumed. He wasn't angry and accepted Cliff's explanation about being enamored with the beauty of the Cathedral. Cliff patted the camera in the case attached to his belt.

"I got some great shots."

We sat down beside Max. A waiter came to the table and both Cliff and I ordered a café américain. Max asked for another beer. I shook my head, saying, "Not now Max, we have an engagement tonight and all of us need our wits about us."

The waiter smiled and said, "Shall I bring three *américains*?"

"No; Just two and *un expresso quatre tir avec un peu de crème* for our friend."

Max frowned, but didn't resist.Cliff asked me what I ordered for Max."It's four shots of espresso with a little cream in it." "That ought to do the trick!"Max leered.It felt good to sit for a while; my feet were killing me.

Standing on marble and hard tile floors for that long made my toes feel like they were on fire. Cliff had some post cards and he was engrossed in writing to his new wife. The warm sun started to make us all sleepy. As the expresso percolated in his body, Max became so wired with caffeine that he jumped up, pointing the way towards where he thought La Vieille Charité was. His sense of direction was all wrong. I rose and turned him around and we headed for the Rue Puits du Denier.

The Le Panier hillside neighborhood is filled with pastel- colored buildings with green, yellow and blue shutters and old oak doors. The ancient working class neighborhood has been transformed into a multiethnic quarter filled with art galleries, fancy gourmet food markets and fabulous bistros. On almost every block of the narrow streets were Algerian food shops or restaurants, the best in all of France.

It was late Fall back in the USA, and in Maryland, where Cliff lived, the temperature had dipped into the forties and most days were cloudy, but in Marseille it was 75°F and the sky was cloudless blue. Luckily Cliff must have read a tourist guidebook, because he brought the appropriate garb. It was already close to 2pm and we needed to get to La Vieille Charité to meet the chemist that HP wanted us to see. The outside architecture of the place gave us a feeling that we weren't in

France, that somehow we had been transported to Malta or Morocco.

We entered the building and the first floor gallery where we found an exhibition of Mexican art. We were engrossed with artwork that, for the most part, we were unfamiliar with. A tall thin man approached us; it was Monsieur Fils-Aime. His glasses were thick and the rims looked to be antique. In his hand was a satchel that reminded me of something a schoolboy in the 1950's would have carried. He was dressed in a lab coat and wore white sox under his sandals. His accent was French; his English understandable. My impression was he was not born in France. He may have been from St. Martin or New Caledonia.

He reached out his hand to Max and Cliff and then bowed to me. He introduced himself and first addressed Cliff, saying, "I am honored to meet you. I have read your book on art materials. It's most enlightening."

Looking at Max he added, "You are a very gifted painter. I saw your work last year in Gordes." Almost as an after thought, he acknowledged my presence by saying that the next time he was in Paris he hoped to be able to visit my gallery.

Fils-Aime continued. "I know you are working on a

classified assignment for our government, purportedly involving forgeries of some of France's most important artists, most notably the paintings of Paul Cézanne and Monet. Beyond that, I don't know anything more regarding details of the investigation. I have been told you are undertaking an operation tonight that may bring the perpetrators to justice. We have been asked to assist you. I have something to show you." He pulled two drawings from his schoolbag.

The first one was of red-roofed buildings set against the sea. "This is an authentic Cézanne drawing of the nearby fishing village of L'Estague. Between 1870 and 1880, Cézanne visited there often."

Fils-Aime then handed Cliff the other drawing. Max, standing beside his friend, immediately recognized it. It was one of the Cézanne-like drawings Francoise had done while in Aix and then had passed on to the sexy cosmetologist in Avignon. It now made sense to him; the woman who so sensually applied makeup to his now-dead girlfriend's face was a courier between Françoise and the cartel.

****

Max didn't say anything at that point. He knew it was a fake, but he was interested in hearing what the scientist had to say.

There were no museum visitors or even the usual guard in the gallery. Fils-Aime walked to the empty wall space between the Diego Rivera and the Frida Kahlo paintings. He held the drawing up towards the bright track lights attached to the museum's ceiling. He quickly pointed out that there were no tears, mends or mold patterns.

As though the scientist was looking at something hard to see, he squinted, saying, "I did an analysis of the sizing on the paper and while it is correct to the mid 1800's, it is odd that it shows no signs of deterioration."

"The paper is old and the watermark correct to the maker of the paper that Cézanne would have worked on. However, it is too clean. In my opinion this paper was only lately taken from a storage box, or it came from a sketchbook that, until recently, had never been opened. Under my microscope I found no dust, no traces of exposure to sunlight, and no oil from a human hand. Paper over a hundred years old, exposed to light, would have yellowed. This paper is brownish."

"If you look closely you'll notice the tones of the

drawing paper appear uneven and stained. This was done in order to give it the appearance of age."

"I exposed the paper to ultraviolet light and found minuscule particles of coffee beans embedded between the fibers of the paper. When we traced the genetics of the bean fragments, we found their origin to be from Vietnam. The French government started the coffee plantations there in the late 1850's, although exportation of the beans back to France didn't really begin in earnest until the first quarter of the 20th century. Clearly, in an attempt to make the drawing appear old, someone has stained the paper with coffee."

"I had one of my colleagues at the CNRS, whose hobby is handwriting analysis, take a look at the signature. It's unusual that Cézanne would have signed a drawing. He saw them as preparatory studies for paintings and, therefore, rarely signed them. The first thing my colleague pointed out was a noticeable omission in the signature on this piece. My friend could find no examples of Paul Cézanne signing his work without a P before his last name. Also, on this drawing the Z is slanted in an unusual way.

"But here's the real clincher; when we did a FTIR sampling of the ink used in the drawing, it indicated the presence of **iron salt, phenol, and a** black dye. Those are ingredients found in modern ink, therefore not appropriate to the inks we know Cézanne used."

"It's a fake. A damn good one and whoever made the drawing had talent."

Max asked, "Did you find traces of latex on the paper?"

We all looked at Max wondering why he asked the question. He didn't say anything more. Later when I asked what made him ask the question regarding latex, he told me Françoise always wore gloves to protect her perfectly manicured, expensively painted nails.

Finally, Fils Aimee looked at Cliff and said, "I have something in my bag that may prove to be useful to our investigation." The scientist reached inside and handed Cliff what looked to be a camera.

"This is a Kodak DC40. It's what we call a digital camera; it doesn't use film. It's in the early stages of development, but I think his new tool will be useful in helping us detect forgeries. Our scientists are experimenting with something they call statistical analysis of digital images using a technique called Wavelet Decomposition."

With a self deprecating smile, he added, "I won't bore you with the details of how it works, unless you are a geek like me and find such things interesting or are fascinated by algorithms, hidden Markov trees or the variances of wide Gaussian Distribution."

"The Department of the French Interior Ministry has asked us to employ this technology to the photo images of the paintings you find tonight. We have also been requested to digitally photograph paintings already known to be authentic in the collection of The Musée d'Orsay, but not the Louvre. We need you to take as many photos of the Cézanne paintings as you can. If you have time, also do a few Picassos and Monets."

Max asked, "How do we get the camera and film back to you?"

"Remember, I told you, there is no film, just a digital stick inside the camera that holds the pictures."

Fils Aimée showed Max how to use the camera. There was no film advance mechanism and the camera automatically focused. The scientist pushed the exposure button and the camera just kept on clicking. Fils Aimée said, "Unlike the film you are used to using, this new digital technology allows you to take a huge amount of images."

"You mean we can take more than 36?" "Yes, many more; because all the images are stored on what's called a disk, not a roll of film with a limited capacity."

Fils Amiee handed the camera to Max, who then gently placed it into his knapsack saying, "As for returning the camera, someone has been assigned to retrieve it from you tonight." Fils- Aime gave us a short bow. We stood there looking at each other and listened to the muffled sound of his sandals as he disappeared down the hall.

****

As we returned to the hotel we didn't talk much. All three of us were tired. I needed a nap. By the time I came out of the bathroom Max was snoring. I set the alarm. The phone woke us up.

HP called our room to tell us he won't be a part of the break-in team. We're shocked. I think Max is going to pull out. HP has made it clear that he can't be involved.

"Look," he said. "If something goes wrong, and I, as a high government official, am caught in what is an illegal operation, it will ruin our chances of shutting down the cartel and the conspiracy."

Max didn't buy it. In a voice of absolute determination, Max said, "You're the government, get a warrant, God damn it!"

Céline's speakerphone was turned on and I could hear what HP was saying. "Max, this is France, not the United States. Liberty began here and it's not going to end here. If we make a legal mistake, we're screwed."

Max was pissed. "Fuck your legal bullshit. We saved your ass's from the Nazi's, and did lots of things that were outside the law for you Frogs!"

I thought all was lost. I put my hand on Max's and whispered in his ear. "Breathe, Max. HP is not the enemy."

For a few seconds he inhaled deeply, and then he calmed down. HP told him there would be a six-man team that was going to meet us in front of the hotel at 9pm. "Get yourselves dinner and the best bottle of Champaign the hotel has to offer. The French Government will pay the bill."

Reluctantly, Max thanked HP and hesitantly agreed to go forward with the plan. I, on the other hand, would have been relieved if the whole fucking scheme was postponed.

Max is taking a shit. We are about to meet Cliff in the lobby for dinner. I'm dressed for dinner; Max is dressed for espionage.

I haven't heard back from my attorney. I need to know if it's safe for me to go to the warehouse. Damn it, why hasn't he called me?

✻✻

At the beginning of my trial I gave this journal to my supposed Russian defense attorney as evidence of my innocence. I thought it would clear me of the charges that led to the unjust, politically motivated prosecution that's landed me in this fucking inhumane Gulag. I am rotting here under false accusations perpetrated by the French and Russian governments. My name, as well as my supposed deeds, have been plastered all across Europe. No one believes my side of the story. I've been framed! I'm not the mastermind of The Cézanne Conspiracy. I had nothing to do with the deaths of Françoise, Robert, or any of the others. And I absolutely have no knowledge of why HP committed suicide.

I was convicted, not because of incontestable evidence or testimony of those involved. All of them were conveniently dead. For all I know, Max may be sitting in another cell, or maybe he's dead too. Everything you hear or read about me is a lie. Everything my jailers tell me is a lie. Just like forgery is a lie, so is this verdict against me.

I was indicted because of doctored evidence that included a fabricated photograph. The prosecution presented a second Polaroid picture of Françoise and her friends on the steps of the Louvre, but this one included a young me. There I was standing next to Françoise, Domino and Robert. Someone, most likely the Russian Federal Security Service, must have taken it from my university's gradation photo, or off of an old employment ID card.

My last night in France was spent in a mafia warehouse in Marseilles.

Six men met us in the lobby of the hotel. They were a formidable looking lot; all were dressed in street clothes. At least two of the brutish characters were heavily tattooed. One had his head shaved; the other sprouted a Mohawk. Two dark-skinned Algerian looking men had hair that reached to their shoulders. The apparent leader of the group looked older than the rest of his crew. He wore a fedora hat and a leather jacket. His hair was pulled back into a ponytail and he sprouted a scruffy goatee with crumbs left over from a croissant, or some other messy pastry. He was short and stocky, and by the way he walked, it was obvious he was wearing elevator shoes. The last one looked like an albino. He had a nasty rosy colored scar that ran from just below his ear, down across his cheek, and disappeared under his chin. His hair was white and his eyes were a pinkish color. He was scary. I suppose

HP hadn't wanted to send in a team that looked like the Sûreté agents who wore suits and ties.

What a contrast. Cliff looked like the professor he is. Max had on his usual attire of paint splattered jeans and a t-shirt, and I, of course, looked like a lady.

The leader of the group introduced himself as Maurice (most likely not his real name) and escorted us to a beat-up old van parked in the alley behind the hotel. There was no step-up, so it was hard for me to get into the truck. Maurice, the little prick, opened the door for me to get in. I could see he was enjoying how high my skirt hiked up.

There were benches along the sidewall of the van to sit on. I scooted towards the front behind the cab. Max and Cliff followed and, with the exception of the two Algerian looking thugs, the rest of the team jumped in. The door was closed, an overhead light came on and we heard the passenger and driver's side doors slam shut.

The van began to move. The team leader asked for the mobile phone that HP had given me. I hesitated; my thought was that maybe my attorney would call. The runt who was in charge sensed my reluctance. With his right index finger, he tapped the opened palm of his left hand for me to give the phone to him. I was hesitant, but I complied. After all, what choice did I have? When I passed it to him, he smiled. It was a wicked smile, the kind that says, I gotcha. I felt uncomfortable. Very uncomfortable!

He asked if we had any weapons on us. Max and Cliff shook their heads no. I pointed to my umbrella. One of the brutes chuckled. The leader gave him a look, the kind of glare that would stop a laughing hyena. I just wanted the van to stop and let me off. This was not the place for a woman like me.

Maurice pulled a map from his inside coat pocket, along with a pack of cigarettes. He searched in his pockets for a match; one of his henchmen snapped a lighter and lit his boss's cigarette. Without asking if I minded; he started smoking. I coughed, but he kept puffing away. The albino pulled the sliding window open. I remember thinking I was surrounded by imbeciles, plus two artists who would be useless if things got rough.

Maurice looked at his map and told us we would be heading for the Port Marceille-Fos and that it would take us about 45 minutes to get to our "Target." As we got close to Fos-sur-Mer I saw oil storage tanks and smelled the stench of refineries. We drove through some industrial areas not far from the Chenal de Caronte. After zigzagging around warehouses and vacant lots we finally reached our destination. The large building was located on a substantial track of sandy scrubland. There was no driveway or parking lot, no signage other than a hand written cardboard notice on the front door of the gray, windowless, dingy building that read "Défense d'entrer."

On the side of the door was a keypad. Maurice pressed a series of numbers and I heard the lock disengage. In hindsight, I should have thought it odd, but at the time I was so frightened that it didn't dawn on me that he had such intimate knowledge of the workings of the building. Maybe he had been there before, or, could it have been that he was a double agent?

It was pitch black inside. The albino turned on his

flashlight, as did the others. Maurice walked directly to the electric panel and pushed the lever up. Immediately the entire open space became flooded with light.

I could tell Max and Cliff were stunned by what they saw. There were a hundred cubicles separated by wire screening. Each space contained works of art representing a single master. Some were paintings, but the majority of artwork was drawings, pastels and watercolors. Some of the work represented the major artists from the renaissance, but the preponderance of what was there were the Impressionists, and those who followed at the turn of the century. Half of the spaces were filled with the likes of Picasso, Dali, Miro and a handful of lesser-known modern artists.

Maurice told the two Algerians to guard the entrance door. The rest of us began walking down the long corridor between the fenced cages. All around us were what appeared to be masterpieces, but of course we knew they weren't.

As we walked between the stalls, our footsteps echoed through the cavernous warehouse. In several cells there were workbenches, easels and drafting tables. We passed a pen where two van Gogh oils hung on the caging wire. One of them was a scene of a yard full of chickens, the other a portrait of Doctor Gachet, the man who helped Vincent during the last three months of his life. Twenty or so empty old frames were attached to the wire dividers. On surplus library tables, watercolors and ink drawings were neatly stacked and separated according to size. In the corner were boxes containing sheets of dirty oily glass, many of them broken but still usable, if recut to fit into a smaller frame.

When we came to the caged Cézannes, I thought Max would shit. On the worktable were the two drawings he had given to the Valerie in Saintes-Maries-de-la-Mer; the ones he did in the old quarry on the outskirts of Aix. The two sketches were side by side. Max's signature was on one, but not on the other. Next to the drawings were paper towels, can lids, cotton swabs and two bottles, one labeled Evian, the other, bleach. Cliff explained. "The cotton swabs were first dipped into clean water, and then into a small amount of bleach. The dampened swabs were ever so lightly stroked over your signature. This was done several times. Over several applications, your identity was painstakingly removed."

"The paper was blotted one more time with a clean, water- dampened paper towel in order to remove the residue left over from the bleach. Bleach is derived from sodium chloride, which is basically common table salt. The manufacturers of household bleach produce their product by bubbling chlorine into a solution of water and sodium hydroxide. During the process, the mixture is converted into a sodium hypochlorite solution. It is nearly impossible to entirely remove the crystals from the paper."

Cliff opened the wooden box that he had brought with him from the university. "We'll set up here." He asked Maurice to clear off the table. The boss motioned to the albino who pulled surgical gloves from his pocket and a sealed bag that contained, what looked like a sterilized sheet. After putting on the gloves he spread the white material on an empty work stool and then Cliff placed the drawings carefully on it.

Clifford removed the highly sophisticated microscope. "This is an Electron Microscope with electromagnetic lenses and specialized detectors. At the minimal magnification I should be able to find salt crystals imbedded into the paper. This will confirm that bleach was used to take your name off and replace it with the fake Cézanne signature."

As a test, he focused the microscope on a section of one of Max's drawings. He waved Max over to look into the instrument. Max saw the almost perfect microscopic crystalized cubes, some fractured at 90 degree angles. They were beautiful.

Cliff pointed out to Max. "This microscope is highly sophisticated and I'll test for inconsistences embedded in the paper and paint samples tonight. I will be able to detect chemicals and organic materials inappropriate to the time period that a particular artist was working."

It was decided the Albino would stay to assist Cliff. Max took the new fangled camera and began photographing drawings, pastels, watercolors and paintings. Because of my expertise as a buyer and seller of many of the artists whose purported work filled the warehouse, it was felt that I should pick out the pieces to be brought to Cliff. After all, I have been a consultant to many private collections in both America and Europe. Maurice accompanied me. I pointed out the artwork, he removed it and brought it to Cliff and then returned to me for another selection. After taking minuscule samples and readouts from the microscope, Cliff sent the work back with Maurice to rehang it in its appropriate cell. We had done this picking up and retuning art for almost an hour. But then Maurice seemed to disappear; I went looking for him.

I walked back towards where Cliff was working. Before I got there I heard the sound of boots trampling against the hard cement floor. I squinted my eyes trying to see into the dark end of the building and, coming out of the dim light into the floodlit area of the warehouse, I saw Boris Volkov, Maurice and HP along with six uniformed gendarmes coming towards me.

I stood there frozen, totally transfixed as they came towards me. I didn't know what to say or do. I was grabbed by two policemen who held my arms tightly. I yelled at HP. He paid no attention and headed towards the area where Cliff and Max stood watching. Volkov spun me around and he, along with three of the officers, marched me out the back door to a waiting police wagon.

A gendarme handcuffed me. As I stepped up to enter the police van, another officer held my elbow. One of my stiletto sandal heels caught the edge of the first step, snapped off and my ankle twisted. I was so pissed; those shoes cost me beaucoup francs. I spat at the officer as he pulled off my other shoe and threw it to the pavement.

They pushed me onto a bench in the police wagon and then one threw a seatbelt across my lap. As the pig reached across to belt me in, he touched my breast. I spat in his face. When the doors were closing, I heard the local Marseille police captain ask HP, "Where should I put the prisoner when we get to the station?"

I heard HP reply, "For her safety, it will be best not to put her with the men. Put the prisoner in the women's holding cell for now. We will be there soon to begin *Madamé's interrogatoire.*"

The door slammed shut. As the vehicle drove along the pot- holed road of the warehouse district, I was bounced up and down. This was no way to treat a woman.

I was placed in a 10-foot square cell with my wrists still handcuffed behind my back. It was cold and there was vomit on the floor. I was determined not to give them the satisfaction of seeing me cry.

Finally two guards came and took me to a room where HP was sitting on a steel chair. Leaning against the wall, smoking a cigarette was a man who looked familiar. One of the guards un- cuffed me, pushed me down on a chair and then left the room with his partner.

HP offered me water. I rubbed my wrists; my yellow gold Harry Winston charm bracelet was scratched. Holding the bracelet an inch from his nose, I yelled at HP, "Who's going to pay for this?" He said nothing.

The other man in the room walked towards me.

There was something about him that scared me.

In a thick Russian accent he offered me a cigarette; I shook my head no. He said, "In a few moments, we will be leaving France. You are taking a trip with me to Moscow."

"No I'm not."

Pleadingly I looked at HP, but he said nothing. I demanded to speak with my attorney.

I woke up on a jet plane handcuffed to the Russian. I looked at my watch; it was 3am. I had been knocked out for 12 hours. Who knows what they did to me during that time. I asked if I could use the toilet, my captor motioned to a stewardess to accompany me. In the small bathroom I saw that, at some point while I was drugged and unconscious, someone had removed my panties.

The airline attendant returned me to my seat. I slid into my place beside the Russian, then, still handcuffed, I uncomfortably reached for my purse. As I bent down to retrieve it from under the seat in front of me I noticed my captor was wearing zippered boots. It was then that I recognized him. He was the same man I saw at the airport when we had picked up Cliff.

My abductor said, "We will be landing soon at

Sheremetyevo where I will turn you over to Major Volkov from Internal Services."

I looked forward to spitting in Volkov's face. I had nothing to do with the cartel or any forgeries. The Russians have always persecuted we French. They have no artists of any importance outside of Chagall, but he ran off to France.

I was taken down the stairs from the plane to be handed over to Volkov. As I was shoved into the waiting limo, he smiled, saying, "Welcome to Moscow. I am glad we finally get to meet. My friend Max has told me much about you, as has my colleague HP. Sadly, you are not here as a tourist, for if the circumstances were different I would take you to Saint Petersburg to visit the Hermitage to see the twenty-three beautiful Cézannes there. Instead you will enjoy a long vacation here in Moscow. My guess is that you will love Russia so much that you will never want to leave."

****

That was six months ago. I should have been tried in France. But it didn't happen that way. I am not guilty of anything. I am not the leader behind the forgery cartel; I am a pawn in a game. The real conspirators have killed everyone involved and locked me away to rot in oblivion.

But a strange, yet wonderful thing has happened to me. My memory disorder has disappeared. And with no make-up, no dresses and my hair cut short, I am not consumed with my identity anymore. Duplicity no longer shapes my life.

A few days ago Volkov was here and he gave me back my journal. So now I'll continue to write. He assumes, because he returned it, that I'll be more forthcoming. He's wrong. I will never cooperate with the Russians or the corrupt officials of France. Sometime, somewhere, someone will launch a real investigation and the truth of my innocence will be proven. I will be exonerated and the real conspirators will be revealed. Volkov is either a fool, or takes me to be one. Yes, I'm in love with Max, but if Volkov thinks dangling tidbits of information concerning Max's whereabouts, or his dalliances with other women, will somehow tempt me into revealing more, then he's even a dumber piece of shit than I originally thought. Supposedly the Russians used listening devices and cameras to monitor Max and me. Of course they doctored the tapes. Even the vodka suckers have technologies. Yesterday he continued to interrogate me. It didn't work. I'm too strong for the commie bastard.

Volkov returned again today and tried a new tactic.

He began by saying; "Your government wanted you out of France. We agreed to take you off their hands. After all, you are dangerous to their economy and so called prestige. The American and European capitalist leaders have covered up your conspiracy. They have protected the West's art museums and rich collectors. Your plan to undermine the art world and thus threaten their finical stability has not succeeded. No one, except a few high-placed government officials in Washington and Paris know the circumstances of what you have done."

"Oh, and by the way, a week after your trial began, your friend Max met an attractive American woman, a photographer who came to Provence to photograph gardens for a book that was recently published by Rizzoli in New York. Max met her in Cézanne's garden. He was there drawing and she was taking pictures of the iris planted along the wall on the side of the great painter's studio."

He must have bought a cheap supermarket romance magazine to help him say the next piece of shit that came out of his mouth. "Your friend Max introduced himself to the photographer. She took the camera away from her eye and smiled at him. She was much younger then Max. Her dark short hair framed a face that reminded my comrades of the American actress Jamie Lee Curtis. She was tall and lanky and wore shorts and a lacy pink blouse. Her skin was the color and smoothness of alabaster and her eyes, cerulean blue. Around her neck were two smaller cameras and a silver necklace."

"Your friend, or should I say want-to-be husband, introduced himself. Jamie Lee said she knew who Max was." 'You're the famous American expatriate painter.'

"Your boyfriend bowed and replied, 'Not, famous, more like infamous.' He had a huge grin on his face. I understand you once told him his smile turned you on."

"Our agents filmed Max as he sat on a bench across from where she was snapping pictures. With our sophisticated listening device we were able to pick up their conversation. I hope it won't upset you too much, but here is what they said."

I put my fingers in my ears. Volkov pressed his pager and a guard entered the room and walked behind me. Violently, causing excruciating pain, he pulled my arms down and yanked them behind my back where he handcuffed my wrists. I spat at him and he started to put tape on my mouth. Volkov stopped him and gestured for the brute he called

Putin to leave the room. He then continued his informational bullshit. I screamed at him saying my treatment was illegal and intimidation and harassment would not be tolerated in France. He laughed and then removed tape and a pager from his jacket. I shook my head as Volkov attempted to tape my mouth shut.

I opened my mouth as wide as possible to avoid my jaw from being constrained. I was sick of hearing his soliloquy, so I tried to conjure up a Beatle song in my head. I heard *Lucy In The Sky With Diamonds*. Unfortunately, neither strategy worked. Volkov put one of his huge paws on top of my head and the other under my chin, like a vice, he forced me to close my mouth. With a smile on his lips, he said, "Shall I request our friend Vladimir return with the tape?"

I acceded to his threat and allowed him to tape my lips closed. He then pulled his chair up beside me, leaned close to the side of my face, and began speaking directly into my ear.

The Russian pig continued his story. "Max said to the Jamie Lee look-a-like, don't let me distract you, go on with your picture taking. I'll just sit here and watch you work."

"That will be more distracting," she said.

Volkov continued torturing me. I wanted him to knock off the Jamie Lee shit. "Max asked about the beautiful photographer's work and she told him about her assignment." Max said, 'I could show you gardens in Provence that most tourists never see."

Slurring through my taped mouth, I told Volkov to fuck himself. He smiled and continued taunting me.

"This beautiful American woman obviously was infatuated with the man you thought was yours after you had Françoise killed and dumped in Monet's pond."

Shaking my head, I mumbled that I had nothing to do with the bitch's death. He put his finger to his lips as a signal to stop my muffled attempts at talking and then continued his tale.

She said to him, "I would like to see the hidden gardens where tourists never go, but to do so with you, the great landscape painter, well, that could be intimidating. I'm sure you would distract me from my work."

Max flirtatiously smiled, "I'd enjoy being your distraction."

I jerked hard trying to pull my arm up to give the Russian the finger. As I thrashed in my chair, the pain of being so tightly restrained made me grimace and I felt that I was about to vomit. Thank God I didn't. If I had, I would have choked to death on my own puke. Of course that didn't stop Volkov. He took great pleasure in antagonizing me. He continued telling me about Max's banter with the woman. "His reply to the gorgeous woman was, 'Oh, come on now, how could this old man be a distraction?'

"Comrade Max was pleased with her reply. 'Oh believe me, you would distract me.' She introduced herself as Samantha Huston, but said her friends called her Sam."

Volkov continued to piss me off. "Ah Celine, you can image your suave boyfriend's smile when he suggested they have lunch together. Max knows how to seduce a woman, you know that. It's just another one of his many talents. He tempted her by saying he'd divulge where to find the most beautiful gardens in Southern France. She of course accepted. What woman wouldn't? He is charming, is he not?"

I stuck my tongue out at my fucking Russian tormentor. "Our agent, who had been filming from almost 50 yards away, readjusted his video camera to get a close up of your man's face. Believe me, Max wasn't shy. To the contrary, he kissed her on the cheek and took her hand."

"They walked along the gravel path. You know the one. As we had observed over the last year, you and Max walked there from time to time. It's the one off the curved road leading into Aix. They walked to the city. He took her to his favorite café, the Café du Roi René on the Cours Mirabeau. I recall you were there with him on one of your visits to Lacoste."

I was never there. The fucker smiled and said, "Oh yes you were. We have photos of you both sitting outside. Would you like me to show them to you?"

The Russians must have had me under surveillance for some time. From his reply, it was obvious he could read my thoughts. "Yes, we have a great deal of photos, video recordings, and wiretaps, of you. Most with Max and, of course, some of your unusual acquaintances."

I spat at him. He moved his head quickly; my phylum missed his cheek by a hair.

He continued. "The Jamie Lee look-a-like and your friend sat outside under a blue canopy. The light dappling through the trees danced on the sidewalk with a young girl who was selling flowers, a gypsy child, not more than seven years old. She moved rhythmically with the flickering sunlight and shifting shadows. Across the street an organ grinder turned the crank and sang old French love songs, songs from before the Second World War."

"Your hoped-for-lover found the American female exquisite and his attraction for her titanic. Not since his first meeting with Françoise has Max felt such a connection to any another woman in his life. I know because he told me."

I recognized what Volkov was up to. He surely knows about my time with Max in New York. His intent was to make a mockery of the fact that I am the only woman Max ever really loved. I was the best lover he would ever have. I have skills that his other women could never possess, a special attribute. I was born with a pussy and a cock --- I am a hermaphrodite.

Volkov pulled his chair closer to me so that his mouth was only inches from my ear. "Max looked at her hand and saw there was no wedding ring on her finger. She agreed to his offer to take her to the gardens at Cordeliers in *Digne-les-Bains*. He would have taken her to Michelin's gardens, but you know what happened to your client. You had him killed, hung by a rope in his own back yard."

I kept my composure. He would get nothing from

me.

"Max picked her up early the next morning in Aix. The drive gave your precious Max time to learn about her. Her husband died eight years ago and after his death she committed herself to her passion for taking pictures. She is now recognized by art galleries and magazine publishers for her immense talent."

"A few years ago she nearly died of cancer. Her former husband was a successful investment banker, and while they were together she lived a genteel life. She still resides in a mansion in Ohio and has a second summer cottage on the shores of Lake Michigan. In addition to her passion and fame as a photographer, she raises horses and designs gardens."

"That's her background, but let me go on with my love story. When they reached Digne they entered the walled garden. It is the one divided into four sections. You've been there; I'm sure you can recall the aromatic lavenders, rosemary, sage, andthyme. The monks hood was blooming and its lavender-blue spikes were alive with butterflies. The pond was teaming with dragonflies that flew like miniature helicopters. As I reviewed the surveillance tapes, it made me think of dragonflies hovering over the lily pads in the botanical garden near Saint Petersburg."

"As I watched the tapes, it was apparent to me that this beautiful American woman was about to capture your old boyfriend, just as Françoise had done. Max is obviously is attracted to beautiful women. I assume, that as you lost your beauty, he must have grown tired of you."

I pretended that I didn't hear him. He looked at me and smiled.

"She took several photos of the rose beds while Max sketched her. After a while they walked to the edge of the garden and the path that leads to the wooden bench under the vine-*covered* pergola. They sat soaking in the warmth and beauty of the gardens. The American took out her notebook and wrote a few lines of poetry. When she finished she fumbled through her camera case and found a pushpin, then tacked her poem to one of the beams. Max got up to read her words and she pulled his sleeve and asked him not to read it because it was for the eyes of dragonflies only.

After Max and his new infatuation left, my officers retrieved the note. Are you wondering what she wrote?"

I continued to listen to Beatle songs in my head.

'All the lonely people, where do they all come from? All the lonely people,

Where do they all belong?'

"When the sun was reaching the center of the sky; the heat began to take its toll on her. American women are more prone to be uncomfortable in heat. Maybe that's why Max suggested they go to the Maison du McDonalds. She looked at him and frowned. He laughed. I know, you French think it's barbaric, but it's the only place in all of France where you can get a cold drink with ice in it."

"As they walked into town she put her arm in his. Quite romantic, wouldn't you say Céline? After all, I'm sure it felt good to him to walk with a classy woman again. A year is a long time for a man to be without a woman. And since you killed Françoise and have disappeared yourself, he obviously needs a replacement for you."

The Beatles left. Their songs failed to extinguish Volkov's thick Russian accent from drilling into my head.

"Max has started a new series of paintings of gardens with ponds in them. These paintings have been flowing like ripe fruit falling off a tree, just one good painting after another. He is now represented by one of your competitors, The

Maggie Gérard Gallery. The title of his new show is 'Maxfield's Gardens.' I was at last week's opening of the exhibition of the pond paintings. The show sold out within minutes of the gallery's doors being opened. I was fortunate to buy one.

There has been a persistent rumor throughout the Parisian art world that his new paintings have something to do with Françoise Gemmer. It is known that Max was her lover and that he was, for a brief time, a suspect in her murder. When the photo of him standing on the bridge over Monet's Lily pond was initially splashed on the front pages of almost every French newspaper, his celebrity soared. He and Françoise are being compared to Rodin and Camille Claudel. You, on the other hand, are compared to Marthe Hanau who defrauded the French financial markets.

"Max's palette has lightened. There's no longer any black in his work and the horizontals of his previous paintings have shifted to verticals. The critic from Le Monde raved about his painting where he threw red ink across the surface and the likeness of a dragonfly appeared on the canvas. When I saw him at the opening he said the painting was inspired by his new girlfriend. It is beautiful."

"Max and Sam spent almost a month visiting the Jardins de Provence. Our surveillance often showed them holding hands and kissing. In one incident we caught them enjoying a cool September night sitting in a café. While they were there, we were able to place a camera in their hotel room. The hotel room was small, as most rooms in France are."

"They were fortunate to have a tiny sitting area off the bedroom. Max noticed two paperbacks on the floor by the small couch, a book of Hemingway's short stories and poetry by Gustaf Sorbin. While waiting for her to return from the bathroom he leafed through the pages. She returned with wine and glasses and opened a bottle of Roussillon wine."

I pretended to be falling asleep.

Volkov kicked my shin and continued to tell his lies. "Don't go to sleep; the best parts of the story are unfolding."

"Sam looked sad, or maybe worried would be a better word. She told him she had something to tell him that might affect his feelings toward her. Max was worried that she might have secrets just like Françoise. I suppose that's why he recoiled."

"I had cancer and it still may be with me. My doctors gave me a clean bill of health, but I have been warned the cancer could come back. I have to return to the states for a screening test next month."

Max took her in his arms. She hung on to him tightly; I am certain he could feel her tears against his cheek.

"Come lay with me in the bed," she asked.

"He removed his shoes and pulled the blanket to the end of the bed. He watched her unbutton her white blouse, revealing a cream-colored camisole top. She pulled her skirt down and laid it across a chair near the bed. Lowering her into his arms, they kissed and her fingers shook as she unfastened the buttons of his denim shirt. Her mouth touched his neck. He audibly sighed."

"She asked Max to hold her through the night. They talked; they touched. Just before dawn, they fell asleep. I am sure Max realized how sensual a night together, without sex, can be."

For a moment, Volkov stopped tormenting me with details of Max's love affair. "Céline, we have been watching you for over a year. We know all there is to know concerning your gallery and your disgusting private life. We are fully aware of your forgeries, your corrupt morals and the deviant nature of your body and mind. You will die in this prison. Outside of a few within our governments, no one will ever know what you've done. To your colleagues and your customers, you have retired from the art business. You have disappeared. No one will be the wiser. Your clientele will assume you're living in some far-flung exotic part of the world. Life in the art world will go on without you. You'll soon be forgotten. No one will miss you."

"Before I go, let me finish the story of Max and the beautiful photographer. On the drive to the airport outside of Nice, few words were spoken; I guess you could describe their journey as reflective. We filmed them going from the parking lot to the ticket counter. Before she was checked through customs, she held on to Max for a very long time. We don't know what they said to each other at that moment. I have to say I do like watching people in airports saying goodbye or welcome home. The kisses and embraces of lovers and families often bring a tear to my eye. I am a Russian, we are a sentimental people."

"As your beloved Max walked through the glass doors to exit the airport, he reached into his knapsack, removed his wallet, and fumbled through it trying to retrieve a few francs to pay for parking. Tucked between the currencies was a notecard. For a brief moment he looked at it, crushed it in his hand, and then tossed it to ground. After Max drove away our agent picked it up."

"There was an impression of your lips on the paper and beside it, in your handwriting, was a wish that will never come true. 'I'll see you in Paris. Love, Céline.'

"Touching is it not?"

The bastard dropped the wrinkled card on my lap. "Here, you might want it as a memento." He opened the cell door and said

"Au revoir." The heavy metal prison door closed behind him. The sound of the steel bolt slammed into its slot and I screamed. "I'm innocent. Don't leave me here!

LA FIN